ANYONE CAN
GROW ROSES

Anyone Can

* * *

* *

Grow Roses

by Cynthia Westcott

COLLIER BOOKS, NEW YORK

COLLIER-MACMILLAN LTD., LONDON

THE MACMILLAN COMPANY, NEW YORK
Collier-Macmillan Canada Ltd., Toronto, Ontario
Printed in the United States of America

In Memory of My Nephew
JOHN CULLEN WESTCOTT

FOREWORD

AS I PREPARE a fourth edition of this small book on roses I believe in the title more firmly than ever. Truly *Anyone Can Grow Roses* with a little love and land where the sun shines part of the day. The love is necessary. With it, roses bloom in impossible soil as hard as bricks, in lands of drought and devastating winds, in regions of great summer heat and of intense cold, even in shady areas with much less than the supposed minimum requirement of sunshine. Without love, roses languish even in the best of climates. By love I don't mean smother love, a continual fussing over your bushes. I merely mean being interested enough to find out their simple requirements, partly from reading but mostly by trial and error in your own garden. If you are willing to learn, the rose will teach you.

A continuing stream of letters from rose lovers in every state and visits to rose gardens in almost every state prove this over and over. In Minnesota you struggle for winter protection; in Florida you strive to keep the organic matter replenished in your soil as you fight blackspot, Cercospora leaf spot and nematodes; in Oregon and California you worry about rust and mildew and in Oklahoma about drying winds; Japanese beetles add to your problems in the East. But you grow roses—wonderful roses!

Once you have started growing roses you can't stop. Nor can you stop proselyting. I started spreading rose gospel in a small way, inviting the neighbors in for tea on a June Sunday. Then, wanting to demonstrate vegetable techniques during Victory Garden Days, I used the roses as a "come-on," inviting the whole town to wartime punch and cookies in the rose garden. As the roses filled and overflowed my small backyard, so did the visitors who came, each second Sunday in June, from a hundred towns and cities. When I moved to New Jersey, people said roses did not grow well there and were far too much trouble. My rose garden was a pebble dropped in the pool of rose inertia. Some went home to start roses, others to plant more roses; then their neighbors tried a few.

Now I have another rose garden, in a retirement development in Westchester County, New York. But I still have Rose Day; 1965 makes the twenty-fifth.

This slight book is meant to be an extension of Rose Day, a discussion of the things that roses have taught me through the years—the things to do, and not to do, to keep rose-growing a pleasure and not a chore. It is largely limited to my personal experience and does not pretend to be complete, nor to offer competition to many fine rose books now in print. In order to be within reach of the "Anyone" of the title there are no expensive color pictures. With a few five-cent stamps on letters requesting catalogues, you can get more pictures of beautiful roses than we could provide in a book at thrice the price. This way, you may still have money enough to order a bush or two.

CYNTHIA WESTCOTT

Springvale
Croton-on-Hudson, New York
March, 1965

CONTENTS

CHAPTER I

GROWING ROSES

Anyone who loves roses can grow roses, granted a few feet of earth where the sun shines part of the day. The ten commandments of rose culture are tempered with common sense according to where you live and your own experience. It really takes longer to talk about them than it does to carry them out.

One autumn in New Jersey we had a windstorm that did far more damage in my section than previous storms officially labeled as hurricanes. The glass of my sun porch was shattered, the lawn littered with shingles from near-by roofs and the tall trees shading the hillside were flung over the road along the back of the lot. My neighbor's yard farther up the hill was equally bare of trees; yet the next morning as we were ruefully surveying our losses his first words were, "Well, now we'll have a good view of your roses." And my first thought was, "At last I'll have enough sun on this hill to grow the creeping roses I've always wanted."

All day as I tugged limbs down off the hill I thought about roses and their resilience, for in that tremendous wind not one of the five hundred in my garden turned a hair. Now I have another garden, in an apartment development for "senior citizens" along the Hudson River. A few weeks ago another windstorm felled numerous large trees on this property but my new three hundred roses emerged unscathed.

Roses are unbelievably tough and long-suffering. In one hurricane, climbing roses on Long Island were covered with salt water yet went on to bloom better than ever the next summer. A terrific New Year's Day ice storm in New Jersey broke many frozen canes yet made little differ-ence to June bloom. Once in August a huge tree fell on a client's bushes, completely smashing two dozen roses. We trimmed the plants near ground level and by October every bush had sent up new canes and most were in bloom.

The worst trick Nature has for roses is a sudden big drop in tempera-ture in autumn before the bushes have hardened off. But even then, when canes are black to the base and you order replacements for roses you are sure you have lost, most of the plants surprise you with a spring resurrec-tion. I lectured in Ohio once in May. Early the previous November, with sap still high in the canes, there had been a severe freeze that split and killed the unhardened wood. In all the gardens I visited, spring pruning had had to be at ground level. But six weeks later, when I arrived, almost every bush was sending up a profusion of strong new canes, a few with flower buds already showing color.

Aside from being resilient when Nature goes on a rampage, roses pro-vide the longest possible blooming season. In the suburban New York area hybrid teas provide bloom for about six months and by choosing a few early-blooming species such as *Rosa primula* or *R. hugonis,* which sometimes start in April, the season can be lengthened to nearly eight months. I have cut buds of floribunda Else Poulsen in early December and once I took sprays of Orange Triumph to brighten evergreens at a Christ-mas Greens Show. Long after chrysanthemums are black with frost there is color in the rose garden.

An old argument against growing roses is that they require too much time and attention. I think that roses are particularly easy to grow and that the idea of their requiring a disproportionate amount of care is just plain silly. For twenty-five years I earned most of my living caring for other people's roses. As a plant doctor I was supposed to be a general practitioner but my clients turned more and more to roses as they dis-

covered how much return they got on their investment when it was protected with a little regular attention. My "doctoring" included preparing
the soil, planting, pruning, feeding, winter protection (until I decided it
was unnecessary), as well as spraying once a week. My assistant and I
sprayed roses (50 to 500 bushes per garden), other shrubs and perennials
in more than fifty gardens each week, with time out for rainy days and
for transportation over a fifty-mile area. Simple arithmetic proves that the
weekly time spent in each rose garden was not excessive.

Roses are not expensive. Some years ago one rose was introduced at $10
and a very few have started at $5 but top price for most new patented roses
is $3.50 with the cost dropping a bit in a year or two. Many excellent
older varieties are still available for $1.35 to $1.50 and if you prorate that
cost over a dozen years (and many roses last your lifetime) the initial investment is infinitesimal. New rose varieties are much less expensive than
new irises. Of course, you can increase the iris by divisions; in fact, you
have to keep dividing it and this sometimes becomes a chore. Once you
have planted a rose, you don't have to worry about its multiplying. However, if you do want to increase it, propagation by cane cuttings is not
much more trouble than dividing and replanting iris.

Most roses deserve some upkeep expense and a few minutes of care
each week but some survive total neglect. I first fell in love with roses at
the age of four, when we moved to a house in Massachusetts honored
with an old rose bush covered with dark pink flowers every June. I never
learned what it was, nor its age when we arrived, but to my certain
knowledge it has been blooming untended for more than sixty years and
is still going strong. When I left my New Jersey garden in 1961 most of
the roses planted in 1933 were still producing despite their use for testing
various sprays and dusts or as "checks" receiving no treatment at all. One
bed, purposely left unsprayed for twelve years, had most of its original
planting.

Roses were on earth long before man. We know from fossils that they
have been here at least thirty-five million years. Maybe they will still be
here after man has destroyed himself. So let's enjoy roses, knowing that
they will usually survive mistreatment and will respond lavishly to every
bit of loving care.

LOCATE ROSE BEDS PROPERLY

1. *Plant away from tree roots, where the sun shines at least six hours a day and where there is reasonably good drainage.*

You can test the drainage by digging a hole 18 inches deep and filling it with water. If it seeps away in a couple of hours there is no need to worry; if it doesn't, either choose another location or have tile drain installed.

Roses are said to require a minimum of six hours of sunshine for good bloom. Many of my New Jersey roses got less than that but they did not do as well as my New York roses in more open land. Roses usually do very well with sun all day but in hot summer weather they keep their color better with some afternoon shade. Morning shade is not so desirable.

Tall trees, such as elms, may allow enough sun to reach the roses but their roots can be a curse. Roses in beds nearest trees grow progressively worse as the season advances and the tree roots continue to steal food and moisture. If roses must be placed near trees, or shrubs or hedges, a barrier of sheet metal can be placed vertically at the edge of the bed but this is not very satisfactory. Even if you manage to solve the root problem you still have that of spray residue on foliage when trees are sprayed for cankerworms or beetles. The spray is always disfiguring to roses and often actually injurious. When roses are near trees being sprayed, at least persuade the operators to wet the roses with a hose immediately before the trees are treated and to wash them down afterwards. I have seen tree experts deliberately turn the spray gun on roses and other garden plants under the delusion that they were being helpful. Residue from spray drift is bad enough but for the operator to purposely put the disfiguring tree spray on roses is unforgivable. It is weeks and weeks before the leaves lose that awful white coating and all too often the rose foliage drops off.

Planting too close to trees and shrubs has other disadvantages. It cuts off free circulation of air and encourages powdery mildew and red spiders. And the roses grow tall and leggy, leaning away from the trees.

PREPARE SOIL THOROUGHLY

2. *Work the soil for roses thoroughly to two spades' depth and incorporate organic matter generously.*

Roses are not fussy about their soil requirements. They thrive in any soil prepared deeply enough to give the roots a chance. Soils that are heavy and wet with too much clay and soils that are too light and sandy can be amended by working in plenty of humus, organic matter, which makes the heavy soil more friable and the light soil more moisture-retentive.

The older rosarian laboriously prepared rose beds by excavating the soil to 3 feet, putting in a drainage layer of cinders or stones, then upturned sod, followed by top soil mixed with manure and finally bottom soil also mixed with manure. He usually incorporated some slow-acting bonemeal.

The modern grower (without much help) removes the top spade depth of soil and improves the next in place. This means omitting the drainage layer but this is more advantageous than otherwise. All too often the old drainage area became a sump hole, collecting water and giving the roses wet feet. The modern grower uses superphosphate more often than bonemeal and he may substitute peat moss and dehydrated manure for old-fashioned cow manure but the results are just as good, possibly better.

In preparing a small rose bed it is easier to remove all the top spade depth of soil at once. If you want to save the lawn, pile it on a piece of canvas or in bushel baskets. A larger rose bed can be worked in sections. In loosening the second spade depth you will probably have to start with a pickaxe or mattock and there will likely be big stones or boulders to be grubbed out. Don't ignore them; get them out! Sometimes when I investigate a puny rose I find that a lazy gardener left a boulder down under the roots. When you have done an honest job of loosening the soil down to at least 18 inches from the surface, then add up to one-fourth as much organic matter. This can be well-rotted cow manure and your own compost but don't worry if neither is available. Get peat moss—the rough bulky type, not the very fine material. Open up the bale and, if there is time, wait for the rains to moisten it. Plan 5 or 6 bushels of peat moss per 100 square feet of bed.

When you are ready, spread half of the peat moss over the bottom half of the bed, the soil already having been loosened. Scatter over this a goodly amount of dehydrated manure (Bovung, Driconure or a similar preparation), a few handfuls of superphosphate (about one per bush to be planted) and some complete fertilizer, either 5-10-5 or a special rose food. Fork all this together thoroughly, then replace the top spade depth of soil, incorporating into this more peat moss, manure, superphosphate and fertilizer.

You may, or may not, want to incorporate some ground limestone into this mixture. Although roses tolerate soils in a rather wide pH range they do best in a somewhat acid soil. We have said for many years that a pH of around 6.0 or 6.5 was optimum but experience leads me to believe that 5.5 to 6.0 is still good. If the pH is below 5.0 or if the peat moss is quite acid, then you should add 3 to 5 pounds of ground limestone for each 100 square feet of bed.

If the soil is quite alkaline, pH 7.5 or above, you can work in 1 to 2 pounds of powdered sulfur per 100 square feet. If the soil is only slightly alkaline, incorporating peat moss and using fertilizer with a base of cottonseed meal may be sufficient without sulfur. In many sections of the country the soil is naturally somewhat acid and there is little need to be concerned with pH for roses. But along the Gulf from New Orleans to Houston and in parts of the semiarid West the soil and irrigation water are both alkaline and pH becomes a problem. In such cases, peat moss is more useful than organic manures that have an initial alkaline reaction.

Soil preparation should be done several weeks before planting to give the beds time to settle. This means late summer for fall planting, and late autumn for spring planting. Letting the bed settle is truly important. Otherwise your roses may sink down too far after planting and some may die. Or the roses will be left in mounded beds that will not hold water during drought periods.

In most sections of the country the final level of the bed after settling should be 1 to 3 inches below the surrounding turf, even if this means removing some soil before planting. In very hot dry sections, like New Mexico, the level should be 3 to 4 inches below the turf to hold irrigation water. In areas with a high water table, like New Orleans and Houston, the beds may have to be raised above the surrounding grass to keep the roots from rotting.

PLANT CAREFULLY

3. *Plant No. 1, field-grown roses carefully, at the right time for your section.*

The right time to plant roses depends on where you live. Spring planting is safest in Minnesota and other cold states, and winter planting, mid-December to mid-February, is best in much of the South. In Florida, November planting is recommended for winter bloom. It has often been stated that you have to grow roses as annuals in Florida but Mrs. G. F. Lampkin of Bradenton grows marvelous roses on the same bushes year after year. She has some that have survived for twenty-five years and she is gradually gaining converts to the idea that roses can be permanent shrubs even in the Deep South.

In the suburban New York area we can plant in either fall or spring. In November the days are usually pleasant and the soil friable. You have first choice of the desired varieties and the plants come directly from the nursery to your garden, with their roots out of the ground the shortest possible time. When rose roots are established before winter the first June bloom is earlier and better than with spring-planted bushes. But some years we have an unusually long, warm autumn and the nurseryman is forced to dig before the wood is sufficiently mature or else to delay digging so long that the ground is frozen before you receive your plants. If you have less than perfect drainage you may lose a fall-planted bush if water freezes into the roots in a very cold winter.

Spring planting is good if you can get the bushes into the ground early enough, preferably by April 15th in my area. Unfortunately, nurserymen are swamped with orders in spring and your bushes may arrive too late to establish a good root system before warm weather. Also in spring you are too apt to be enticed by the pretty pictures you see on packaged roses that have been lying around in the heat of stores. You buy them only to find that the roots are broken or moldy, that the buds have started too soon, and that there are long pale shoots that break off as you handle the plant. This is not an indictment of packaged roses per se. I have seen some fine roses in packages in storage. It all depends on the grade of the rose and how long it has been sitting around out of storage before you get it.

When roses come to you by mail or express, plant on arrival if you can. If that is impossible you can hold the unopened bundle in a cool place for a day or two or three. If there must be a longer delay, unpack the bushes and bury them in a trench. Some people prefer to bury all roses received for a few days to plump up the buds; such heeling-in is a good precaution if stems look dry and shriveled.

When ready to plant, take out a few roses and put them in a pail of water; keep the rest wrapped or in the soil. Never let the roots be exposed to sun and wind even momentarily. Some people stand their roses in a pail of water overnight before planting but they should never be soaked longer than that for fear of rotting.

Dig a hole large enough to accommodate the roots without crowding. Some nurserymen send bushes with roots cut quite short; others send plants with roots so long they may require a little shortening to get the proper spacing between bushes.

Inspect the rose carefully; make sure there are no root-knot nematode nodules on the roots or any signs of crown gall. The latter usually appears as an enlargement, with a somewhat roughened surface, at the crown but sometimes there are only small galls on the roots. Crown swellings may be merely callus formation around a wound but it does not pay to take a chance of its being the bacterial disease (see Crown Gall, Figure 14). A plant afflicted with crown gall may, or may not, die within the next year or two. If it does, the bacteria may live in the soil without any host plant for a couple of years, during which time a new healthy rose put in the same location may contract the disease. All reputable nurseries want to sell you sound, healthy stock but sometimes, in the rush of grading and storing, or in getting out orders, a diseased plant slips through. The nursery will replace a rose with crown gall so don't be afraid to report it. By all means keep that plant out of your soil; don't cut off the gall and hope for the best; don't even attempt treatment with one of the materials offered for this disease. They are not yet sure cure.

In planting your bush, cut off all broken roots and cut off all roots that are too long for your *large* hole. Don't coil the long tips back or around. If possible, spread the roots out over a soil mound in the bottom of the hole. Some bushes have a heavy tap root that makes the mound impractical but usually it helps in planting at the proper depth and in spreading the roots out and down at the right angle.

There has always been argument among rosarians as to depth of planting. Older directions for the Temperate Zone call for placing the bud union, the bump from which the canes start, 2 inches below ground level. Our modern idea is to plant practically at ground level, barely covering the bud union. And some of us, even in the North, are beginning to plant slightly higher. In the South and in California high planting, an inch or more above soil level, is the rule.

Such shallow planting, allowing sun to reach the bud union, encourages more basal breaks, new shoots from the base. I have had more failures from too-deep rather than too-shallow planting but in very cold regions deep planting is insurance against sudden cold weather before roses have been hilled with soil for winter. It means that one or two buds live on even though the cane is killed back to ground level. Directions that come with the subzero Brownell roses, originally bred for cold regions, say to place the bud union 3 inches below ground level. I have found this too deep for the suburban New York area and have learned to disregard instructions aimed at more northern states.

With the rose bush held firmly in place over its soil mound, work friable soil in around the roots so there are no air spaces. It helps to have two people at the planting job, one to hold the rose at the right level, the other to work in the soil, but you can hold with one hand and firm in soil with the other if necessary. When the hole is three-quarters filled, tramp on the soil, one foot on each side of the bush. This is important! A rose so loose you can jiggle it in the soil may not survive. If you did not judge the distance right, you may find that stepping around the bush has carried the bud union down too low. *Dig* it out and start over; be sure not to *pull* it out of that compacted soil, thereby breaking off fine feeding roots. Not all rosarians approve of tramping but I have had good results for more than forty years.

After tramping, fill the hole with water and let it soak completely away before adding the rest of the soil, which is kept loose and not

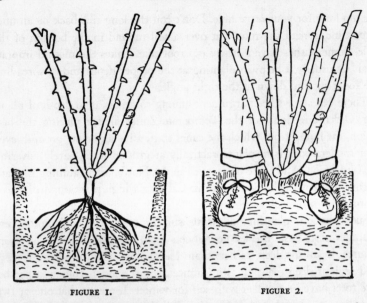

FIGURE I.   FIGURE 2.

FIG. I. Planting a rose; roots spread out over an earth mound; bud union at almost
ground level. FIG. 2. Planting: soil tramped in firmly.

firmed. If you are planting in the fall, mound up with soil for winter.
If you are planting in the spring make a temporary soil mound 8 inches
or so high around the bush. This last precaution is often overlooked but
it is very necessary in giving the rose a good start. It keeps drying winds
from shriveling the canes before the roots get their water conduction
system established. Remove the extra soil in a week or two, as the buds
start to grow. If the plant remains dormant and the buds do not break
promptly try cutting the canes back harder and keep the bush well
watered. Don't give up too soon. Some bushes sulk for awhile but come
along later.

The distance between your bushes depends again on where you live
as well as on the type and variety. In warm climates the bushes grow
larger and 3 feet is about right for most hybrid teas although some
varieties can use 4 feet for best growth. In New York and New Jersey
2 feet is now average for hybrid teas. Distances between polyanthas and
floribundas vary from 1 foot for little Margo Koster to 4 to 6 feet for

Betty Prior. Most climbers are planted 6 to 8 feet apart but some pillar roses, trained upright around a post, can be planted a bit closer.

If your rose planting must be delayed until May, potted roses, in full foliage and coming into bloom, are a better buy than remainder stock of dormant roses. The latter do not have time to get roots established before hot weather. Container-grown roses cost a little more and are often available only on a cash-and-carry basis but they have more chance of surviving late planting. In the East, the containers are usually of roofing paper. Dig a hole somewhat larger than the pot and place in it some friable soil mixed with compost or peat moss. Carefully open up the bottom of the container and place it in the hole so levels of soil in the pot and the bed are the same. Then slit the tar paper down the side and carefully remove it without disturbing the earth around the roots. Don't try to straighten out the roots; leave the soil intact and firm in more to fill the sides of the hole. Do not mound up but keep well watered.

I have never approved of planting left-over potted roses that have stayed around in the nursery all summer in small pots. There is a new trend, however, that is quite exciting. Nurseries are potting up roses late, in large containers, and bringing them into bloom for early fall sales. These are fine sturdy bushes and decidedly not "left-overs."

Sometimes you are planting dormant roses in perennial beds or in separate locations around the garden. In that case you can, if necessary, dig a hole when you are ready to plant, making it deep enough to work some organic matter and fertilizer in the soil down under the roots. But be sure to cover this with straight soil so that no fresh manure or fertilizer actually touches the roots.

If you want to move roses already established it is best to do it in autumn when the bushes are nearly dormant or in spring before growth starts. Prune the canes back about halfway before digging and work some peat moss or other organic matter in the new location as you replant. If you must transplant during the growing season try to dig the bushes with some earth around the roots, prune back fairly drastically, and spray with Wilt-pruf to prevent too much evaporation from the foliage before the water-conducting system starts working in the new location. Mid-season transplants are seldom an ornament the rest of the year but they often are as good as new by the next summer.

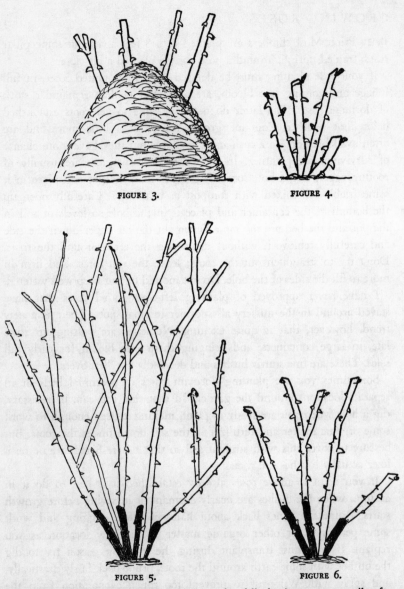

FIGURE 3.

FIGURE 4.

FIGURE 5.

FIGURE 6.

FIG. 3. Rose mounded with earth for winter after fall planting or temporarily after spring planting. FIG. 4. Fall-planted rose after first spring pruning. FIG. 5. The same bush before pruning the second spring. FIG. 6. The same rose after pruning the second spring.

PRUNE WITH COMMON SENSE

4. *Prune in spring, cutting back to sound wood and making all cuts close to a bud.*

Roses purchased for fall planting are usually cut back at the nursery; if not, they are cut back to about 12 inches on planting. All pruning of established bushes should be deferred until spring. Callus formation is slow in autumn and wound fungi and pith borers may enter the cut stems. Roses leaf out from the top buds with any warm spell during the winter only to freeze back later. If you prune in the fall many of the buds needed to make new shoots for summer bloom may be destroyed; if you delay pruning until spring, the only buds killed in late winter or early spring frosts are on the upper part of the cane and this you will be cutting off anyway. The only exception to the rule of no fall pruning is when there are extra long canes that would whip too much in winter winds. These can be shortened to the level of other bushes in the rose bed.

The time for spring pruning again depends on where you live. In Florida, pruning may be as early as December; along the Coast and in California it may be January or early February; in Georgia mid-February; in Tennessee, early March; in New Jersey late March or early April; in Massachusetts around April 10th.

Never start pruning until all soil and other material used for winter protection has been removed for you must examine the canes to the base. Prune first for disease control, cutting out canes with cankers or serious wounds or split bark. Cut out dead canes at ground level. Then shape the bush according to its type.

Cut back to sound wood with a clean slanting cut just above a good eye (bud) going in the same direction as the bud and as close to it as you can get without injury to it. If you leave more than ¼ inch of stub, wound fungi will get started. To keep the bush shapely, cut to an outside bud where you can, but that part is not too important. Cut out weak spindly canes, branches that cross each other in the interior of the bush, and any candelabra type of growth. If you are lucky, you will have left at least three stout canes.

For many years rosarians believed that if you wanted very large exhi-

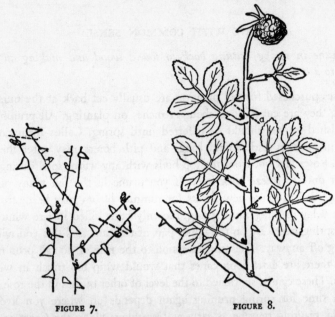

FIGURE 7.   **FIGURE 8.**

FIG. 7. Dotted lines show proper placing of pruning cuts.   FIG. 8. Cut off dead bloom at *a*, a flower for the house at *b*.

bition blooms you whacked your remaining canes down to only two or three eyes, or about 6 inches from the ground. The theory was that all the strength of the bush went into a few blooms. Modern exhibitors realize that more foliage is required to manufacture food for flowers and prune moderately, with canes left 12 to 18 inches high where the winter has allowed it. Nature, however, often decides the pruning height and some springs you have to cut back almost to the bud union. Don't despair; don't dig the bushes out too quickly thinking they are dead. Almost always they come back with vigorous new growth.

In true high pruning, possible only where winters are mild, canes are left 3 or 4 feet high but the twiggy growth is cut out as well as interlacing branches. Each year one or two of the oldest canes are cut out at the base to encourage new wood.

For most of spring pruning you need curved-edge pruning shears, as large as will fit comfortably into your hand. These are less likely to injure canes than the straight-edge, snap-cut type. Inadequate or dull shears mean jagged cuts that encourage disease or the entrance of pith borers. A clean cut is quickly callused over. Have your shears sharpened by a professional before the season starts and return them for a fresh edge when they get the least bit dull. For the past several seasons I have been very happy with a Wilkinson sword pruner, imported from England but now available at many garden centers. It requires very infrequent sharpening.

The larger canes should be cut with lopping shears or a keyhole saw. It takes practice to cut out an old or dead cane at ground level without nicking the bark of an adjacent good cane.

It may be wise to paint the cut surface of very large canes but I still think it unnecessary to paint most cuts, despite all advice to the contrary. For years I pruned over twelve thousand roses for my clients each spring without ever painting a cut or ever losing a bush to borers, although I have had to cut individual canes nearly to the base to get below borers. In observing other gardens I have found that tree paints used for pruning cuts are often injurious, killing the cane back several inches from the painted surface. A pruning compound is available in aerosol form, for roses as well as trees, but I think the result is pretty disfiguring to the bushes. If you have lots of spare time and insist on painting cuts, orange shellac is probably the safest and least noticeable material. The Rockwells, in their *Complete Book of Roses*, report that they do not protect most cuts but apply grafting wax to the largest canes.

The United States Department of Agriculture has made some quite convincing experiments showing that lime sulfur applied as a dormant spray has no effect on subsequent blackspot. I am inclined to agree but think that lime sulfur applied immediately after pruning may kill some infective material spread during the pruning operation, and may act somewhat as a protectant fungicide. I know that it is definitely helpful in controlling rose scale. Use the commercial liquid, 1 part to 9 of water, and apply only to roses still nearly dormant, where the buds have not broken more than ¼ inch. For roses on trellises, or near houses or other painted surfaces that will be stained black with lime sulfur, you may have to substitute a dormant oil for scales, or malathion in summer when young scales are crawling, but neither is as efficient as lime sulfur.

No matter how good a pruning job you do on dormant roses you will probably have to do some supplementary cutting as the season advances. A sudden freeze in early autumn kills many canes outright; you can see this dead tissue and cut it at first pruning. But a later freeze may leave the bark green and kill the interior. The buds start normally and the cane may carry on until flowering; then it dies back due to the increased demands of the vascular system. Unless canes are cut below all brown pith in spring there will almost always have to be more cutting back during the summer. This is normal and you need not worry about acquiring a new dieback disease when you see yellow leaves.

The higher you prune in spring the more quickly your rose bush will come into bloom. A rose has apical dominance and the top buds are coming out of dormancy while the lower buds are sound asleep. This becomes important if you are planning an event in connection with roses and the season is late. One year the hard-pruned roses of a public garden had scarcely a bloom on their Rose Day while my own lightly pruned garden was full of bloom for its open house the same week. I have had two clients in the same town entertaining in their gardens the same week. One, who had pruned moderately hard, had only one or two flowers; the other, who had pruned unusually high, had bloom on every bush.

Hybrid perpetual roses are usually pruned somewhat higher than hybrid teas, perhaps down to 2 feet. They are hardier than other roses and may not kill back much over winter but they do have to be cut down in spring to prevent their getting too tall and leggy.

Some people prune *floribunda* roses rather severely to make them conform to a pattern and provide a mass display all one height. I prefer to choose floribundas for special locations agreeable to their natural heights and to let them grow unchecked except for cutting out winter-killed tips and old flower sprays in spring and old dead canes in summer. Floribunda and polyantha roses are constantly pushing up new canes from the base and having some of the older canes die back to the ground. This exchange is a little more conspicuous in midsummer when red spiders cause some defoliation but it is nothing to worry about.

Climbing roses are pruned according to their type. Old-fashioned ramblers that bloom on new canes, such as Dorothy Perkins, Crimson Rambler and the newer Chevy Chase, are pruned in summer immediately after flowering, taking out all or much of the wood that has bloomed, and tying the new canes to a support. Lots of us don't get around to doing this and we end up with a tremendous mass of briers that defies all attempt at order. After several years of neglect the only way to achieve neatness is to chop off the whole tangle and let the plant start over.

Large-flowered climbers and ramblers bloom mostly on old wood. Those of moderate growth, like recurrent bloomer Dream Girl or Blossomtime, or climbing hybrid teas, need only the dead tips of canes removed at spring pruning. Rampant growers, like Dr. W. Van Fleet and Silver Moon, sometimes require drastic treatment to keep them from taking over the whole place. One or two of the oldest canes may be removed each season at ground level to make room for new canes. The laterals, which are shoots coming out at right angles from the main canes, are shortened to 4 to 12 inches after flowering. With June-flowering climbers you may, if you wish, forget about cutting off dead blooms and enjoy the rose hips in autumn. For recurrent bloom on varieties like New Dawn and Dr. J. H. Nicolas you must keep cutting off fading flowers if you want continuous production. That is true, of course, for all types of roses; continuity of bloom depends on cutting off the present crop of flowers as soon as they start to fade.

This removal of dead blooms as well as cutting flowers for the house should still be considered a pruning operation and carried out with the same care to cut *close* to a bud, which means just above a leaf. The bud which will grow out to the next flowering shoot is in the axil of a leaf, so always cut to a leaf that shelters a live bud, not to one where the bud is missing or dead. Never make a cut halfway between leaves. The cane will die back to the leaf axil (node) and in that dying stub canker fungi get started. For the same reason never twist off a fading flower at the top of a stem; always cut back to the first leaf with a good bud. Cut flowers from new bushes with very short stems, usually just back to the first leaf. Float them in rose bowls or use flat arrangements. Established roses can be cut back to the second leaf from the base of the stem. This provides two buds to produce flowering shoots for later bloom. Cut only a few stems this low; leave the rest fairly long. Remember that it takes from five to seven leaves, not leaflets, to manufacture enough food for each flower.

If you want that flower to be particularly large for exhibition or if you want roses for the house produced singly on long stems, you practice disbudding, which means pinching out the side buds with your thumb and finger while they are still very tiny. If you wait until they are good-sized the food required for your one big flower has already been diverted. Unless a rose show schedule has a special class for roses grown naturally (and this can be very lovely) your exhibition hybrid tea rose *must* be disbudded and you are penalized for evidence of recent disbudding. Grandiflora roses may be shown disbudded like a hybrid tea or as a spray like a floribunda.

Often it is possible to disbud enough roses for fine cut flowers and still leave enough not disbudded for effective and continuous garden display. Study your varieties and their habits. Margaret McGredy produces many buds and makes a fine splash in the garden; leave her there, not disbudded. McGredy's Yellow and Mrs. Sam McGredy can be profitably disbudded for specimen bloom. If you go all out for blue ribbons it is possible to cut back all the canes somewhat a certain number of weeks before a Show and bring your flowers to perfection at about the right time. See Chapter IV for further information along this line.

Floribunda roses are not disbudded. Some of the flowers in a cluster will fade while the rest are still attractive. Remove these as you have time, but after the entire cluster has finished cut it back to a good bud in a leaf axil below the cluster; don't start the new growth from the small secondary stems.

Throughout the season be alert for *suckers* coming from the understock. Cut out this growth before it kills your good budded rose but don't confuse it with the basal breaks (new shoots) of the real rose. A common fallacy is that all roses having leaves with seven leaflets are understock but many hybrid teas produce some seven-leaflet leaves and some understocks have leaves with only five leaflets. People talk about roses "reverting" but that is not true; the budded rose dies and the understock takes over and blooms. The sucker differs from the good rose in the color and texture of foliage as well as in the flower. Multiflora understock, widely used by eastern growers, has dull light green foliage and produces small white flowers in clusters, something like those of blackberries. This rose, so widely advertised as a living fence, is fine for farms and to prevent accidents on highways but has no place in the small suburban garden. California understock is usually Dr. Huey, often called Shafter. It has reddish foliage and will grow into an attractive red-flowered climber if allowed to overpower the budded rose. Quite recently roses produced for Florida consumption have been produced on Fortuniana understock. This is the double white Cherokee rose and would be doubtfully hardy north of Florida.

Some growers make life unnecessarily hard for their roses by whacking them back right after the big June bloom, thinking that this makes a better fall display and eliminates spraying for Japanese beetles. Granting that roses are somewhat smaller and less profuse in midsummer, that they have fewer petals at high temperatures, I know of no evidence suggesting that giving up all summer bloom makes the fall display one bit better. On the contrary, loss of all that foliage may even detract from the autumn output and the rose may find it hard to get going again after an enforced rest in summer. You have to keep spraying the leaves you have left anyway, to control both blackspot and beetles, as well as red spiders and other pests, so cutting back is merely wasted time depriving you of summer flowers and your roses of their rightful food.

FEED JUDICIOUSLY

5. *Fertilize established roses soon after pruning, as they are coming into bloom, and again in summer, but not after August 15th, in the North.*

Newly planted roses need no food beyond that already incorporated into the soil. Feed established roses as soon as convenient after pruning, applying up to a trowelful of a complete commercial fertilizer for each bush. Scatter it between the plants, never letting it touch canes or foliage, and work it into the soil lightly, without disturbing roots. There are many special rose foods with an organic base. These are excellent but for my area the 5-10-5 fertilizer (meaning 5 parts nitrogen, 10 parts phosphorus, 5 parts potash per 100 pounds) sold for vegetables has been quite satisfactory for roses and much less expensive. For many years I made three applications in clients' gardens: after pruning; in late May as plants were coming into bloom; and in July or early August. Some years ago I switched to a single ground feeding of 5-10-5 mixed with some de-

FIGURE 9.   FIGURE 10.

FIG. 9. Watering with a Waterwand. FIG. 10. Fertilizer worked in lightly with side of All-Purpose Hoe.

hydrated manure (Bovung or Driconure). This is applied right after pruning and is followed by foliar feeding every other week. I merely add 2 teaspoons of Rapid-Gro to each gallon of the pesticide spray I have to apply anyway. This saves time and energy and the results are fine for a display garden; more food would be necessary for exhibition roses. The highly concentrated fertilizers designed for foliar feeding may also be applied through the soil, using the coarse hose applicator meant for lawns, or a watering can, but this takes more chemical and more time for equal effect.

A moderate feeding program that stops early enough to allow plants to ripen thoroughly before cold weather usually means a long-lived bush. Exhibitors in fall rose shows often feed rather heavily in late summer. This increases the number of blue ribbons, decreases the chance of winter survival. More fertilizer is required where roses have a long growing season. Recommendations for Florida, for instance, call for applications every 4 to 10 weeks. The Agricultural Extension Service of your own state can help you plan a feeding program tailored for local requirements.

WATER PRUDENTLY

6. *Water thoroughly, when necessary, always making sure the foliage has time to dry off before evening.*

Roses like to drink even better than to eat and every feeding should be followed by copious watering unless a rain is due soon. If watering is by overhead sprinkler or water-fan be sure and finish early enough in the day so plants can dry off before night. This is to prevent blackspot which gets started if the leaves are continuously wet for six hours. Safer than overhead watering is a soil-soaker hose, though this is a bit messy to get in and out of mulched beds. If you have time to spare in the evening —enough to water each plant individually—try a Waterwand, a 4-foot aluminum rod that attaches to the hose. Held at the base of a bush it dispenses a large volume of water at low velocity without washing away the soil or wetting the foliage. Another hose attachment is the Water Bubbler, a perforated aluminum ball with baffles inside. It, too, waters deeply without washing out the soil but, because it has no stiff rod, I find it more arduous to use. If you have no special apparatus you can remove the nozzle from the hose and let the water splay out over a wide board into the bed.

If you are able to water regularly and thoroughly throughout the summer and if you keep spent blooms cut off promptly you can keep your roses producing even in midsummer when they are inclined to rest a bit. But unless you are able to water *regularly* all season it may be safer to bring your roses up "tough." Don't start with a great excess of water early in the year and encourage a lot of tender growth if you expect to go away for a month or two or if the use of water is likely to be restricted in your area. If there is plenty of organic matter in the soil and a good mulch, roses will survive extended periods of drought if they are not too succulent at the start.

If your roses are planted close to hedges, shrubs or trees be extra generous about watering. Where there is such root competition roses come off second best.

I never realized how much difference copious water makes to the color and size of roses until the spring when it rained every weekend and most of the time in between. We spent our time cussing out the weather because so little gardening could be done but the June display of roses was the finest ever seen in New Jersey.

MULCH AND RELAX

7. *Mulch with buckwheat hulls, bagasse, ground corncobs, pine needles, sawdust or other material soon after first feeding.*

A good mulch eliminates much of the work in growing roses by keeping down weeds and reducing the watering required. My personal preference is for buckwheat hulls. They are light, easy to handle, can be applied dry, and the dark color, that of rich soil, is most pleasing. Four large bags, 200 pounds, cover 260 square feet 1-inch thick and it should not be applied in any greater amount. Fill pails from the bag and pour the hulls on the ground *under* the bushes (not down through them). Be sure the foliage is dry, for the hulls stick to wet leaves. Despite their lightness, buckwheat hulls stay in place, do not cake, and allow water to penetrate freely to the soil below. The hulls may also kill the grass if you spill a pile over the edge of the rose bed and do not brush it back. Occasionally a weed will come up through the hulls and once in a while a buckwheat plant appears but it takes only a few minutes to pull these out and the time saved over ordinary weeding is enormous. It goes without saying that the rose bed should be carefully weeded and leveled before the mulch is first applied.

If you live where no winter protection is necessary the mulch may be left in place and enough new hulls added the next spring to keep the 1-inch depth. If the hulls are applied deeper than this or are mounded up around the canes for winter or are worked into the soil in spring there may be a detrimental effect. Use them strictly as a mulch, not a soil conditioner. If you must mound your bushes with soil for winter, take off most of the mulch and store it in the original bags for reuse in spring—*unless* it is full of blackspot leaves; if such is the case burn the mulch and buy fresh for next year. A clean mulch reduces disease by providing a mechanical barrier between infective material left on the ground and developing leaves overhead, although naturally it offers no protection against spores developing in overwintered lesions on canes.

Cocoa shells, marketed in bags like buckwheat hulls, also provide a dark, attractive mulch but for the first week or two the garden smells like a chocolate factory. Cottonseed hulls and peanut shells are sometimes used in the South. The latter should be fumigated to prevent transport of parasitic nematodes.

Sugarcane bagasse, now available in the North, makes a satisfactory mulch if appearance is not of prime importance. It is light colored and a bit messy but it works down into and enriches the soil. The ground corncob mulch has many devotees and in certain areas it is very inexpensive. The one year I tried corncobs they were shockingly conspicuous compared to buckwheat hulls but as they got dirty they were less obnoxious. As the corncob mulch rots down it makes a fine soil conditioner but extra nitrogen must be added so that the soil is not robbed of nutrients during the breaking-down process. Corncobs kept too wet or piled too high around canes may rot them. Sawdust makes a similar mulch; it, too, requires extra nitrogen.

Chopped tobacco stems are sometimes used as a mulch and supposed to have some insecticidal effect but I think this angle is much overrated. Pine needles provide a most pleasing mulch in long-leaf pine regions. Wood chips are sometimes available.

Grass clippings provide a cost-free mulch but are somewhat unsightly and tend to mat down. Apply gradually, in thin layers so that they do not heat up too much.

Organic manures should be used for mulching with discretion; they must not keep the canes too moist or warm or encourage too soft growth. In my opinion, peat moss is far more useful inside a rose bed than on top as a mulch. It either absorbs too much water, reducing the supply to the roots below or it cakes on top so that water runs off the bed instead of into it.

The earlier a mulch is applied in spring, after the ground warms up a bit, the less energy you'll have to spend in weeding, provided the soil has been carefully cultivated and all incipient weeds removed before the mulch is applied. Apply your fertilizer first, because it is easier to scatter this over and work it into bare ground. If you then change to foliar feeding you don't have to worry about the mulch. If you want to do later ground feeding, scatter dry fertilizer around the bushes on top of the mulch, stir it gently down through with a cultivator, then water well to carry it into the soil.

After promoting the idea of a mulch I must now confess that in my

new "senior citizen" garden without help, without enough energy to lift
50-pound bags, I am getting along without a mulch and the roses don't
mind a bit. They are planted so that the leaves of one bush almost touch
those of the next. This keeps the ground shaded and cool, reduces
evaporation and discourages weeds. Occasionally I do a little shallow
cultivation after rains or watering. This is the old idea of a dust mulch,
supposed to be outmoded. It does keep the soil aerated and I found that
in my New Jersey garden the beds that had been mulched continuously
for many years had gotten quite acid, probably from lack of oxygen with
no cultivation. They were, however, still blooming fairly well and it only
goes to show that there is no one best way to grow roses; they are wonderfully adaptable.

TREAT FOR DISEASES AND PESTS REGULARLY

8. *Start summer spraying or dusting soon after roses come into full
leaf and repeat about once a week until mid-autumn.*

Although long experience has convinced me that more roses are killed
by misguided efforts of gardeners than by insect pests and plant diseases
there is no denying that most roses do need regular protection with some
combination fungicide-insecticide. Likewise there is no denying that
a spray or dust so strong that it knocks the leaves off is worse than no
treatment at all.

Some disease may be expected even in a brand-new garden, placed a
long distance from other roses. Bushes purchased from the West Coast
may bring along mildew mycelium in dormant buds on the canes. Roses
purchased from other parts of the country are very likely, unless the
grower did a spectacular job of control, to bring in blackspot mycelium
in almost invisible lesions on the canes. If you have grown roses for a
long time and are discouraged because of disease you are not going to
accomplish anything by getting rid of all your old bushes and putting in
new unless you embark on a rigid spray schedule. And if you do that
you can probably keep most of your old bushes and bring them back to
full productivity. I have often taken over a rose garden defoliated by
blackspot season after season and inside of two years, without replacing
the bushes, brought it back to glowing health without a single spotted

leaf. It is merely a question of regular treatment with a combination pesticide suited to your location and rose varieties. Treatment need not take long—an hour or so a week will do up to five hundred roses—but it must be regular.

There is no perfect insecticide or fungicide or combination thereof, nor any perfect method of applying chemicals. All have advantages and disadvantages. The right combination for you and your roses may depend somewhat on you and your allergies. Some people react with dermatitis to certain chemicals or they can't stand the smell. Some rose varieties are allergic to copper; almost all object to sulfur or malathion on a very hot day. Find the combination that means the least work and most comfort for yourself, gives the best control of the most important rose enemies in your section with the least injury to your roses and then stick with it, using it religiously every week (more or less) right through the summer. For disease control your treatment should be applied before, rather than after, rains but if you spray or dust often enough to have a protective coating on foliage at all times you don't have to worry about weather reports. Charts to help you recognize rose pests and diseases, details on chemicals, and how and when to use them are given in Chapter VI on Rose Enemies.

BEWARE WINTER PROTECTION

9. *Your best winter protection is a healthy plant. Soil mounds and other coverings are needed only in very cold regions.*

I used to protect roses for winter in the time-honored way, with a soil mound applied at the end of November, sometimes putting manure between the hills after the ground had frozen hard. There came a year when the temperature dropped wickedly on Thanksgiving Day and the ground stayed solidly frozen thereafter. So I advanced the protection time to early November, putting on soil mixed with sifted compost, half a pail poured into the center of each bush to make a natural mound. It grew to be quite a chore to do this for the many clients who had no extra soil available nor any annual or vegetable bed from which to steal. I found myself carting around and giving away my own hard-won compost with Henry, my assistant, grumbling more and more about the unnecessary work. So we experimented. One year I left a third of my own roses unprotected; the next winter one-half were left alone. There was no difference at spring pruning.

My chief civic service in New Jersey was the planting and maintenance of the roses at the Montclair Garden Center. They were planted in the fall and mounded up immediately with soil from the beds. The next spring the soil was leveled off and the beds mulched with buckwheat hulls. That fall we removed the mulch from one-half the garden and hilled those bushes with soil brought in from a vacant lot. The other half was left unhilled, with the mulch intact. There was no difference between the halves in winter survival. The extra soil was removed and the mulch replaced. But all summer, despite the mulch, we had to spend hours on the beds that had been hilled, getting out weeds growing from seeds brought in with that extra soil. There were almost no weeds where we had left the mulch in place without special winter protection. The idea of working hard in November just to provide more labor the next summer was too much. I decided then and there never to hill another rose and I never have (except, of course, right after planting). I have had no cause to regret this decision.

After a very severe winter I asked members of the North Jersey Rose Society to fill in a questionnaire about their methods of winter protection and amount of winter injury. Their answers showed no correlation, although there was some connection between roses fed late in the season and subsequent dieback and a definite relation between poor drainage and winter injury.

I started my Springvale Rose Garden in the spring of 1962 with about two hundred bushes, planting about fifty more that autumn. The latter were mounded after planting but the spring roses were entirely unprotected, even though they were planted high with the bud union exposed. We had a very severe winter with terrific winds. Over New Year's the temperature dropped so fast the water pipes froze in our buildings. The roses came through beautifully. I only lost two of the unprotected roses and these had severe crown gall. I lost six of the new mounded roses but they were at the bottom of a slope, near the exit of a drain pipe and had had wet feet all winter. None of the roses were hilled the next winter; there were no losses and very little dying back.

Summer pest control is vital for winter protection. If bushes are defoliated by blackspot, or red spiders, and have to put out one or two or three new crops of leaves there is little vitality left for winter survival. If bushes are continually chopped back so that there is too little foliage to manufacture food to fill the canes with carbohydrates for the winter there may be injury. If roses are heavily fed and watered late in the season so that there is unhardened succulent growth going into winter there may be injury. Generally speaking, however, a rose is a hardy shrub that does not need to be coddled.

In the course of graduate studies at Cornell University I worked on brand canker, a disease of climbing roses suddenly prevalent in the test garden there. It killed many of the plants, caused a great deal of dieback on the rest. After four years of investigation, trying out all kinds of summer spraying and winter protection, we learned that control was very simple. All we had to do was to eliminate all winter protection (soil, leaves, evergreen boughs or wrapping in burlap) and thus eliminate the moist conditions favorable to the fungus, which worked only in winter, not in the heat of summer. We learned to remove the climbers from their supports in autumn while the canes were still pliant and to hold them down on the grass with crossed stakes but with no covering.

Standard or tree roses do need special winter protection, except in mild climates. The tender rose is budded at the top of a hardy stem and the only way to get soil protection for the good rose is to dig a trench, loosen the roots of the standard on one side, tip the whole thing over and cover with soil. Tree roses should be planted only where such a trench is possible unless you are willing to replace them after a severe winter. In some seasons they survive if wrapped in straw and waterproof paper, or in pliofilm with evergreen boughs tied around, but this is a gamble.

These observations on winter protection are mostly for the suburban New York area. I don't know how far north hybrid teas are safe without a soil mound nor how high it must be. Probably 8 to 10 inches of soil is sufficient in Massachusetts but in very cold states like Maine, New Hampshire and Minnesota, up to 15 inches may be recommended with evergreen boughs or oak leaves on top. In Minnesota they sometimes make wooden coverings and I have read of one cold-temperature rosarian who digs his roses, puts them in a piano box, and has them hauled to the local storage plant to be kept in the crisping room all winter.

If you live in the Middle Atlantic states and don't quite trust your roses without the winter protection I now consider unnecessary, stick to the earth mound. Bring soil from some other part of the garden; don't scrape it up from between the bushes and so expose the roots. Don't, in the regions where we have alternate freezing and thawing, add manure, leaves or other material that will keep the canes warm and moist enough to encourage canker fungi. Don't add salt hay even though that stays dry. It is the dickens to remove in the spring, it encourages field mice, and the worst case of brown canker I ever saw in my life was where the bushes had been swaddled with salt hay in a rather mild winter. Using leaves for insulation seems to be all right in the far north where everything stays solidly frozen over winter.

There are various devices on the market to aid in winter protection. Wire-mesh enclosures hold soil in place and reduce the amount required. These are satisfactory if the mesh is large enough to allow complete drainage; don't use impervious materials. Plastic rose cones are available which will keep the bushes dry but you must then cut back drastically to fit a vigorous bush under the cone. My advice is to experiment with your roses and see if they really require all that labor and expense in your area.

LOVE YOUR ROSES

10. *Love your roses enough to know when they are healthy and happy and don't disturb them with unnecessary attention.*

Carrying out the first nine commandments is no great chore. It may take half a day (a whole day if your soil has rocks like mine) to prepare a bed properly and give your roses the right start in life. But all the annual activities—pruning, feeding, watering, mulching, spraying—can be handled in well under an hour a year per bush and an annual cost of fifty cents or less per bush. Of course, if exhibiting roses becomes your chief hobby, you will gladly spend more time and money in exchange for blue ribbons.

Carrying out the tenth commandment is more difficult, especially if

you have a gardener. You may tell him he has so much to do in the rest
of the garden that you will personally care for the roses but some day
when you are out, and with the kindest of intentions, he will go in
and fork up the beds to get rid of weeds, mound up the beds by edging
with a spade, throw fertilizer down over the foliage, apply a strong dose
of bordeaux mixture that looks horrible and makes the leaves fall off,
cut back the roses in summer "so you will have fall bloom," chop down
all the canes in autumn, or heap everything with fresh manure or leaves
for winter. I see these things over and over again in the course of plant
doctoring. I'll enlarge on a few of the more important "don'ts."

Don't mound up the beds

It is a rare gardener indeed who does not edge beds with a spade, cutting
more and more toward the roots of the roses on the outside and mounding
more and more soil over the crowns. The roses are smothered on the one
hand and exposed to drought conditions on the other; they can never be
properly watered. In some places, as in Houston and New Orleans with a
high water table, a raised bed may be preferable but it should be a *flat*
plateau, extending at least a foot beyond the plants, and not a mountain
with the bushes stuck in at the side.

Many years ago I met a yard man who could properly edge a rose bed
and he taught me how. Once each spring you do use a spade, cutting a
straight line along the edge of the bed, guided by a string stretched between two stakes. But the spade is used only for cutting down into that
uneven sod; you do not lift up the sod and soil and throw it over the rose
crowns. You withdraw the spade and keep cutting down the line. Then
you go back on your knees and take out the grass clumps by hand,
shaking the earth back in place and keeping the bed level. After that
first lining up it is relatively easy to keep a neat edge with grass shears
the rest of the season provided the bed is an inch or two below sod level.

Don't disturb the roots

Roses obtain food and water by a system of fibrous roots extending
through the soil. Any violent cultivation disturbs these roots yet far too
often I see gardeners forking through the rose bed or hoeing with a heavy
hand. Keep it shallow; loosen the surface not more than an inch or two.

Or use a mulch so there will be no temptation to dig around the bush. Remember that your roses are shrubs. Once planted they should last a lifetime. Don't fork around a rose any more than you would around a forsythia or rhododendron.

Don't use too strong sprays

The only reason for spraying for blackspot or beetles or spider mites is to keep enough leaves on the bush to manufacture food for flowers and to store for winter. Any spray so strong it makes the leaves turn yellow or drop off or burns them so they cannot function properly defeats its own purpose. Spreaders and stickers sometimes increase the injury from sprays. Materials safe in New York may not be safe all year in Florida. You must never increase the amount of a pesticide over that indicated on the label but you may have to decrease it to avoid injury in your location. Spraying is nothing to be left to the gardener. You can't trust him to read the labels and make up the mixtures accurately. He can, perhaps, pump a sprayer under your direction but with a good hose-end sprayer, the kind with an extension tube and deflector, you can do the job yourself with very little time and effort. The physical act of spraying each bush makes it possible to check it weekly for its state of health. You can soon tell when it looks abnormal, just as a mother can tell when her child feels ill, and then you can start figuring out the things you have done which you ought not to have done.

CHAPTER II

CHOOSING ROSES

Now that you have some idea of the cost, in time and money, of keeping up a rose garden, you can think about buying roses. Many of us start our rose purchases by seeing a pretty picture in a catalogue without knowing whether or not it will be a good long-term investment. The American Rose Society helps to make that investment gilt-edged with a leaflet, "Guide for Buying Roses," revised annually. You can get this mine of information by writing to the Society, 4048 Roselea Place, Columbus, Ohio 43214 and sending a five-cent stamp.

This leaflet indicates the average height of each rose variety (low, medium or tall), the color class (there are sixteen) and whether or not the rose is fragrant. Most important, the Guide gives the national rating of each variety as compiled from reports of member societies in all sections of the country. A point score of 10 means a perfect rose (there is none so far); 9 to 10 means an outstanding variety (we have a few); 8 to 9 means excellent (we have many here); 7 to 8 means a good average rose; 6 to 7 only fair; and 5 to 6 of questionable value. Check the

31

gorgeous pictures in catalogues with the rating list, and, if you are a beginner, start with roses having a score of at least 7.0.

Since 1930, when the first plant patent was granted to the rose New Dawn, many roses have been so protected. The number is over 2400 as I write this, with more being processed each year. Such roses cost a little more because each propagator pays royalty to the holder of the patent. Legally this includes you if you try to root cuttings in your own backyard but the law has not been enforced that strictly. A patent is no guarantee of merit; it merely grants exclusive rights to a breeder or introducer who thinks that particular new rose is worth the cost of getting the patent.

The letters AARS after a rose do indicate merit. They mean that All-America Rose Selections, Inc., an organization of introducers and commercial growers, has selected this rose as outstanding on the basis of pre-introduction tests for at least two years in different parts of the country. In these official test gardens (twenty-four in sixteen states in 1964) roses are judged for novelty, vigor, habit, disease resistance, foliage, floriferousness, bud form, flower form, substance, color when the flower opens, color as it fades, fragrance, and length and sturdiness of stem. Standards are high. Usually two or three roses are selected each year but in 1951 no rose was considered sufficiently worthy and so the judges named the ten best AARS roses introduced up to that date. The All-America Rose Selections thus far are:

1940—Dickson's Red, Flash, The Chief, World's Fair.
1941—Apricot Queen, California, Charlotte Armstrong.
1942—Heart's Desire.
1943—Grand Duchess Charlotte, Mary Margaret McBride.
1944—Fred Edmunds, Katherine T. Marshall, Lowell Thomas, Mme. Chiang Kai-Shek, Mme. Marie Curie.
1945—Floradora, Horace McFarland, Mirandy.
1946—Peace.
1947—Rubaiyat.
1948—Diamond Jubilee, High Noon, Nocturne, Pinkie, San Fernando, Taffeta.
1949—Forty-niner, Tallyho.

1950—Capistrano, Fashion, Mission Bells, Sutter's Gold.

1952—Fred Howard, Helen Traubel, Vogue.

1953—Chrysler Imperial, Ma Perkins.

1954—Lilibet, Mojave.

1955—Jiminy Cricket, Queen Elizabeth, Tiffany.

1956—Circus.

1957—Golden Showers, White Bouquet.

1958—Fusilier, Gold Cup, White Knight.

1959—Ivory Fashion, Starfire.

1960—Garden Party, Fire King, Sarabande.

1961—Duet, Pink Parfait.

1962—Christian Dior, Golden Slippers, John S. Armstrong, King's Ransom.

1963—Royal Highness, Tropicana.

1964—Granada, Saratoga.

1965—Camelot, Mr. Lincoln.

1966—American Heritage, Apricot Nectar, Matterhorn.

Most of these roses have withstood the test of time and are still available; some have fallen by the wayside.

It does not make much difference where your rose is grown provided it is on the right understock for your section and you get it in good condition for your best planting time. I have had equal luck in my gardens with roses from California, Georgia, New Jersey, New York, Ohio, Oregon, Pennsylvania, Rhode Island, and Texas. Even if you buy from a local nursery the rose you select may have been grown for it in some distant state. The environment in which it is produced makes no difference to the inherent hardiness of a variety.

While the *source* of your rose is not important its *grade* and *condition* are very important. The official No. 1 grade calls for three or more 18-inch canes; No. 1½ must have two 15-inch canes; No. 2 should have two 12-inch canes. You may not know the original cane length because the rose is usually cut back before shipping but at least you can count the number of firm canes. Beware of bargains! An advertisement may truthfully say that the roses are two-year, field-grown, budded but neglect to state the grade. It is foolish to buy anything but the best when that is

so inexpensive. Three roses for a dollar are not half as good value as one
$1.50 rose.

Roses grown commercially for outdoor planting are budded onto
an understock. In most eastern and Texas nurseries this is a form of
Multiflora; in California it is usually Shafter (Dr. Huey) or Ragged
Robin (Gloire des Rosomanes); in the South it is occasionally Odorata
and recently, in Florida, it may be Fortuniana. The latter two are not
hardy in the North. Seedlings (preferably) or rooted cuttings of the
understock are planted in spring and grown until summer, when the
bark is slit and a bud of the desired variety, selected from a flowering
shoot, is inserted and tied in place. The next spring the understock is
cut off above the bud. When the latter develops shoots the tips are
pinched off to form well-shaped plants. Bushes are dug and sold that
autumn or stored for spring sales. To the cost of this long-term production, including pesticides to keep the bushes healthy, must be added cold
storage and marketing, as well as years when the land is revitalized
by being planted to cover crops. You are getting full value when you
pay top price for a rose. This price usually includes replacement if the
rose does not bloom the first year even though you may have been at
fault in planting.

Sometimes cheap roses are cutback greenhouse stock that has outlived
its indoor usefulness. I have seen some of these do fairly well in outdoor
gardens but they are a poor risk. Greenhouse roses are grafted, not
budded, and usually on Manetti understock that does not have the same
habit as outdoor roses. Likewise the varieties may not be well suited for
garden culture. Better Times, for instance, is a very popular greenhouse
rose but it has a poor rating as a garden rose.

After you have made up a list of roses from pictures, ratings, and
awards try to see them growing in a public park or municipal rose garden. If such a garden is near you, visit it several times during the season
and choose varieties that put on a good show in your section despite
weather and disease. There are huge rose gardens, like the Park of Roses
at Columbus, Ohio, the International Rose Test Gardens at Portland,
Oregon, the wonderful display at Jackson & Perkins, Newark, New York
and in Hershey, Pennsylvania and fine rose plantings at the various botanical gardens but there are many smaller displays that are well worth

visiting. The public gardens cited below are those listed (in 1964) by All-America Rose Selections as display gardens but they have, for your enjoyment and education, many varieties besides those with the AARS tag.

AARS DISPLAY GARDENS

ARIZONA

Valley Garden Center Municipal Rose Garden, Northwest 15th Avenue at Palm Lane, Phoenix.

CALIFORNIA

Arcadia County Rose Garden, 405 S. Santa Anita Avenue, Arcadia.

Berkeley Municipal Rose Garden, Euclid Avenue and Bayview Place, Berkeley.

Corcoran Memorial Rose Garden, 1702 Whitley Avenue, Corcoran.

Fresno Municipal Rose Garden, Roeding Park, Fresno.

Descanso Gardens, 1418 Descanso Drive, La Canada.

Exposition Park Rose Garden, Los Angeles.

Oakland Municipal Rose Garden, head of Jean Street, Oakland.

White Park Rose Garden, Market Street between 8th and 9th, Riverside.

State Capitol Grounds Rose Garden, 15th and Capitol Avenue, Sacramento.

San Jose Municipal Rose Garden, Dana and Naglee, San Jose.

Huntington Botanical Gardens, 1151 Oxford Road, San Marino.

Santa Barbara Memorial Rose Garden, 700 E. Canon Perdido Street, Santa Barbara.

Visalia Garden Club Public Rose Garden, Tulare County General Hospital, Tulare.

Rose Hills Memorial Park Pageant of Roses Garden, 3900 S. Workman Mill Road, Whittier.

COLORADO

Denver Botanic Gardens, City Park, 18th & Colorado Boulevard, Denver.

Longmont Memorial Rose Garden, Roosevelt Park, Longmont.

CONNECTICUT

Elizabeth Park Rose Garden, Hartford.
Norwich Memorial Rose Garden, Rockwell Street at Judd Road, Norwich.
Hamilton Park Rose Garden, Waterbury.

DISTRICT OF COLUMBIA

Shoreham Hotel Rose Garden, 2500 Calvert Street, N.W., Washington.

GEORGIA

Piedmont Park, Atlanta.
Ida Cason Callaway Gardens, Pine Mountain.

IDAHO

Municipal Rose Garden, Julia Davis Park, Boise.
Caldwell Municipal Rose Garden, North Kimble, Caldwell.
Memorial Rose Garden, Lewiston.
Lakeview Municipal Rose Gardens, Lakeview Park, Nampa.
Rotary Rose Garden, Ross Park, Pocatella.

ILLINOIS

Marquette Park, 3540 W. 71st Street, Chicago.
Gardener's Memorial Garden, 1707 St. John's Avenue, Highland Park.
Cook Memorial Rose Garden, 413 N. Milwaukee Avenue, Libertyville.
Peoria Park District Rose Garden, Glen Oak Park, Peoria.
Sinnissippi Park Sunken Gardens, 1300 N. 2nd Street, Rockford.
Robert B. McCormick Memorial Gardens, McCormick Estate, Wheaton.

INDIANA

Lakeside Rose Garden, 1500 Lake Avenue, Fort Wayne.
International Friendship Gardens, Michigan City.
Munseetown Rose Point, Tuhey Park, Muncie.
E. G. Hill Memorial Garden, Glen Miller Park, Richmond.

Iowa

Iowa State University Rose Gardens, Ames.
Huston Park Rose Garden, 3rd Avenue, S.E. & 15th Street, Cedar Rapids.
Municipal Rose Garden, 236 W. Central Park Avenue, Davenport.
Greenwood Rose Garden, Greenwood Park, 4812 Grand, Des Moines.
Weed Park Memorial Rose Garden, Muscatine.
State Center Rose Garden, State Center.
Waterloo Municipal Rose Garden, 2522 West 4th Street, Waterloo.

Kansas

Kansas State University Rose Garden, Manhattan.
Reinisch Rose Garden, Gage Park, Topeka.

Louisiana

Louisiana State University Rose Test Garden, Department of Horticulture, Baton Rouge.
Municipal Rose Gardens, Bolivar Boulevard, Bienville Plaza, New Orleans.

Michigan

Michigan State University Horticultural Gardens, East Lansing.
Cooley Gardens, Townsend & Main Streets, Lansing.

Minnesota

Minneapolis Municipal Rose Garden, W. 42nd Street & Emerson Avenue S., Minneapolis.

Missouri

Cape Girardeau Rose Display Garden, Capaha Park, Perry Avenue & Parkview Drive, Cape Girardeau.
Kansas City Municipal Rose Garden, 5200 Penn Street, Loose Park, Kansas City.
Missouri Botanic Garden, 2315 Tower Grove Avenue, St. Louis.

MISSISSIPPI

Jackson Municipal Rose Garden, Livingston Park, Jackson.
Mississippi State College Rose Garden, State College.

MONTANA

Missoula Memorial Rose Garden, Sunset Park, Missoula.

NEBRASKA

Lincoln Municipal Rose Garden, 27th & C. Streets, Lincoln.

NEVADA

Reno Municipal Rose Garden, Idlewild Park, Reno.

NEW MEXICO

Community Rose Garden, Lea General Hospital, Hobbs.
Los Alamos Memorial Rose Garden, Community Center, Los Alamos.
Roswell Municipal Rose Garden, Main & 11th, Roswell.

NEW YORK

Cranford Memorial Rose Garden, Brooklyn Botanic Garden, 1000
    Washington Avenue, Brooklyn.
Niagara Frontier Trial Rose Garden, Humboldt Park, Buffalo.
Cornell Rose Garden, Ithaca.
New York Botanical Rose Garden, Bronx Park, New York City.
Municipal Rose Garden, Maplewood Park, Rochester.
Dr. Edmund M. Mills Municipal Rose Garden, Thornden Park, Syra-
    cuse.
Sterling Forest Gardens, Tuxedo.

NORTH CAROLINA

Sunnyside Rose Garden, East Seventh Street, Charlotte.
Raleigh Municipal Rose Garden, Pogue Street, Raleigh.

OHIO

Memorial Rose Garden, Pioneer Street at Goodyear Avenue, Akron.
Ault Park Municipal Rose Garden, Ault Park, Cincinnati.
Columbus Park of Roses, High Street at Acton Road, Columbus.
Ohio State University Rose Garden, Columbus.

OKLAHOMA

Johnstone Park Municipal Rose Garden, City Park, Bartlesville.
Norman Municipal Rose Garden, Main Street and Jones Avenue, Norman.
Municipal Rose Garden, Will Rogers Park, 3500 N.W. 36th Street, Oklahoma City.
Tulsa Municipal Rose Garden, 22nd Street & S. Peoria Avenue, Tulsa.

OREGON

Corvallis Community Rose Garden, Avery Park, Corvallis.
George Owen Park Municipal Rose Garden, Jefferson Street, Eugene.
International Rose Test Gardens, Washington Park, 228 S.W. Wright Avenue, Portland.
Lewis & Clark College Memorial Rose Garden, 0615 S.W. Palatine Road, Portland.

PENNSYLVANIA

Malcolm W. Gross Rose Garden, Allentown.
Hershey Rose Garden, Hershey.
Longwood Gardens, Kennett Square.
Municipal Rose Garden, Buchanan Park, Lancaster.
Renziehausen Park Arboretum, R.D. #1, McKeesport.
Morris Arboretum Rose Garden, 9414 Meadowbrook Avenue, Philadelphia.
Philadelphia Zoological Society Rose Garden, 34th Street & Girard Avenue, Philadelphia.
Mellon Park Rose Garden, Phipps Conservatory, Schenley Park, Pittsburgh.

Pottstown Municipal Rose Garden, High & Rohland Streets, Pottstown.
Reading Municipal Rose Garden, City Park, Reading.
Pennsylvania State University Rose Garden, University Park.

SOUTH CAROLINA

Timrod Park Rose Garden, Timrod Drive, Florence.
Edisto Rose Garden, Edisto Memorial Gardens, Orangeburg.

TENNESSEE

Municipal Rose Garden, Warner Park, Chattanooga.
Memphis Municipal Rose Garden, Audobon Park, Memphis.

TEXAS

City of Amarillo Municipal Rose Garden, Memorial Park, 24th &
Washington Streets, Amarillo.
Corpus Christi Rose Society Garden, Hewitt Estates Park, Corpus
Christi.
Dallas Garden Center, Fair Park, Dallas.
El Paso Municipal Garden, Copia & Aurora Avenue, El Paso.
Fort Worth Botanic Garden, 3220 Botanic Garden Drive, Fort Worth.
Municipal Rose Garden, Civic League Park, W. Beauregard & Park
Street, San Angelo.
Jefferson Gardens, 723 Donaldson Avenue, San Antonio.
Tyler Municipal Rose Garden, Tyler.

UTAH

State House Museum Gardens, Fillmore.
Municipal Memorial Rose Garden, 96 N. 1st Street, East. Nephi.
Provo Municipal Rose Garden, 600 North & 500 West, Provo.
Salt Lake Municipal Rose Garden, 1050 E.S. Temple, Salt Lake City.

VIRGINIA

Arlington Memorial Rose Garden, 16th & N. Edison Streets, Arlington.
Terrace Park, Southwest Museum, Big Stone Gap.
Mountain View Fishburn Garden, 714 13th Street, S.W. Roanoke.

WASHINGTON

Aberdeen Municipal Rose Garden, Samuel Benn Park, Aberdeen.
Cornwall Park Rose Garden, Bellingham.
Fairhaven Park Rose Garden, Bellingham.
Chehalis Municipal Rose Garden, City Hall, Chehalis.
Woodland Park Rose Garden, 700 N. 50th Street, Seattle.
Rose Hill, Manito Park, W. 4-21st, Spokane.
Point Defiance Park Rose Garden, Tacoma.

WEST VIRGINIA

Ritter Park Rose Garden, McCoy Road, Huntington.

WISCONSIN

Alfred L. Boerner Botanical Gardens, Whitnall Park, 5879 S. 92nd
Street, Hales Corners.

CLASSIFICATION OF MODERN ROSES

There are literally *Roses for Every Garden* as Dr. R. C. Allen implies
in the title of his excellent book. If you cannot give your plants the regular
attention most hybrid teas deserve you can still find some roses suited to
your mode of life.

The classification of roses has always been difficult and every attempt at
simplification has resulted in some inconsistencies. The American Rose
Society uses *Modern Roses,* first published in 1930, as a standard reference
in deciding classification problems. This edition of *Anyone Can Grow
Roses* follows *Modern Roses V,* published in 1958.*

Roses are usually separated into two main divisions: Bush Roses, which
are upright, grow without support, and are seldom over 6 feet tall; and
Climbing or Trailing Roses, which produce long canes and require some
sort of support. This sounds simple but there are gradations. Some climbers can be grown as shrub roses and some shrubs act like climbers.

The rose groups or classes recognized in *Modern Roses V* are given

* *Modern Roses 6* was published just as this manuscript went to press.

here alphabetically, together with the abbreviations (in parentheses) used in that book and in the listing of varieties in this chapter.

ALBA (A). Forms of *Rosa alba* or hybrids; fairly vigorous, non-recurrent (without repeat bloom) shrubs with white, blush or delicate pink double flowers with a hyacinth fragrance and large, pitcher-shaped scarlet hips. The leaves are soft gray-green with 5 to 7 rather blunt leaflets. Robust hooked prickles (thorns), usually mixed with bristles, are distributed irregularly over clear green canes; a few forms are thornless. *Rosa alba,* the White or York Rose, is believed to be a natural cross between *R. gallica* and *R. corymbifera.* It is included in Gerard's Herball, published in 1957, and may have been brought to England by the Romans prior to 100 A.D., but there is no evidence before the twelfth century.

BOURBON (B). Descendant of *Rosa borboniana* that came to France from the Isle of Bourbon, a hybrid between *R. chinensis* and a repeat-blooming form of the Damask rose. Shrubs are of varying vigor, mostly recurrent (repeating bloom) with large, well-formed, white, pink, red, or purple flowers, borne individually or in small clusters. The canes are bright green with purple shading. The rather large leaves, with 5 to 7 leaflets, have a purplish edge when young. Souvenir de la Malmaison is probably the best known of this group.

CENTIFOLIA (C). Varieties of the cabbage or "hundred-leaved" rose, *R. centifolia.* This appeared in Holland in the sixteenth century and probably originated there although some claim it was known to the Greek Theophrastus in 300 B.C. The blooms are very double, cupped, fragrant, solitary, on long, slender pedicels.

CHINA (Ch). Derivatives of forms of *Rosa chinensis,* the China rose, the first "perpetual" form to reach the western world. Flowers are 2 inches or more across, crimson or pink, sometimes other colors, not fragrant or slightly so, recurrent, foliage evergreen or partially so. The leaflets are usually 3 to 5 and the prickles are few, usually hooked.

CLIMBER (Cl). As used in *Modern Roses V,* Climber denotes a rose of fairly vigorous growth bearing characteristically large flowers, single, rather than in clusters, and potentially recurrent. Many roses formerly classed as Large-flowered Climbers (LC) are now classed as Large-flowered Ramblers (LR) because they do not repeat. This includes some, like Mrs. Arthur Curtiss James, that are borne singly on old wood. Climbing forms of hybrid teas, polyanthas, and floribundas are classified as the bush type and should be exhibited with these at rose shows.

DAMASK (D). Supposedly varieties of *Rosa damascena,* a gallica hybrid or subspecies of uncertain origin. Flowers are double, very fragrant, red, pink, or white, sometimes striped, usually in clusters. There are two types. The summer Damask, pink to white, blooms but once. The autumn Damask, Rose des Quatre Saisons, blooms again in autumn and is the form used by Roman florists.

EGLANTERIA HYBRIDS (E). Hybrids between *Rosa eglanteria,* the English sweetbrier, and other roses. Bushes are tall, hardy, with foliage scented like apples; flowers are small, single, often pink or peach, sometimes red or white.

FLORIBUNDA (F). Hybrid polyantha, the result of crossing hybrid teas with polyanthas. An immensely popular class, very free-flowering, with relatively large blooms mostly in clusters, hardy, of wide color range, and with heights and styles suited to every purpose.

GALLICA (G). Varieties and hybrids of the French Rose, *Rosa gallica,* mostly compact shrubs of upright growth, moderate height, pink, red, purple or striped flowers, non-recurrent, with a tendency to spread by underground shoots; ancestors of many modern roses.

GRANDIFLORA (Gr). A new class created for roses with the free-flowering habits of the floribundas and the perfection of form of hybrid teas; often taller than hybrid teas with more vigor; flowers borne singly as well as in sprays.

HYBRID MUSK (HMsk). Name given to a class created in England by Pemberton and a similar group originated in Germany by Lambert. The true musk rose, *Rosa moschata,* played only a minor part in the crosses. Vigorous recurrent shrubs of everblooming pillars bear medium to large flowers in many colors; recurrent.

HYBRID PERPETUAL (HP). The result of interbreeding several types, with Damask, Hybrid China and Bourbon roses playing a large part.

The first distinctive varieties were introduced in France in 1837 and called Hybrid Remontant, a better name than Hybrid Perpetual because many varieties do not repeat after their profuse June bloom. Bushes are vigorous, hardy, with tall, upright growth, wrinkled dull green foliage, and large, usually very fragrant flowers that are white, pink, red to deep maroon, but never yellow. Frau Karl Druschki, the most universally beloved rose of this group, has now been reclassified as a hybrid tea.

HYBRID RUGOSA (HRg). Derived from *Rosa rugosa,* very hardy, tall, to 6 feet or more, everblooming habit; distinctly rugose (wrinkled) foliage, shining dark green. The shrubs are especially useful near the seashore and the enormous hips are suitable for preserves. The hybrids may or may not resemble the parent species.

HYBRID TEA (HT). Originally crosses between hybrid perpetuals and teas. La France, generally considered the first such variety, was introduced in 1867 and is still in commerce. In 1900 Pernet-Ducher established a new group of hybrid teas, Pernetiana, by crossing them with the yellow Austrian Brier (*Rosa foetida*) thereby giving us the bold yellow and orange tones that so enhance modern roses, as well as enhancing their susceptibility to blackspot. Hybrid-tea buds are usually long and pointed; the flowers, single, semi-double, or double, are borne singly or few together. They are hardy through most of the United States, requiring some winter protection in the more northern regions. The so-called subzero hybrid teas, introduced by the Brownells in 1939, have *Rosa wichuraiana* blood to increase their hardiness, decrease their susceptibility to blackspot.

KORDESII (K). A new race, first introduced in 1952, stemming from *Rosa kordesii,* a new species resulting from spontaneous doubling of chromosomes in a rugosa hybrid (Max Graf) in the nursery of Wilhelm Kordes in Germany. The hardy climbers or shrubs have large flowers of many colors, borne in clusters, and are dependably recurrent.

LARGE-FLOWERED RAMBLER (LR). See Rambler.

MINIATURE (Min). Fairy roses, mostly descendants of *Rosa chinensis minima.* Flowers are less than an inch across, borne singly or in clusters, mostly of hybrid tea form; bushes are hardy, seldom more than

1 foot high. Miniatures are suitable for rock gardens, edging or sunny windows.

Moss (M). Sports or seedlings of various forms of the Centifolias. They are distinguished by a conspicuous mosslike growth on sepals, calyx, flower stems, and sometimes leaflets. The mossy buds are most attractive and the flowers are fragrant.

Noisette (N). Tender climbing roses, typically cluster-flowering and recurrent. The first Noisette was Champneys Pink Cluster (*Rosa chinensis* × *R. moschata*) raised by John Champneys of Charleston, S.C., given by him to Philip Noisette and introduced by the latter's brother in Europe in 1814. The best known variety of this class is Marechal Niel.

Polyantha (Pol). Originated as hybrids of *Rosa multiflora* and *R. chinensis* but not confined to this parentage. The plants are usually small with large clusters of small "pompom" flowers, chiefly red, orange or pink, seldom fragrant. The bushes are hardy, very recurrent. Of approximately 250 varieties listed in *Modern Roses V* scarcely a dozen can be found in modern catalogues, Margo Koster and Cecile Brunner being most readily available.

Rambler (R). Climbing roses of vigorous but typically lax growth, bearing large clusters of small flowers once a year. Crimson Rambler, introduced from the Orient in 1893, is the most prominent example of a rambler derived from *Rosa multiflora;* Dorothy Perkins, an American hybrid brought out in 1901, is the forerunner of hybrids of *R. wichuraiana.* Both types bloom mostly on new wood produced the previous season and both are very susceptible to powdery mildew.

Other Wichuraiana hybrids are relatively free from powdery mildew and have large flowers. Those that bloom but once are now classified as Large-flowered Ramblers (LR) even though many of them bloom on old wood. Those with recurrent bloom are classed as Climbers (Cl).

Semi-Climber (SeCl). Pillar roses, less vigorous and with shorter canes than typical climbers. Most forms can be trained either as climbers or as shrubs.

SHRUB (S). This is a catch-all group, roses differing from bedding forms but not typically climbers or ramblers. Many species roses and their hybrids are included here.

TEA (T). Pink and yellow forms of *Rosa odorata,* the tea-scented rose brought from China to England in 1810 and 1824. In the South and on the Pacific Coast there is a revival of interest in the old teas for they are very recurrent and grow without much care, being tolerant of blackspot and intolerant of pruning. Although bred for mild moist climates, several are hardy in the North. Flowers are of medium size, without bold colors (soft pink, light red or yellow), profuse through a long season, fragrant, and completely charming.

Tree or standard roses do not form a distinct class but are manufactured from any of several groups. A hybrid tea, hybrid perpetual, floribunda or polyantha is budded at the top of a straight trunk, 2 to 4 feet tall. This trunk, usually *Rosa rugosa,* is often on another understock to prevent suckering. Occasionally more than one variety is budded onto the trunk. Weeping standards are formed by budding Wichuraiana ramblers onto tall Brier trunks.

A FEW GOOD ROSES

Any list of rose varieties is ephemeral. Popular new roses continually replace the old reliables. The nurseryman must be attuned to demand to stay in business and cannot continue to stock varieties for which he has little call. A few nurseries specialize in "old roses" produced a couple of centuries ago but some find roses produced a couple of decades ago are already lost by the wayside. *Modern Roses V* lists 7562 varieties plus 333 species but many of these are included for their historical interest and are not presently available.

The varieties listed here are my personal friends, grown in my own garden, except for a few tender roses known in numerous southern sojourns. So far as I can determine, the list includes only those available from some nurseryman at this writing. The list was made up after perusal of dozens of 1964 catalogues but it is no guarantee that all these varieties will still be sold in future years. In order to have space for some of the better new varieties some of my older friends have had to be omitted, along with those no longer sold.

In each listing the variety name is followed by the abbreviation for the rose class: A for Alba; B—Bourbon; C—Centifolia; Ch—China; Cl—Climber; LCl—Large-flowered Climber; D—Damask; E—Eglanteria; F—Floribunda; G—Gallica; Gr—Grandiflora; HCh—Hybrid China; HMsk—Hybrid Musk; HP—Hybrid Perpetual; HRg—Hybrid Rugosa; R—Rambler; LR—Large-flowered Rambler; S—Shrub; SeCl—Semi-Climber; T—Tea.

Following the type the color group is given according to the American Rose Society classification and then the ARS national rating, where one has been given. An asterisk (*) indicates a new rose whose rating may change. Roses honored with an AARS award are so indicated. In parentheses are given the name of the breeder or originator, the U.S. firm introducing the rose, the date of introduction, and the patent number for roses so protected.

Many of the introducing firms are included in the list of Nurseries Specializing in Roses (see p. 89). If your local nursery does not stock a rose you may be able to purchase it from the introducing firm. In a few cases of hard-to-get roses I have indicated possible sources. You may always call on the American Rose Society for help. If you are interested in heredity and want to know the parentage of rose varieties or if you are a cytologist interested in chromosome numbers, consult *Modern Roses 6*.

AGNES. S. Medium yellow, 7.4. (Saunders, 1900; int. Central Exp. Farm, 1922.) Hybrid rugosa shrub, 6 feet or more, covered with coppery yellow buds and large, creamy yellow, very fragrant flowers; profuse bloom for a month, starting in mid or late May; foliage light, wrinkled, pest-free except for aphids; very hardy.

ALOHA. Cl.HT. Medium pink, 6.3. (Boerner; int. Jackson & Perkins, 1949; Pat. 948.) A truly everblooming pillar, with cupped, fragrant, rose-pink flowers, deeper on the reverse side. I rate this higher than the ARS 6.3.

AMERICAN BEAUTY. HT. Light red, 7.2. (Ledechaux, 1875.) The most famous greenhouse rose of yesterday, usually classed as a hybrid perpetual; very large, cupped, rose-red to shaded carmine, very fragrant, with some recurrent bloom; long stems. This is still available as a garden rose. Climbing American Beauty has the bush form as one of its parents but is not recurrent.

AMERICAN HERITAGE. HT. Yellow blend. AARS 1966. (Lammerts; int. Germain's, 1965.) Creamy yellow, tinted with scarlet, vermilion and crimson; many petals. Leaves have red markings.

ANGELS MATEU. HT. Apricot blend, 7.4. (P. Dot; int. Conard-Pyle, 1934; Pat. 174, expired.) Double, globular flower in an exciting orange-rose color, raspberry fragrance; abundant bloom; fine for garden display.

APRICOT NECTAR. F. Apricot blend. AARS 1966. (Boerner; int. Jackson & Perkins, 1965.) A worthy descendant of Spartan, with soft apricot blooms 4 to 5 inches across; dark green, disease-resistant foliage; medium height.

AZTEC. HT. Orange red, 7.6. (Swim; int. Armstrong Nurseries, 1957; Pat. 1648.) Stunning orange-scarlet flower, large, double, high-centered, fragrant; glossy, leathery foliage.

BABY BETSY McCALL. Min. Light pink, 8.2*. (Morey; int. Jackson & Perkins, 1960; Pat. 1984.) Small, ovoid bud, double pearl-pink blooms, several together, slightly fragrant, lasting well, fairly continuous. One of my favorite miniatures.

BABY GOLD STAR. Min. Deep yellow, 7.1. (P. Dot; int. Conard-Pyle, 1940; Pat. 407, expired.) Semidouble golden yellow flowers; plant rather large for the class.

BABY MASQUERADE. Min. Red blend, 8.1. (Tantau; int. Jackson & Perkins, 1956; Pat. 1580.) Adorable product of Masquerade × Tom Thumb and exactly like its full-size parent in coloring—yellow, red, pink; flowers double, to 1½ inches; plants tall, to 20 inches; free recurrent bloom. Fun to have indoors or out.

BANZAI. HT. Red blend, 7.6*. (Mme. M. L. Meilland; int. Conard-Pyle, 1961; Pat. 2142.) Rose red to deep pink with cream at extreme base of petals; borne in flattish clusters like a floribunda; continuous bloom.

This plant is fine for a hedge and garden display, also for low-bowl arrangements indoors. The large, double, flat-centered flowers have a luminous quality. This is a different rose, well worth trying.

BARONESS HENRIETTE SNOY. T. (Bernaix, 1897.) Pointed buds, large double flowers, peach-pink shaded cream, with carmine-pink reverse; vigorous, disease-free bush; free bloom.

BARONESS ROTHSCHILD. HP. Medium pink. (Pernet, 1868.) Very large, double, cupped, soft rose flowers; profuse in June, sometimes recurring through the summer. Tall, vigorous, hardy bush.

BELINDA. HMsk. Light pink, 7.8. (Bentall, 1936.) Very large, soft pink to rose clusters of small, fragrant flowers on a tall bush that may spread to 6 feet. Fair recurrent bloom; attractive foliage.

BELLE PORTUGAISE (Belle of Portugal). LR. Light pink. (Cayeux, 1903.) Very vigorous climber with prolonged and profuse spring bloom. Flowers are large, 4 to 6 inches across, semidouble, flesh pink; foliage is glossy. Supposedly not hardy in the North but I have seen a bush near Roanoke, Virginia, where the winters are often cold, covering the side of a house with canes as big as my arm. Almost naturalized in California.

BETSY MCCALL. F. Medium pink, 7.5. (Boerner; int. Jackson & Perkins, 1956; Pat. 1603.) Reminiscent of its Fashion parent but restrained; appropriately named for a paper doll.

BETTY PRIOR. F. Medium pink, 9.0. (Prior; int. Jackson & Perkins, 1938; Pat. 340, expired.) A most desirable, almost foolproof rose. Very tall, to 6 feet or more, vigorous; pointed bud carmine, single flower like a pink dogwood but reverse of petals deeper pink; profuse continuous bloom to late autumn, in loose clusters. Mildew tolerant and seldom requiring spraying, this rose is excellent for a hedge, specimen shrub, or for color against background evergreens. Allow plenty of room, 4 feet or so, between bushes.

BLANCHE MALLERIN. HT. White, 7.1. (Mallerin; int. Conard-Pyle, 1941; Pat. 594, expired.) Large, full, satiny-white, fragrant flowers from long-pointed buds on good plants.

BLAZE. Cl. Medium red, 8.1. (Kallay; int. Jackson & Perkins, 1932; Pat. 10, expired.) A Paul's Scarlet with good repeat bloom but not literally everblooming. Brilliant, vigorous, deservedly popular.

BLITHE SPIRIT. HT. Light pink. (David Armstrong & H. C. Swim; int. Armstrong Nurseries, 1965.) Cheerful bright pink blooms, not too double, on long stems on a tall plant.

BLOSSOMTIME. SeCl. Medium pink, 8.3. (O'Neal; int. Bosley Nursery, 1951; Pat. 1240.) Enchanting flower of hybrid tea form, deeper pink on the outside, fragrant; moderate climber or shrub; good recurrent bloom.

BUCCANEER. Gr. Medium yellow, 7.3. (Swim; int. Armstrong Nurseries, 1952; Pat. 1119.) The double fragrant flower is a wonderfully bright, non-fading buttercup yellow but the bush is too tall and willowy for me.

BURNABY. HT. Light yellow, 8.1. (Eddie; int. Peterson & Dering, 1954; Pat. 1314.) Large, high-centered pale yellow to cream (although classed now as white) flower on long stem; exhibition type; moderate bloom. This rose seems to do best in the West Coast but thrives in some eastern gardens.

CAMELOT. Gr. Light pink. AARS 1965. (Swim & Weeks; int. Conard-Pyle, 1964; Pat. 2371.) Luminous coral-pink, large, to 5 inches, flowers, blooming singly or two or three on a stem; strong plant; shiny dark green leaves.

CANDY STRIPE. HT. Pink blend, 7.5. (Edward McCummings; int. Conard-Pyle, 1963; Pat. 2278.) Delicious sport of Pink Peace, bright pink, striped like peppermint candy, large, fully double, fragrant, most attractive; upright bush; good foliage; rather free blooming.

CAPRI. F. Orange red, 7.4*. (Gladys Fisher; int. Melvin E. Wyant, 1960; Pat. 1453.) Coral to pink double flowers, 3-inch, fragrant; profuse bloom; glossy foliage; vigorous plant.

CARROUSEL. Gr. Dark red, 9.0. ARS Gold Medal 1956. (Duehrsen; int. Elmer Roses, 1950; Pat. 1066.) Striking red flowers, similar to hybrid teas but produced more profusely on a taller bush.

Cecil. HT. Medium yellow. (B. R. Cant, 1926.) Large (4-inch), single (5 petals) shining gold stars on a medium low bush with dark green glossy foliage. Still offered by Tillotson's.

Cecile Brunner, the original Sweetheart Rose. Pol. Light pink, 7.7. (Vve. Ducher; int. Pernet-Ducher, 1881.) A tea-polyantha growing vigorously to 3 feet in the South, rather dwarf in the North. Small, exquisite pink buds and double flowers with a yellow base; fine for corsages. Climbing Cecile Brunner bears a profusion of pink flowers in clusters in mild climates.

Charlotte Armstrong. HT. Light red and deep pink, 9.0. AARS 1941. (Lammerts; int. Armstrong Nurseries, 1940; Pat. 455, expired.) A marvelous rose and parent of many other good roses. The color is variable, more deep rose than red. The bud is long, flower very large, to 6 inches across, double, fragrant, on long stem; bush tall, 4 to 5 feet, free flowering. An exhibition rose, good in all parts of the country.

Cherokee Rose. See *Rosa laevigata*.

Chicago Peace. HT. Pink blend, 8.0*. (S. C. Johnson; int. Conard-Pyle, 1962; Pat. 2037.) A sport of Peace and even better, with deeper coloring, more substance, the same excellent foliage and nearly continuous bloom on a vigorous bush. A must for every garden; the bud is unbelievably perfect and the huge open flower lasts well, fades gracefully.

Christian Dior. HT. Medium red, 7.7*. AARS 1962. (Francis Meilland; int. Conard-Pyle, 1961; Pat. 1943.) Large, double, high-centered, crimson-red, fragrant flower; vigorous upright plant with few thorns; fairly continuous bloom. Somewhat subject to mildew and not quite so good in humid coastal areas; performs well in the South and Southwest.

Christopher Stone. HT. Medium red, 8.1. (H. Robinson; int. Conard-Pyle, 1936.) A fine bright scarlet that keeps producing in hot summers; good form, 35 petals, showing golden stamens when open; damask fragrance; sturdy bush.

Chrysler Imperial. HT. Dark red, 8.8. AARS 1953. (Lammerts; int. Germain, 1952; Pat. 1167.) Bud long, tapering; flower large, double, high-centered, crimson red, very fragrant, fine for exhibition; foliage large, dark, semiglossy; sturdy bush.

CIRCUS. F. Yellow blend, 7.8. AARS 1956. (Swim; int. Armstrong Nurseries, 1956; Pat. 1382.) Large clusters of yellow flowers marked pink, salmon, and scarlet on a medium low bush with semiglossy foliage.

CITY OF YORK. LR. White, 8.6. ARS Gold Medal, 1950. (Tantau; int. Conard-Pyle, 1945.) Pale yellow buds and large semidouble, cupped, creamy white flowers with most attractive yellow stamens, in clusters of 7 to 15; extremely fragrant and producing a tremendous amount of bloom; very vigorous with handsome glossy foliage. I still consider this the finest white rose I have ever grown or seen and cannot understand why sales were so low the introducers soon dropped it from their list. It does take room, spreading 20 feet or more, but it can be used as a ground cover as well as over fences and makes a fine green background that never has to be sprayed. The memory of its marvelous June burst more than makes up for lack of repeat bloom, but sometimes you get a bonus. I write this in September and my bush has five laterals in good flower at the moment. City of York was the most photographed rose in my New Jersey garden and so is the one planted here at Springvale. It is still available (1964) from Earl Ferris, Roy Hennessey, J. J. Kern, Ilgenfritz, and Thomasville. And I am happy to announce that Conard-Pyle has reconsidered its rejection and is now budding for 1965 sales.

CLAIR MATIN. Cl. Medium pink. (Mme. M. L. Meilland; int. Conard-Pyle, 1963; Pat. 2186.) A graceful climber reminiscent of Clytemnestra in its clusters of small flowers, pink with a tinge of buff. There is a delightful sweetbrier fragrance and repeat bloom through the summer. The foliage is excellent, glossy dark green, bronzy when young, but there is some tendency to mildew.

CLYTEMNESTRA. HMsk. Light pink. (Pemberton, 1915.) A low pillar or climbing rose, to 4 or 5 feet, good for fences and walls. Coppery buds open to small, ruffled, buff-pink flowers; recurrent bloom enhanced by glossy foliage. The planting around the large pool at the Brooklyn Botanic Garden, particularly lovely in September, made me acquire this for my own garden. Listed by Hennessey and Kern.

Cocorico. F. Orange red, 8.4. (F. Meilland; int. Conard-Pyle, 1953; Pat.
1193.) Bright orange-red flowers, 2½ to 3 inches with 5 to 9 petals,
holding color in hot weather; bush upright, foliage glossy.

Columbus Queen. HT. Medium pink, 7.7*. (D. L. Armstrong & H. C.
Swim; int. Armstrong Nurseries, 1962; Pat. 2170.) Long-pointed
urn-shaped buds, light pink flowers with darker reverse and long, thorny
stems; tall bush.

Comtesse Vandal (Countess Vandal). HT. Pink blend, 7.5. (M. Leen-
ders; int. Jackson & Perkins, 1932; Pat. 38, expired.) An old favorite
of fine exhibition form; orange-copper tapering buds open to large, high-
centered flowers (30 petals), pink to salmon with a gold base; fragrant.

Condesa de Sastago. HT. Orange blend, 7.4. (P. Dot; int. Conard-Pyle,
1932.) Another fine old rose, often as tall and vigorous as Peace with
the same large, glossy dark green foliage. Distinctly a bicolor when opening, with rich gold on the reverse of copper-red petals, it changes with
the seasons and with age to almost raspberry pink; nearly continuous
bloom in summer; attaining great size in autumn.

Confidence. HT. Pink blend, 8.3. (F. Meilland; int. Conard-Pyle, 1953;
Pat. 1192.) A beautiful pastel exhibition and garden rose; large buds,
opening to 6-inch flowers, fragrant, high-centered, very light pink tinged
with yellow and white; produced freely on long stems on a vigorous bush.
A few June blooms may be marred by thrips.

County Fair. F. Medium pink, 7.5*. (Swim; int. Armstrong Nurseries,
1960; Pat. 1897.) My favorite for a low pink hedge; flowers nearly
single, glowing pink with yellow stamens; charming long-pointed buds.
An inexpensive rose, sold on its own roots for hedge use. Said to be good
in semi-arid regions although susceptible to rust.

Crimson Duke. HT. Medium red, 7.4. (Alain Meilland; int. Conard-
Pyle, 1963.) Large, double, high-centered fragrant bloom; upright
bush, large leathery foliage.

Crimson Glory. HT. Dark red, 9.1. (Kordes; int. Dreer and Jackson &
Perkins, 1935; Pat. 105, expired.) Long the most popular red rose in

America. The dark red, very velvety, wonderfully fragrant flowers have perfect form, do not blue with age nor fade in summer sun. The bush is vigorous but spreading, often wider than tall, so give it enough space.

CRIMSON ROSETTE. F. Dark red, 7.8. (Krebs; int. Howard & Smith, 1948; Pat. 901.) Clusters of dark crimson, rather small double flowers, flat like a rosette; a decorative garden form.

CROWN JEWEL. F. Orange red. (Boerner; int. Jackson & Perkins, 1964.) A floribunda to rival Spartan; I have been entranced the two seasons I have had it under test. The orange-red color is soft, not harsh, with a coral tone. Ovoid buds open to flat, very double, 3½-inch flowers, long-lasting, slightly fragrant, still pleasing in old age; borne singly or in clusters. Good dark green foliage on a vigorous bush, 3 to 4 feet.

CURLY PINK. HT. Medium pink, 7.8. (Brownell, 1948; Pat. 842.) The best of the subzeros that I have tried. A very double two-toned pink, with pale inner surface recurved over the deeper pink reverse; of good form and size throughout the summer. Fine for arrangements; try it in a soft blue vase. Allow more space for this bush than for the average hybrid tea.

DAINTY BESS. HT. Light pink, 8.4. (Archer, 1925.) A large single rose, 5 petals, soft rose-pink with prominent wine-colored stamens. The pointed buds and dainty flowers are charming for arrangements; often a winner at shows.

DIAN. Min. Light red & deep pink, 7.9. (Moore, int. Sequoia Nursery, 1957; Pat. 1808.) Double, soft red, slightly fragrant flowers; small, dark glossy foliage; bush to 15 inches.

DONALD PRIOR. F. Medium red, 8.3. (Prior; int. Jackson & Perkins, 1938; Pat. 377, expired.) A fine bedding rose, half as tall as Betty Prior; large, semidouble, scarlet-crimson flowers in large clusters; damask fragrance; continuous bloom.

DON JUAN. Cl. Dark red, 8.1. (Malandrone; int. Jackson & Perkins, 1958; Pat. 1864.) Flowers very large, double, cupped, velvety dark red, fragrant and very long lasting; recurrent bloom. Foliage dark, glossy; height 8 to 10 feet.

DR. J. H. NICOLAS. Cl. Medium pink, 7.1. (Nicolas; int. Jackson & Perkins, 1940; Pat. 457, expired.) In the right location, full sun with room to spread many feet horizontally, this climber is literally everblooming, covered with hundreds of very large (5-inch) rose-pink flowers all summer. In semishade, Dr. Nicolas by no means fulfills its potentialities.

DR. W. VAN FLEET. LR. Light pink, 8.7. (Van Fleet; int. Peter Henderson, 1910.) A hardy, vigorous climber to 20 feet, that can be planted and forgotten. The dark glossy foliage seldom requires spraying (unless leafhoppers or rose-slugs are too abundant). Profuse June bloom on old wood; flowers soft flesh-pink, of hybrid tea form on long stems, slightly fragrant.

DREAM GIRL. SeCl. Pink blend, 7.3. (Jacobus; int. Bobbink & Atkins, 1944; Pat. 643, expired.) Everblooming climber or pillar of moderate habit but good succession of bloom; flowers pinkish in hot weather but developing lovely salmon, peach or apricot tones when it is cool; spicy fragrance; shiny disease-resistant foliage that seldom requires spraying. Listed by Tillotson's.

DUCHESSE DE BRABANT. T. Light pink. (Bernede, 1857.) Still beloved after more than a century and hardy in the North even though a Tea. Pearly pink to rose, cupped, double, fragrant blooms. Tillotson's also lists a white form.

DUET. HT. Medium pink, 7.9*. AARS 1961. (Swim; int. Armstrong Nurseries, 1960; Pat. 1903.) Pink, with dark pink or light red on the reverse, 4½-inch, open flower, long lasting, on long stems; an excellent garden decorative. The bush is tall, to 5 feet or more, the foliage leathery dark green.

DUQUESA DE PENARANDA. HT. Orange blend, 7.2. (P. Dot; int. Conard-Pyle, 1931.) Another old favorite I cannot bear to omit from this list. Striking orange bud, very large cinnamon-peach flower; rich green glossy leaves.

ECLIPSE. HT. Medium yellow, 8.1. (Nicolas; int. Jackson & Perkins, 1935; Pat. 172, expired.) Named because it first bloomed on Eclipse Day, August 31, 1932. Distinguished by a remarkably long gold bud, which opens to a large rich yellow, somewhat fragrant flower.

EDITOR McFARLAND. HT. Medium pink, 7.1. (Mallerin; int. Conard-Pyle, 1931.) Not a great favorite in the North, this old reliable does particularly well in the South where it has the endurance of Radiance and large, bright pink flowers. A light pink sport is offered by Thomasville Nurseries.

ELEANOR. Min. Pink blend, 7.9*. (Moore; int. Sequoia Nursery, 1960; Pat. 2175.) Small, double, pink with coral blooms.

EL CAPITAN. Gr. Medium red, 8.0*. (Swim; int. Armstrong Nurseries, 1959; Pat. 1796.) Fiery red, velvety flowers on long stems; plant vigorous, well-branched.

ELSE POULSEN. F. Medium pink, 8.3. (S. Poulsen, 1924.) One of my best friends, lovely from the time bronzy leaves appear with daffodils in April until snow in December. Else is wonderful as a hedge or against evergreens. She can be pruned to 3 feet but her natural height is about 5 feet. Pointed deep rose buds, in clusters, open to semidouble, clear pink flowers. The bronzy new foliage is somewhat subject to mildew.

EMILY. HT. Light pink, 7.3*. (Baines; int. F. Cant, 1949, Tillotson's, 1958.) Large, exhibition type silvery pink buds and high-centered flower. Said to have a tendency to split or ball but most of my blooms are perfect, on long stems.

ETOILE DE HOLLANDE. HT. Medium red, 8.1. (Verschuren, 1919.) This Dutch favorite still performs well in most parts of the country and especially in the South where some newer reds fail. The bright, very fragrant flowers start earlier than other reds and make a fine mass display. The bush has moderate vigor; the foliage is rather thin.

FASHION. F. Pink blend, 9.0. AARS 1950. ARS Gold Medal 1954. (Boerner; int. Jackson & Perkins, 1949; Pat. 789.) Starting a new color in roses, clusters of lively coral-peach flowers, 3 to 3½ inches, slightly fragrant, in great bursts of bloom on sturdy bushes, 4 to 5 feet wide and tall. One of the best floribundas but I do not recommend it next to clear pink.

FASHIONETTE. F. Pink blend, 7.6. (Boerner; int. Jackson & Perkins, 1958; Pat. 1563.) A darling rose, color of Fashion but more like a hybrid tea in shape, on a more restrained bush. Good for cutting and for corsages.

FIRE KING. F. Orange red, 7.8*. AARS 1960. (Meilland; int. Conard-Pyle, 1959; Pat. 1758.) Flowers double, 2 to 3 inches, bright vermilion red, in clusters on an upright bush. This is a striking garden decorative where the color is appropriate. Almost continuous blooms, flowers appearing somewhat burnt on aging.

FIRST LOVE. HT. Light pink, 8.0. (Swim; int. Armstrong Nurseries, 1951; Pat. 921.) I fell in love with this rose when it was just a number and I couldn't agree more with its name. The delicate, two-toned pink recurved pointed petals with silvery sheen express exactly the charm of a young girl ready for her first dance. The buds, borne singly on long stems, are particularly distinctive. The bush is tall, somewhat spreading; the bloom is nearly continuous.

FLORADORA. F. Orange red, 8.2. AARS 1945. (Tantau; int. Conard-Pyle, 1944.) The indescribable color, listed as cinnabar-red, and the swirling petals reminiscent of the Floradora Sextette, make every visitor stop to exclaim. An upright bush, 3 to 4 feet, with fine shiny foliage.

FRAU KARL DRUSCHKI. HP. White, 8.0. (Lambert, 1901.) Long hailed as the finest hybrid perpetual, then classed as a hybrid tea because of its parentage. But don't, for heaven's sake, plant it with other hybrid teas; it is a rampant grower that has to be cut back several times a season to keep it in bounds and to encourage repeat bloom. My Springvale bush, only 2 years old as I write this, is 5 feet high and wide. It had 100 blooms at once in June, a few at a time ever since. The large flowers have perfect form and this variety often has been best in show. The buds are tinged with pink but open into snow-white blooms.

FRAU DAGMAR HARTOPP. HRg. Light pink, 8.0. A fine, 2- to 4-foot shrub with crinkled, rich green foliage. The single satiny pink flowers (5 petals) start in May and repeat all summer. The hips are large, deep red.

FRENSHAM. F. Dark red, 8.6. AARS Gold Medal 1955 (Norman; int. Conard-Pyle, 1949.) Large trusses of deep scarlet, semidouble flowers,

3 inches across; vigorous bush to 4 or 5 feet; foliage somewhat subject to mildew.

FROLIC. F. Medium pink, 7.9. (Swim; int. Armstrong Nurseries, 1953; Pat. 1179.) Continuous profuse bloom; flowers double, to 3 inches, bright clear pink, in large sprays; vigorous tall bush.

FRÜHLINGSMORGEN. S. Pink blend, 8.7. (Kordes, 1942.) A lovely spring-blooming shrub, starting in early May with fragrant, 4-inch single flowers (5 petals), yellowish, edged with pink and having a lavender cast; maroon stamens. The blue-green foliage on arching stems (to 8 feet) is handsome all summer and the brilliant red fruits look just like crabapples.

FUSILIER. F. Orange red, 7.8. AARS 1958. (Morey; int. Jackson & Perkins, 1957; Pat. 1709.) Clusters of vivid scarlet-orange, double, somewhat globular flowers, 3 to 3½ inches across, on a medium bush; dark, glossy foliage.

GAIL BORDEN. HT. Pink blend, 7.6. (Kordes; int. Jackson & Perkins, 1957; Pat. 1618.) Bud ovoid, orange-yellow; flower very large, double (50 to 55 petals) high-centered, firm, rose-pink with reverse gold, on long strong stem; somewhat fragrant; vigorous bush with heavy foliage like Peace.

GARDEN PARTY. HT. Yellow blend, 7.9*. AARS 1960. (Swim; int. Armstrong, 1959; Pat. 1814.) Almost white, flushed with pink and gold, exhibition form on long stems; abundant almost continuous bloom; tall, vigorous bush. I would personally rate Garden Party at least 9.0 from its performance at Springvale but it does have some tendency to mildew and apparently is less desirable on the West Coast.

GARNETTE. F. Dark red, 7.8. (Tantau; int. Jackson & Perkins, 1951.) Small, double, garnet-red flowers in clusters, very long-lasting when cut; medium bush; good dark foliage. A favorite rose from the florist, almost as good in the garden.

GENERAL JACQUEMINOT (General Jack, Jack Rose.) HP. Medium red, 7.8. (Roussel, 1853). A clear, intensely red, very fragrant flower, not too double, on a strong stem; large, dark green foliage; occasional repeat bloom. A rose famed in song and story and still the standard for its class; ancestor of many red hybrid teas.

GERANIUM RED. F. Orange red, 7.2. (Boerner; int. Jackson & Perkins, 1947; Pat. 811.) An unusual floribunda in its striking likeness to a geranium in color, form and pronounced odor, which some consider a repellant for Japanese beetles. The double flowers, to 4 inches, should be cut promptly as they fade, otherwise the bush is rather unsightly.

GINGER. F. Orange red, 8.0*. (Boerner; int. Jackson & Perkins, 1962; Pat. 2293.) An excellent result of crossing Garnette and Spartan seedlings. The orange vermilion, 4-inch blooms often cover a vigorous bush, 3 feet or more high and wide. They are fragrant, to boot.

GOLD CUP. F. Deep yellow, 7.1. AARS 1958. (Boerner; int. Jackson & Perkins, 1957; Pat. 1683.) Golden yellow clusters of large, double flowers, somewhat fragrant; fine dark, glossy foliage.

GOLDEN CLIMBER. See Mrs. Arthur Curtiss James.

GOLDEN FLEECE. F. Medium yellow, 7.3. (Boerner; int. Jackson & Perkins, 1955; Pat. 1512.) Large, 4½-inch, fragrant, cupped, buff-yellow flowers in clusters up to 20. No longer offered by the introducer but listed by Tillotson's.

GOLDEN GIRL. Gr. Medium yellow, 7.4*. (Meilland; int. Conard-Pyle, 1959.) Pointed buds, large, high-centered, golden yellow double flowers, usually borne singly on long stems on a bushy plant. Much like a hybrid tea but with more bloom; a highly satisfactory rose.

GOLDEN SHOWERS. LCl. Medium yellow, 7.4. AARS 1957. (Lammerts; int. Germain, 1956; Pat. 1557.) Charming pointed buds and large (4-inch) double daffodil-yellow, fragrant flowers produced singly or in clusters. Good recurrent bloom and very attractive shiny foliage; can be used as a pillar or climber or trained as a shrub. I rate this much higher than the ARS 7.4.

GOLDEN WINGS. HT. Medium yellow, 8.5. (Shepherd; int. Bosley Nursery, 1956; Pat. 1419.) A wonderful rose, most desirable for a specimen shrub or a tall and spreading hedge but *never* to be planted with other hybrid teas; it grows 5 to 6 feet tall and just as wide, covered with single, 5-petaled flowers. They resemble those of Mermaid, pale sulfur yellow with prominent stamens but the foliage is dull rather than glossy. The bush is extremely hardy, without the slightest dying back even in severe winters (around New York).

GOLDEN SLIPPERS. F. Yellow blend, 7.2*. AARS 1962. (Von Abrams; int. Peterson & Dering, 1961.) Brilliant orange luminescent flowers, described as Indian yellow outside, flecked with vermilion inside, 3½ inches across, opening from charming red and gold buds. The bush is supposed to be low and compact but my two are 3½ feet high, nearly as wide.

GOLDILOCKS. F. Medium yellow, 7.3. (Boerner; int. Jackson & Perkins, 1945; Pat. 672, expired.) A fine bedding rose or for a hedge; clear yellow, slightly fragrant flowers of good form in clusters; continuous bloom on a vigorous bush, of medium height, with leathery, glossy foliage. The climbing form is also good.

GOOD NEWS. HT. Pink blend, 8.0. (Meilland; int. Conard-Pyle, 1940; Pat. 426, expired.) Very large double flower, silvery pink with apricot glow in center, color deepening in cool weather; vigorous upright bush. A fine exhibition rose, especially for autumn shows when there is less chance of thrips marring its perfection.

GRANADA. HT. Pink blend, 7.8*. AARS 1964. (Lindquist; int. Howard Rose Co., 1963; Pat. 2214.) Luminous multicolored flowers, in shades of rose with yellow at base; medium-sized—4 to 5 inches, open, with 18 to 25 petals; borne singly and in clusters; fragrant from its Tiffany parent. Vigorous upright growth; free blooming.

GRAND DUCHESS CHARLOTTE. HT. Medium red, 8.1. AARS 1943. (Ketten; int. Conard-Pyle, 1942; Pat. 774, expired.) A fine upstanding rose whose buds have been called chestnut and burnt carmine and flowers tomato red and begonia rose. All I know is that it is a very good rose of a gay and appealing off-red shade.

GRAND OPERA. H.T. Pink blend 7.5*. (Schwartz; int. Melvin Wyant, 1964.) A cross of Peace with Masquerade resulting in 4- to 5-inch cream-colored blooms edged with pink and turning pink with age; intermittent bloom.

GRUSS AN AACHEN. F. Light pink, 7.3. (Geduldig, 1909.) Double flowers, 3½ inches, flesh-pink fading to nearly white; profuse bloom on a rather low but vigorous bush. Despite its age this rose can hold its own with the newer floribundas.

GRUSS AN TEPLITZ. HT. Red, 7.1. (Geschind; int. P. Lambert, 1897.) Rather small, double flowers, crimson with darker edges, spicy fragrance, produced continuously on a tall (to 6 feet) bush; good for hedges.

HARISON'S YELLOW. S. Medium yellow. (Harrison, 1830). A brier rose, with small, bright yellow double flowers, fragrant, covering long canes; profuse spring bloom; vigorous bush to 6 feet; may be injured by certain sprays.

HAWAII. HT. Orange red, 7.5. (Boerner; int. Jackson & Perkins, 1960; Pat. 1823.) A glorious rose in color and form, resembling a sunburst; fragrant; glossy foliage.

HEAT WAVE. F. Orange red, 7.8. (Swim; int. Armstrong Nurseries, 1958; Pat. 1786.) Large, bright, Chinese red, double, cupped to open flowers, holding color in summer heat; dark, semiglossy foliage.

HECTOR DEANE. HT. Red blend, 7.5. (McGredy; int. Jackson & Perkins, 1938; Pat. 361, expired.) Extremely fragrant flowers, orange-carmine-salmon-pink, freely borne on long stems on a vigorous bush. Hard to find but still listed by J. J. Kern. Try it for fragrance.

HEINRICH MÜNCH. HT or HP. Medium pink. (W. Hinner; int. Münch & Haufe, 1911.) Typical large HP bush although classed HT in *Modern Roses V*. Flowers, very large, very double, very fragrant, delicate pink; some repeat bloom.

HELENE SCHOEN. HT. Medium red, 7.5*. (Von Abrams; int. Peterson & Dering, 1962.) A beautiful rose to honor the first woman president of the American Rose Society. Full, high-centered, 6-inch, rich red blooms on long strong stems; vigorous upright bush.

HELEN HAYES. HT. Yellow blend, 7.0. (Brownell, 1956; Pat. 1509.) Tall, vigorous bush covered with large, high-centered, fragrant double flowers, yellow splashed with orange and pink; glossy foliage.

HELEN TRAUBEL. HT. Pink blend, 8.7. AARS 1952. (Swim; int. Armstrong Nurseries, 1951; Pat. 1028.) This bush has everything! Vigorous, spreading, with long graceful stems; beautiful pointed buds ripening to large apricot-pink flowers, 20 to 25 petals, color varying with the weather.

HENRY NEVARD. HP. Medium red, 8.1. (F. Cant, 1924.) Truly fragrant, very red (crimson-scarlet) large, double flowers; dark, glossy leaves; sturdy, tall bush with fair recurrent bloom. If you have room for but one hybrid perpetual, this is it.

HIGH NOON. ClHT. Medium yellow, 7.9. Regional AARS 1948. (Lammerts; int. Armstrong Nurseries, 1947; Pat. 704.) Pillar rose, to 8 feet, best in mild climates but hardy in New Jersey; clear, shining yellow buds and flowers on nearly thornless stems; recurrent bloom.

INDEPENDENCE. F. Orange red, 8.0. (Kordes; int. Jackson & Perkins, 1951; Pat. 1036.) A glorious rose, flowers of hybrid tea form and size, firecracker red, in clusters; vigorous bush, to 4 feet; glossy foliage, bronzered when young. Cut off the fading flowers that detract from the bright scarlet of fresh petals.

INDIANA. HT. Medium red. (Alain Meilland; int. Conard-Pyle, 1965.) I have grown this fine rose under number for two years and must include it, even in advance of formal introduction. The rich red flowers are fully double, 5 to 6 inches across, still attractive when full-blown. The bush is vigorous, 3 to 4 feet, with large, dark green foliage.

INSPIRATION. Cl. Medium pink, 7.6. (Jacobus; int. Bobbink & Atkins, 1946.) Large, semidouble, fragrant pink flowers in loose clusters; recurrent bloom; moderate growth for pillar or trellis; hardy.

IVORY FASHION. F. White, 8.0. AARS 1959. (Boerner; int. Jackson & Perkins, 1958; Pat. 1688.) Ovoid ivory bud, very large white flowers (to 4½ inches), semidouble (15 to 18 petals) produced occasionally singly but more often in spectacular clusters; upright vigorous bush with fine leathery foliage. A truly distinguished rose almost never out-of-bloom.

INVITATION. HT. Apricot blend, 7.6*. (Swim; int. Conard-Pyle, 1961; Pat.
    2018.) A truly fragrant rose of exhibition form, salmon-pink with
base of petals yellow; upright bush; leathery, glossy foliage.

JIMINY CRICKET. F. Orange blend, 7.6. AARS 1955. (Boerner; int. Jack-
    son & Perkins, 1954; Pat. 1346.) Tangerine buds, coral-orange to
pink flowers, slight fragrance; foliage glossy bronze to green; vigorous
growth with prolific blooming habit; cut flowers last well.

JOHN F. KENNEDY. HT. White. (Boerner; int. Jackson & Perkins, 1965;
    Pat. 2441.) Fine white, of perfect form, a fitting memorial to our
late president. Sometimes with a hint of chartreuse.

JOHN S. ARMSTRONG. Gr. Dark red, 7.9*. AARS 1962. (Swim; int. Arm-
    strong Nurseries, 1961; Pat. 2056.) A rose to shout about; I would
rate it at least 9.0. Abundant and continuous bloom on tall, very sturdy,
very hardy bushes. Very dark buds (with edges so black they sometimes
appear frost-bitten) open to dark red velvety flowers, 4½ inches or more,
double, something like a camellia in form; borne singly or few in a
cluster; very long lasting, on the bush or indoors. Leathery, semi-glossy,
dark green foliage with new growth reddish.

JUNE BRIDE. Gr. White, 7.5. (Shepherd; int. Bosley Nursery, 1957; Pat.
    1770.) Bud long-pointed, flowers large (4 inches), double, high-
centered, creamy white, borne singly or in clusters; foliage leathery,
crinkled; upright tall bush.

KAISERIN AUGUSTE VIKTORIA. White, 6.7. (Lambert, 1891.) An old favorite,
    still desirable although now with a rather low rating. Cream bud,
long-pointed; snowy white, very fragrant, double flower with slight
lemon tint at center; intermittent bloom; foliage a rich soft green.

KARL HERBST. HT. Dark red, 7.8*. (W. Kordes; int. Brady, 1956.) Large,
    fragrant, dark scarlet exhibition blooms; better in cool weather.

KATHERINE T. MARSHALL. HT. Medium pink, 7.2. AARS 1944. Boerner;
    int. Jackson & Perkins, 1943; Pat. 607, expired.) Bud deep salmon-
pink; large double flower glowing coral-pink with gold at base of petals;
long stems; upright bush to 3½ feet. A lovely rose.

KATIE. Cl. Medium pink, 7.7*. (O'Neil; int. Melvin Wyant, 1959.) Long-pointed bud; large, double, cupped flowers, silvery pink with deeper reverse, borne singly and in clusters; long lasting, fragrant, good intermittent bloom; glossy foliage.

KING BOREAS. F. Medium yellow, 6.9. (Brownell, 1941.) A fine yellow floribunda with abundant bloom and general effect of Goldilocks but with flowers more like a hybrid tea, 2 to 3 inches across, petals slightly recurved, pale yellow when fully open, slight tea fragrance; vigorous bush of medium height; very hardy.

KING'S RANSOM. HT. Deep yellow, 7.7*. AARS 1962. (Morey; int. Jackson & Perkins, 1961; Pat. 2103.) Medium, ovoid bud and clear yellow, high centered double flower, borne singly and in clusters; profuse continuous bloom, unfading in summer heat; tall bushes, to 4 or 5 feet; dark, shiny foliage. I rate this higher than 7.7.

KORDES' PERFECTA. HT. Pink blend, 7.6. (Kordes; int. Jackson & Perkins, 1958; Pat. 1604.) A most unusual rose, sometimes looking like a mistake, especially as a bud, sometimes winning blue ribbons; large double flower, petals creamy white edged and flushed with crimson in a bicolor effect; pleasing dark, glossy foliage; upright bush.

LADY ELGIN. HT. Yellow blend, 7.6. (Meilland; int. Conard-Pyle, 1957; Pat. 1460.) An exhibition rose; ovoid, reddish apricot bud; large tawny orange double flower on long stem, fragrant.

LADY HILLINGTON. T. Yellow blend. (Lowe & Shawyer, 1910.) Deepest yellow of all Tea varieties; bud long pointed, flower fragrant; bronze foliage; often as hardy as a hybrid tea.

LA FRANCE. HT. Light pink, 6.4. (Guillot Fils, 1867.) Generally considered the first hybrid tea and still good; long bud; large silvery pink flower, reverse bright pink; very double; very fragrant. Listed by Roy Hennessey.

LA JOLLA. HT. Pink blend, 7.5. (Swim; int. Armstrong Nurseries, 1954; Pat. 1103.) Exquisitely beautiful pastel rose; large, very double, high-centered, soft pink veined with deeper pink, center cream and gold; upright bush; dark glossy foliage.

LAVENDER GIRL. F. Mauve, 7.0. (Meilland; int. Conard-Pyle, 1958; Pat. 1672.) A sell-out when first introduced at the extravagant price of $5. Large, cupped, rosy purple flowers, reverse magenta changing to lavender, in clusters, with spicy fragrance; medium bush.

LAVENDER PRINCESS. F. Mauve, 7.1. (Boerner; int. Jackson & Perkins, 1959.) Pointed orchid buds and lavender, double flowers in large clusters.

LILAC DAWN. Fl. Mauve, 7.3. (Swim & Weeks; int. Armstrong Nurseries, 1964; Pat. 2225.) Lilac or lavender pink, 2½ to 3-inch blooms in clusters on short stems; long-lasting; semiglossy foliage. One of the better roses in the mauve class.

LILY PONS. HT. Light yellow. (Brownell, 1939; Pat. 420, expired.) A nearly white subzero with large double flowers, lemon yellow at center, fragrant, on long stems; vigorous, hardy bush.

LITTLE DARLING. F. Yellow blend, 8.4. (Duehrsen; int. Elmer Roses, 1956; Pat. 1581.) The name describes this charming but possibly too willowy floribunda. Flowers are of exquisite form, creamy yellow with soft coral and a hint of orange, deeper pink with age, to 3 inches across. Dark, glossy, leathery foliage.

LOTTE GUNTHART. HT. Medium red. (David Armstrong; int. Armstrong Nurseries, 1965.) Named for the Swiss Mme. Gunthart, renowned painter of roses. An unusual flower, very double but very flat with myriads of small, overlapping velvety red petals, medium size (5 inches).

LOUIS PHILIPPE. Ch. Dark red, 7.7. (Guerin, 1834.) The mere thought of Louis Philippe makes me want to spend another winter along the Gulf Coast where it flowers with the azaleas and camellias. Medium-sized, double, deep crimson flowers, with a spicy scent, are formed profusely. Good either as a hedge or bedding rose and found in nearly every garden of the Deep South.

LOWELL THOMAS. HT. Deep yellow, 7.7. AARS 1944. (Mallerin; Conard-Pyle, 1943; Pat. 595.) An aristocrat for exhibition but with every-day dependability, an excellent yellow for home gardeners. Clear canary yellow, large, high-centered flower from a long, pointed bud; upright bush, 3 to 4 feet.

LUCKY PIECE. HT. Orange blend, 7.8*. (Winifred Gordon; int. Melvin Wyant, 1962; Pat. 1948.) A lucky sport of Peace with large globular bud, very double flower with orange and light red or pink tones on gold; moderate fragrance; leathery dark green foliage; intermittent bloom. This rose resembles Chicago Peace and some of the blooms are just as good.

LULU. HT. Medium pink, 7.5. (Easlea, 1919.) Nearly single, with 8 petals. I am always enchanted by Lulu's unusually long buds and salmon-orange to coppery pink flowers. Still listed by Roy Hennessey.

MABELLE STEARNS. S. Pink blend, 7.6. (Horvath; int. Wayside Gardens; Pat. 207, expired.) A hardy dooryard rose for cold climates; a low bush but spreading to 6 feet or more with abundant bloom. Flowers are double, peach pink with silvery reflexes, very fragrant, in clusters.

MAMAN COCHET. T. Pink blend. (Cochet, 1893.) A favorite tea for California and other mild climates; flower large, to 4 inches, double, pink with yellow base; fragrant.

MA PERKINS. F. Pink blend, 7.9. AARS 1953. (Boerner; int. Jackson & Perkins, 1952; Pat. 1143.) Flowers large, double, salmon to shell pink, fragrant; vigorous bush to 3 feet; improves with age; good in the South as well as North.

MARECHAL NIEL. N. Yellow, 6.8. (Pradel, 1864.) This large-flowered golden yellow climber is beloved throughout the South for its profuse bloom and enchanting perfume. Not for the North except in greenhouses.

MARGO KOSTER. Pol. Pink blend, 7.9. (Koster, 1935.) One of the few true polyanthas now available; low compact plant, seldom over 12 inches; clusters of very small orange-red, ranunculus-shaped flowers; continuous bloom; excellent shiny foliage; good for edging; fine for miniature arrangements. I don't know why this is classed as a *pink* blend; it should not be used anywhere near a true pink. It is, however, charming with dwarf blue ageratum.

MARY WALLACE. LR. Medium pink, 7.8. (Van Fleet; Int. ARS, 1924.)
Flower very large, semidouble, luminous warm pink; profuse June
bloom; vigorous climber; 8 to 12 feet; glossy green foliage. I never
realized just how good this rose was until I saw it blooming all over
arches and fences in Maine after a winter that had killed many hybrid
teas.

MASQUERADE. F. Red blend, 7.8. (Boerner; int. Jackson & Perkins, 1949;
Pat. 975.) A controversial rose but with most visitors succumbing to
this amusing harlequin with red, yellow, pink, lemon and sometimes
orange flowers from yellow buds marked with vermilion. A vigorous
bush, tall and spreading, with dark, leathery foliage.

MATTERHORN. HT. White. AARS 1966. (Armstrong and Swim; int.
Armstrong Nurseries, 1965.) Tall plant with high centered, ivory
to white flowers on long stems; glossy, bright green foliage.

MAX GRAF. HRg. Pink. (Bowditch, 1919.) A trailing rose for banks and
terraces; will bloom in partial shade. Flowers large, single, bright
pink; profuse June bloom; nonrecurrent but glossy foliage attractive all
season; a fine, hardy ground cover.

McGREDY'S SUNSET. HT. Orange blend, 7.5. (McGredy; int. Jackson &
Perkins, 1936; Pat. 317, expired.) I am partial to most McGredy
roses and to this one for its deep sunset colors, chrome yellow shading to
scarlet, and glossy bronze foliage. It is fragrant, too.

McGREDY'S YELLOW. HT. Medium yellow, 7.5. (McGredy, 1933.) Beautiful, long-pointed buds; large, clear, pale yellow flowers, fine for
exhibition or cutting for the house. This variety compares favorably with
modern yellows; it is no longer widely available but still listed by Fred
Edmunds and Inter-State and is sometimes procurable as a potted rose.

MEMORIAM. HT. Light pink, 7.8*. (Von Abrams; int. Peterson & Dering,
1961; Pat. 2280.) Fine exhibition bloom on a rather low bush. Formerly
classed as white rather than pink the flower is very like Royal Highness;
very large, perfect, not produced too freely.

MERMAID. Cl. Light yellow, 8.3. (W. Paul, 1918.) A climbing or trailing
rose with very large, single flowers, 5 to 6 inches across, pale sulfur

yellow with amber stamens; shining deep green foliage; recurrent bloom. This rose, with tea in its parentage, is best in mild climates, where one plant can cover a whole garage, but no northern gardener should miss it, even if it kills back to the soil mound in winter.

MIRANDY. HT. Dark red, 7.7. AARS 1945. (Lammerts; int. Armstrong Nurseries, 1945; Pat. 632, expired.) A huge bud and extra large, double (40 to 50 petals), garnet-red flower; very fragrant. As with other outsize roses, there are not too many blooms.

MISSION BELLS. HT. Pink blend, 7.8. AARS 1950. (Morris; int. Germain, 1949; Pat. 923.) Deep salmon bud, shrimp-pink flower, 5 inches across; slight tea fragrance; coppery green foliage; stems long, nearly thornless.

MME. COCHET-COCHET. HT. Pink blend, 7.7. (Mallerin; int. Conard-Pyle, 1934; Pat. 129, expired.) Long a favorite for exhibition, also good in the garden, freely blooming on long stems, at its best in autumn. A long, tapering bud opens to a very large, semidouble flower, coppery rose-pink, tinted coral; large, vigorous bush.

MME. GREGOIRE STAECHELIN (Spanish Beauty). ClHT. (Dot; int. Conard-Pyle, 1929.) Huge fragrant pink flowers, stained crimson on outside of petals, on long stems. Starting earlier than most climbers and giving abundant bloom for about 3 weeks. Not recurrent, even though classed as a hybrid tea. Vigorous to 14 feet, with large, very attractive, pear-shaped hips. Listed by Tillotson's and Roy Hennessey.

MME. HARDY. D. White, 9.1. (Hardy, 1832.) Considered the most fragrant and beautiful of the old white roses; medium large, full, cupped flowers in spreading clusters on a sturdy, hardy bush.

MME. HENRI GUILLOT. HT. Red blend, 8.4. (Mallerin; int. Conard-Pyle, 1938; Pat. 337, expired.) Another of those gorgeous off-red shades; flower large, orange to coral red (also described as raspberry pink) on long stem with large glossy foliage; fine for cutting and exhibition.

MOJAVE. HT. Orange blend, 7.4. AARS 1954. (Swim; int. Armstrong Nurseries, 1954; Pat. 1176.) Named for sunset on the Mojave

Desert. Tapering buds on long stems; flowers glowing orange, shot with flame; vigorous plant.

MONTEZUMA. Gr. Orange red, 8.6. (Swim; int. Armstrong Nurseries, 1955; Pat. 1383.) Vivid flower, varying from glowing scarlet-orange to salmon-pink according to season and location; large, double, high-centered flower, hybrid tea form, on long stems; single or few in a cluster. An excellent rose!

MOONSPRITE. F. White, 7.7. (Swim; int. Armstrong Nurseries, 1956; Pat. 1450.) A darling rose, aptly named; medium flowers, to 2½ inches, very double, creamy white with pale gold center, in rounded clusters on low to medium bush, to 2½ feet; semiglossy foliage.

MOUNT SHASTA. Gr. White, 7.7*. (Swim & Weeks; int. Conard-Pyle, 1963; Pat. 2132.) A fine rose from excellent parents (Queen Elizabeth and Blanche Mallerin). Very large, long-pointed bud, snow white, double, large (to 5 inches) flowers, borne singly or in clusters; leathery foliage; upright bush.

MR. LINCOLN. HT. Medium red. AARS 1965. (Swim & Weeks; int. Conard-Pyle, 1964; Pat. 2370.) Very double, deep velvety red blooms, 40 or more petals, to 6 inches across, long lasting, with some fragrance; glassy dark green foliage; strong bush, producing rather freely.

MRS. ARTHUR CURTISS JAMES (Golden Climber). LR. Medium yellow, 7.7. (Brownell; int. Jackson & Perkins, 1933; Pat. 28, expired.) You must have patience with this wonderful climber for it takes 2 or 3 years to get the fine sunflower-yellow flowers, of hybrid tea size and shape, borne singly on long stems; glossy foliage. Keep the vigorous canes trained horizontally and do not prune out much old wood.

MRS. CHARLES BELL. HT. Light pink, 7.5. (Mrs. C. J. Bell; int. Pierson, 1917.) One of the hardy, foolproof Radiance group but such a delicate shell pink, shaded soft salmon, that it pleases even the connoisseur. A tall bush, with disease-resistant foliage. Listed by Tate, Thomasville, and Melvin Wyant.

MRS. DUDLEY CROSS. T. Yellow blend. (W. Paul, 1907.) One of the more reliable teas for southern gardens; yellow buds, flowers gradually developing pink tints; thornless. A rather rank grower that resents being pruned.

MRS. JOHN LAING. HP. Pink. (Bennett, 1887.) Clear soft pink, double, very large, very fragrant flower; profuse spring, some recurrent bloom; very hardy bush.

MRS. PIERRE S. DU PONT. HT. Deep yellow, 7.4. (Mallerin; int. Conard-Pyle, 1929.) A medium bush covered with gold buds opening to yellow flowers unfading in summer sun; dependable for bloom in hot weather; holding up against more recent introductions.

MRS. R. M. FINCH. F. Medium pink, 8.0. (Finch, 1923.) A fine old rose hard to beat for everblooming charm, cheerful and lavish in almost impossible situations; clusters of rosy pink flowers fading to nearly white in summer. Listed by Tillotson's.

MRS. SAM McGREDY. HT. Orange blend, 7.9. (McGredy, 1929.) All McGredy roses have distinction but Mrs. Sam is tops; I'll match her against all comers. A large and spreading bush with stunning reddish-bronze foliage and large coppery-salmon flowers produced freely on long stems; good for exhibition; fine for the garden. Don't let this rose disappear from the market! Still listed by Inter-State and Melvin Wyant.

NADINE. Fl. Dark red, 7.6*. (Schwartz; int. Melvin Wyant, 1962.) Very dark maroon red, 3 to 4 inches, with many small petals; spicy fragrance; long-lasting; 1 to 3 on a stem; bronzy small foliage.

NEIGE PARFUM. HT. White, 6.9. (Mallerin; int. Jackson & Perkins, 1942.) A large, double, white, sometimes tinted cream, with unforgettable fragrance, perfect form. Listed by Tillotson's.

NEW DAWN. Cl. Light pink, 8.8. (Somerset Rose Nursery; int. Dreer, 1930; Pat. 1.) A sport of Dr. W. Van Fleet, blush pink like its parent but with recurrent bloom; vigorous, to 15 feet or more; fine, glossy foliage requiring little attention.

NEW YORKER. HT. Medium red, 7.9. (Boerner; int. Jackson & Perkins, 1947; Pat. 823.) The reddest red you can imagine; large velvety flowers, double, high-centered, fragrant.

Nocturne. HT. Dark red, 8.1. AARS 1948. (Swim; int. Armstrong
    Nurseries, 1947; Pat. 713.) A beautiful rose with long, streamlined
buds, and very dark red, fragrant blooms; good for cutting and exhibition; upright bush.

Oklahoma. HT. Dark red. (Swim and Weeks; int. Weeks, 1964.) Tall
    bush with firm, full, fragrant, dark red blooms on long stems.

Opal Jewel. Min. Medium pink, 7.5. (Morey; int. Jackson & Perkins,
    1962; Pat. 2292.) One-inch rose-pink flowers on small plants with
dense green foliage; some fragrance.

Orange Flame. HT. Orange red, 7.4*. (Mme. M. L. Meilland; int. Conard-
    Pyle, 1962; Pat. 2141.) Large, pointed ovoid bud opening to very
large flower, 6 to 7 inches, with dusky tones on orange-red petals; very
long lasting; moderate tea fragrance. Leathery, glossy dark green foliage;
tall bush. A most desirable rose but it is subject to mildew. It is not as
productive as Tropicana but can be planted next to it for alternate bloom.

Orange Triumph. F. Red blend, 8.1. (Kordes; int. Dreer, 1937.) Although
    reclassified as a floribunda, perhaps because the bush is 3 or 4 feet
tall and wide, the flowers are polyantha size, semidouble in large clusters;
salmon-red with orange shadings but never a true orange. Always in
bloom and making brilliant garden color almost to December. Excellent
for indoor arrangements. The bushes may be defoliated by red spiders
in midsummer but they are quickly reclothed with leaves.

Otto Linne (Gartendirektor O. Linne). Pol. S. Light red & deep pink,
    8.4*. (Lambert, 1934.) An old rose now coming back into favor,
offered by Conard-Pyle and Roseway. Large clusters of dark carmine pink
flowers, small, on bushes 2½ to 3 feet. Very shiny bright green leaves
with 7 or more leaflets.

Patricia Macoun. R. White, 7.7. (Central Experimental Farm, 1945.)
    A moderate climber or 6-foot shrub, extra hardy for northern states;
clusters of pure white flowers, 2 inches across, with golden yellow stamens.

Paul Neyron. HP. Medium pink, 7.8. (A. Levet, 1896.) Enormous, very
    double rose, soft lilac pink, very fragrant; some recurrent bloom;
tall plant.

PAUL'S SCARLET CLIMBER. LR. Medium red, 9.1. (W. Paul, 1916.) Until the advent of Blaze, the most universally beloved climber and still popular for its prolonged and profuse June bloom. It may occasionally repeat if the laterals are pruned back after flowering; vigorous and very hardy.

PAX. HMsk. White, 7.9. (Pemberton, 1918.) A graceful shrub to cover banks or fences. Medium-sized ivory flowers, with prominent yellow stamens, pronounced fragrance, produced repeatedly through the summer; excellent shiny foliage. Tillotson's now offers this in place of City of York. It is by no means a substitute but has virtue of its own.

PEACE. HT. Yellow blend, 9.6. AARS 1946. (Meilland; int. Conard-Pyle, 1945; Pat. 591, expired.) Probably the most popular and best-known present-day rose. Bud large, ovoid, yellow with watermelon pink edging; flower very large (6-inch), double, high-centered, firm, changing from yellow to pink suffused with yellow and white. The bush is tall and vigorous with heavy, large, lustrous, dark green leaves. A few people don't like Peace and if you are in that sad minority that condemns a rose simply because it is too big and buxom try Sutter's Gold.

PEACE, Climbing. ClHT. 7.2. (Brady; int. Conard-Pyle, 1950; Pat. 932.) Very vigorous growth, to 20 feet or more, but relatively few blooms. Do not prune back until it attains full size.

PEACH GLOW. F. Pink blend, 7.2*. (Boerner; int. Jackson & Perkins, 1960; Pat. 1999.) Medium-sized, double, cupped, pink to peach flowers, several together or singly; moderate fragrance.

PEDRALBES. HT. White, 7.4. (Nadal; int. Jackson & Perkins, 1935.) Classed as white, this fine rose is as often cream, with yellow buds. Large, semidouble flowers are freely produced on a vigorous, medium tall bush. One of the loveliest classes I have seen at a Rose Show was for Pedralbes grown naturally, without disbudding. Listed by J. J. Kern.

PICTURE. HT. Light pink, 8.0. (McGredy, 1932.) Constantly blooming, ideal for bedding and cutting. I like to plant this with The Doctor to produce several ordinary-sized rose-pink blooms, double with high centers, for each one of his extraordinary affairs.

PIGMY LAVENDER. F. Mauve, 7.1*. (E. S. Boerner; int. Jackson & Perkins, 1961; Pat. 2195.) Very dwarf plant but with profuse bloom; flowers 3 inches, lavender with touch of pink, cupped, double.

PINK BOUNTIFUL. F. Medium pink, 8.2. (J. H. Hill Co., 1945; Pat. 601, expired.) Deep rose-pink buds, good for corsages, and vivid pink double flowers; plants hardy, well-branched, 3 to 4 feet. Useful in the perennial border to provide constant summer color.

PINK CHIFFON. F. Light pink, 7.5. (Boerner; int. Jackson & Perkins, 1956; Pat. 1564.) Aptly named; the 3-inch double flowers are rosy at the center, gossamer pink on the outside; free-flowering on a rather low bush; glossy foliage. Some men can't see any reason for introducing this delicately textured rose; others regard it as highly as I do.

PINK DUCHESS. Pink blend, 7.6*. (Boerner; int. Jackson & Perkins, 1959; Pat. 1834.) Very deep rich pink with a hint of gold; the same size, substance and form of Peace, even more double, with the same type of foliage.

PINK FAVORITE. HT. Medium pink, 8.2. (Von Abrams; int. Peterson & Dering, 1956; Pat. 1523.) Loosely cupped flowers with 21 to 28 petals, "Neyron rose" pink, freely produced on a sturdy bush with most attractive glossy, bright green foliage. I recommend this rose; you can get it from J. J. Kern, Melvin Wyant, or Fred Edmunds.

PINK GROOTENDORST. HRg. Medium pink, 7.3. (F. J. Grootendorst, 1923.) A shrub rose, to 5 feet, with profuse June bloom and recurring somewhat through the season. Flowers resemble small pink carnations with fringed, clear pink petals; in clusters; light green foliage.

PINK HEATHER. Min. Light pink, 7.9. (Moore; int. Sequoia Nursery, 1959; Pat. 2082.) Delightful rose with many slender petals, deep rose with a blue cast; blooms in clusters; bush height 8 to 12 inches.

PINKIE. F. Medium pink, 7.6. (Swim; int. Armstrong Nurseries, 1947; Pat. 712.) A dwarf rose, 15 to 20 inches, fine for edging. The entrancing pointed, deep pink buds open to pale pink, semidouble flowers, 2 inches across, in large clusters; almost continuous bloom.

PINK PARFAIT. Gr. Pink blend, 7.8*. AARS 1961. (Swim; int. Armstrong Nurseries, 1960; Pat. 1904.) Exquisitely formed medium-sized light pink blooms from First Love crossed with Pinocchio. Freely flowering as a garden decorative and fine in front of Duet, which is slightly taller. Also good for arrangements.

PINK PEACE. HT. Pink Peace, 7.7. (Meilland; int. Conard-Pyle, 1959; Pat. 1759.) Not at all like Peace but a must for outstanding fragrance. The bushes are very vigorous, tall and spreading, and produce many extra large flowers, deep dusty pink with a slight hint of magenta. They are more like Radiance than Peace in form and the leaves are dull not shiny. Wrongly named but highly recommended.

PINK PRINCESS. HT. Light pink, 7.7. (Brownell, 1939; Pat. 459.) A sub-zero rose bred for resistance to blackspot; profuse bloom on a very large bush; flowers rather small, rose to flesh-pink, double, fragrant.

PINOCCHIO. F. Pink blend, 7.8. (Kordes; int. Jackson & Perkins, 1942; Pat. 484.) Hardy, easy to grow, in bloom from June to hard frost. Exquisite globose buds, salmon-pink flushed with gold, good for corsages and miniature arrangements; 2-inch double flowers, that turn pale and spot on aging.

PIXIE GOLD. Min. Medium yellow, 7.6*. (P. Dot; int. Conard-Pyle, 1961; Pat. 2091.) Small, pointed golden bud; pale yellow open flower, 10 to 12 petals, usually borne singly. Taller than true miniatures—to 24 inches and nearly as wide.

PIXIE ROSE. Min. Light red and deep pink, 8.2*. (P. Dot; int. Conard-Pyle, 1961; Pat. 2095.) Highly desirable; deep rose pink, freely blooming, singly or in clusters; long lasting; 40 to 45 petals; vigorous bush, to 24 inches, with branched growth habit.

POINSETTIA. HT. Medium red, 7.6. (Howard & Smith; int. Dreer, 1938.) Bright, unfading scarlet, as red as the poinsettia itself; large, double.

POLKA. F. Medium pink, 7.4*. (M. L. Meilland; int. Conard-Pyle, 1960; Pat. 1939.) Lively pink with a hint of orange; flowers 3½ inches with 40 to 45 petals. Good for garden color, especially in cool weather.

POLYNESIAN SUNSET. HT. Orange red. (Boerner; int. Jackson & Perkins, 1965.) Large, brilliant, coral-orange double flowers with definite fragrance.

PRESIDENT HERBERT HOOVER. HT. Pink blend, 7.7. (Coddington; int. Totty, 1930.) A tall bush with exhibition blooms produced rather sparingly on long, erect stems; mixed scarlet, yellow, cerise and flame; tea fragrance.

QUEEN ELIZABETH. Gr. Medium pink, 9.0. AARS 1955. (Lammerts; int. Germain, 1954; Pat. 1259.) First of a new class, very tall, with blooms borne singly or in clusters. Large flowers, high-centered to cupped, rose-pink, fragrant; dark, glossy, leathery foliage; very vigorous bush. A fine rose for the house, the Rose Show, or the garden.

QUEEN O'THE LAKES. HT. Dark red, 7.5. (Brownell, 1949; Pat. 1003.) Of the Brownell roses I rank this next to Curly Pink. Intense red, large, double flowers, exhibition form, fragrant; vigorous bush with fine foliage.

RADIANCE. HT. Light pink, 7.9. (J. Cook; int. P. Henderson, 1908.) People turn up their noses at this foolproof rose that grows so easily in the South, is so hardy in the North, and is so disease-tolerant it survives without spraying. I prefer Red Radiance but I doff my hat to any rose so good any gardener can have it. Flowers are large, double, cupped, cameo-pink, deeper toward the center; fragrant.

RED PINOCCHIO. F. Dark red, 8.6. (Boerner; int. Jackson & Perkins, 1947; Pat. 812.) Almost better than Pinocchio; velvety red flowers, carmine to scarlet, semidouble, 2½ to 3 inches, cupped, formed in clusters; free-flowering; especially good in the South where the bushes are tall and spreading.

RED RADIANCE. HT. Light red and deep pink, 7.9. (Gude Bros., 1916.) As much a lazy man's rose as Radiance and better, especially in autumn when the half-open flowers and reddish new foliage positively glow. One of the best roses for the South, blooming long after first frost in the North. This is a rosy red; do not plant it next to a scarlet red like the New Yorker, or any of the new orange reds.

ROBIN HOOD. HMsk. Light red and deep pink. (Pemberton, 1927.) Fine
for a hedge, a graceful shrub, or along a fence. Large clusters of
small, cherry-red to deep pink flowers produced massively in June, re-
currently through the summer. Very attractive, shiny foliage with small
leaflets; very hardy. Sold as a hedge, 6 plants for $4.45, by Conard-Pyle.

ROSA. Here under the genus name are some of the species roses that have
a place in landscape plantings. Some bloom several weeks earlier
than hybrid teas. Most you can plant and forget, except for pruning out
the oldest wood every year or two as you do any shrub. Some take kindly
to fertilization and spraying but some object to chemicals used either for
food or protection from pests. Hybrids, resulting from the crossing of
two species, are marked with an ✕.

Rosa alba. Jacobite Rose; White Rose of York. Flowers nearly double,
white, fragrant, several together; June bloom. Maiden's Blush, a
soft pink, is an *alba* hybrid.

R. banksiae. Banks Rose. From China. Climber, to 20 feet. Variety *R.
banksiae banksiae* has small double white flowers that are fragrant.
Lady Banksia or yellow Banks Rose, *R. banksiae lutea,* is the rose of the
Old South, still blooming in dooryards from February on through spring.
The flowers are deep yellow, double but not very fragant.

R. blanda. Labrador Rose. Native in northeast N. America. Flowers soft
pink, single, 2 to 2½ inches across, on nearly thornless branches. A
shrub rose, 3 to 6 feet, good in sun or part shade, on banks, or as fore-
ground for other shrubs.

R. ✕ *borboniana.* Bourbon Rose. Cross between China Rose and French
Rose. Flowers 3 inches, double or nearly so, pink, red or purple,
borne singly or few in a cluster; recurrent.

R. bracteata. Macartney Rose. A climber from China, naturalized in
southeast N. America. Flowers large, white, single or few on short
stalks, June to October; foliage half-evergreen, bright, resistant to blackspot. A parent of Mermaid.

R. canina. Dog Rose, Brier Rose. Much used as grafting stock in Europe,
   sometimes naturalized in N. America. Large shrub, 5 to 9 feet; single pink flower; cranberry-size fruit.

R. carolina. Pasture Rose. Native of eastern N. America from Canada to
   the Gulf Coast. Bright pink flowers, often solitary, on a 3- to 6-foot
shrub, spreading by means of suckers.

R. centifolia. Cabbage Rose, Provence Rose. The rose of 100 "leaves,"
   petals. The term cabbage does not refer to size but to the globular
tight formation of overlapping petals. Flowers solitary on slender pedicels, soft pink, 3 inches in diameter; fragrant; bushes grow to 6 feet.

Moss roses are a variation of the cabbage rose with a mosslike covering
of the buds and flower stems. Old Pink Moss, Communis, was noted in
France in 1696; other varieties originated there the first half of the 19th
century. Communis, Salet, Crested Moss, Mme. Louis Leveque and other
moss roses are still available from firms that handle old roses. Do not
prune moss roses until after flowering; otherwise you lose the bloom.

R. chinensis. China Rose; Bengal Rose. Flowers 2 inches across, crimson
   or pink, rarely whitish; recurrent; foliage evergreen or nearly so.

R. chinensis minima (R. lawranceana; R. roulettii). Fairy Rose. A very
   dwarf form was found about 1920 by a Colonel Roulet in a pot on
the window sill of a Swiss cottage; cuttings were taken of the plants, from
century-old stock, by the botanist Correvon. From this Rosa Rouletti
(double flowers with rose-pink petals, only ¾ inch in diameter, plant
only 6 inches high) have come many other miniatures. A number of patented varieties originating with Jan de Vink in Holland and some from
Pedro Dot in Spain have been introduced here by the Conard-Pyle Company. Many more have been bred and introduced by Ralph Moore of
Sequoia Nursery.

R. chinensis mutabilis. Flowers sulfur yellow, changing to orange, red
   and finally crimson, 2 inches across.

R. chinensis viridiflora. Green Rose. Large flowers with petals transformed
   into small narrow green leaves. A curiosity, not a beauty.

R. damascena. Damask Rose. Double red, pink or white flowers, sometimes striped, usually in clusters, June or July bloom; upright shrub
to 5 feet.

R. damascena semperflorens. Autumn Damask; Rose des Quatre Saisons.
Tending to bloom in autumn as well as June; probably one parent
of hybrid perpetuals.

R. damascena trigintipetala. Kazanlik. Red, semidouble flowers, grown
in the Balkans for Attar of Roses.

R. damascena versicolor. York and Lancaster Rose. Small, semidouble
flowers with some petals white, some pink, or striped; hardy; cultivated before 1700.

R. eglanteria. Sweet Brier Rose. Eglantine. Naturalized in our pastures
but of European origin, our common "wild Rose." Pink flowers, 2
inches across, solitary or few in a cluster; foliage fragrant; shrub, to 8
feet.

R. foetida. Austrian Yellow. Austrian Brier Rose. Bright yellow flowers,
2 to 2½ inches, of unpleasant, sickly sweet odor; globular fruit.

R. foetida bicolor. Austrian Copper. Bush is gorgeously covered with
orange-scarlet flowers with yellow reverse. Foliage is somewhat subject to blackspot but does not take kindly to some sprays.

R. foetida persiana. Persian Yellow. Double yellow flowers in June. Very
susceptible to blackspot and may be injured by copper sprays; sulfur
is safe unless it is too hot.

R. × fortuniana. Supposedly *R. banksiae × R. laevigata.* Flowers large,
double, white. Now used as understock for some Florida roses.

R. gallica. French Rose. Probably ancestor of European garden roses.
Flowers deep pink to red, 2 to 3 inches, on stout pedicels; fruit sub-
globose to turbinate, brick red; stems prickly. Many varieties are still
sold: Cardinal Richelieu with purplish flowers; President de Seze, very
fragrant, magenta center petals surrounded by pale lilac; Rosa Mundi,
striped white, pink and red, often confused with the true York and Lancaster; Tuscany Superb, dark velvety crimson, very fragrant.

R. hugonis. Father Hugo Rose; Golden Rose of China. A lovely early-blooming shrub, to 6 feet or taller, spreading by means of suckers; single yellow flowers, 2½ inches; globose, deep scarlet fruit. This rose does much better on poor soil; do not pamper.

R. laevigata. Cherokee Rose. A rampant climber from China, naturalized in the Southeast, where it can be seen blooming through the trees and hedgerows from February through spring. Flowers, white, solitary, 2½ to 3½ inches; fragrant. There is a pink Cherokee available from some nurseries.

R. moschata. Musk Rose. From southern Europe and North Africa. Small white flowers, usually 7 in a cluster, with musk fragrance. The Pemberton hybrids, Clytemnestra, Prosperity, and Robin Hood, have a place in many gardens, along with Bentall's Belinda.

R. moyesii. From western China. Flowers are a warm velvety, reddish terracotta, 2 inches across; bush apt to be leggy, best combined with other shrubs.

R. multiflora. Japanese Rose. Small flowers like blackberries, usually white, many in a cluster, recurving or climbing branches; small, grayish green foliage; attractive bright red fruit. Widely used as an understock and when hybrid teas "revert" it is because multiflora suckers have crowded out the budded rose. Advertised as a living fence but not for the suburbs. One bush may grow 10 feet wide and keeping it trimmed to a hedge will be a hard, thorny, almost impossible task.

R. multiflora carnea. Pink Japanese Rose. Flowers double, light pink.

R. multiflora platyphylla. Seven Sisters Rose. Large trusses of double flowers, 1½ inches across, with 7 colors—lilac, rose and dark carmine tones—blooming at the same time.

R. × noisettiana. Noisette Rose; Champney Rose. Climber or shrub for mild climates; flowers white, pink, red or yellow in clusters. The best known variety is Marechal Niel.

R. × noisettiana manetti. Manetti Rose. Horticultural variety long used as understock, mostly for greenhouse roses.

R. nutkana. Nootka Rose. Native from Alaska to Oregon and Utah. Shrub, to 5 feet, with pink flowers, 2 to 2½ inches.

R. × odorata. Tea Rose. From western China. Flowers double, 2 to 2½ inches, white, light pink to salmon or yellowish, on short stems. Most varieties are for mild climates, have relatively little blackspot, require little pruning.

R. × odorata ochroleuca. Amber Tea Rose; Park's Yellow Tea-scented China. Introduced in England in 1824 as the original Tea Rose. Pale yellow, double flowers.

R. palustris. Swamp Rose. A native from Nova Scotia to Minnesota, south to Florida and Mississippi, preferring swampy, moist ground. Flowers in clusters, pink, 2 inches in diameter, June to August; shrub grows to 8 feet.

R. primula (often mistakenly sold for *R. ecae*). Extremely early; yellowish white flowers formed along stems with decorative thorns; leaves small, stiff, incense-scented; bush 3 to 5 feet.

R. roxburghii. Chestnut Rose; Burr Rose. A 6-foot shrub from E. Asia, unusual for its prickly fruit resembling chestnut burs and bark that peels like a sycamore; pale pink single flowers; foliage like a locust tree.

R. rubrifolia. Redleaf Rose. Bronze-red foliage very decorative for landscape use; flowers small, pink; shrub to 6 feet.

R. rugosa. Rugosa Rose. A shrub, 5 to 8 feet high, from Asia but sometimes naturalized in our Northeast; very hardy; fine for the seashore where it thrives in sand and salt air. Foliage distinctly rugose (wrinkled), shining dark green; flowers 2½ to 3½ inches, pink, purple or white; blooming May to September according to variety; attractive red fruit. Most rugosas are beloved by Japanese beetles but some hybrids are seldom attacked.

R. sericea omeiensis. Omei Rose. From western China. Unusual in that the small white flowers have only 4 petals and the tall canes bear winglike translucent thorns that glow like fire when young; foliage is fernlike; lush green.

R. setigera. Prairie Rose. A native shrub, 6 to 10 feet, from Canada to
Florida and west to Wisconsin, Nebraska and Texas; very hardy;
adjusted to adverse conditions and used in hybridizing roses for the far
North. Flowers 2 inches across, almost scentless, deep rose to whitish, few
in a cluster; June and July bloom; showy bright red hips; branches recurved or climbing; useful on fences or as pillars.

R. spinossissima. Scotch Rose. A rather low shrub, 3 to 4 feet, from Europe
and western Asia, sometimes naturalized in N. America. Flowers
1½ to 2 inches, pink, white or yellowish, formed along stems in May and
June, fragrant; black fruit; fine-cut foliage; good as a hedge; spread by
suckers.

R. spinossissima altaica. Altai Rose. Flowers large, white, blooming with
lilacs.

R. virginiana (R. lucida). A native shrub, to 6 feet, from Newfoundland
to New York and Pennsylvania. Flowers single or few in a cluster;
bright pink, June and July; red fruit remaining until spring; shiny, dark
green foliage; brownish stems with few thorns.

R. wichuraiana. Memorial Rose. A prostrate rose from E. Asia, favorite
as a ground cover for its creeping branches, half-evergreen foliage.
Flowers white, 1½ to 2 inches, fragrant, few in a cluster; July to September.

R. xanthina. Manchu Rose. Upright shrub from N. China and Korea
with long, arching stems, 6 to 10 feet; double yellow flowers, solitary on long stems, following *R. hugonis* in bloom.

ROSE GAUJARD. HT. Red blend, 7.4*. (Gaujard; int. Armstrong, 1963;
Pat. 1829.) Large, long-pointed buds, very double flowers, velvety
cherry red and silver white. Upright plant; good repeat bloom; pleasing
foliage.

ROSENELFE (Rose Elf). F. Medium pink, 8.2. (Kordes; int. Dreer, 1939.)
Camellia-like flowers, pink with a silvery sheen, 2½ inches across;
vigorous, medium tall bush.

ROUNDELAY. Gr. Dark red, 8.0. (Swim; int. Armstrong Nurseries, 1954;

Pat. 1280.) Lovely dark red, camellia flower, medium-sized, borne singly or in clusters on upright bush.

ROYAL HIGHNESS. HT. Light pink, 7.9*. AARS 1963. (Swim & Weeks; int. Conard-Pyle, 1962; Pat. 2032.) Truly royal; upright bush with pale pink exhibition bud and bloom (almost sculptured in alabaster) on long strong stem; long lasting; some fragrance; excellent, glossy, leathery, dark green foliage.

RUBAIYAT. HT. Light red and deep pink, 8.2. AARS 1947. (McGredy; int. Jackson & Perkins, 1946; Pat. 758, expired.) More pink than red, mostly deep rose; very large, double, high-centered, fragrant on a long stem. In the South the bush seems to be as vigorous as Radiance, which is saying a lot.

RUMBA (or Rhumba). F. Red blend, 7.5*. (S. Poulsen; int. Conard-Pyle, 1962; Pat. 1919.) Very double, very small blooms in rather flat clusters; poppy red with orange centers, sometimes orange, aging to chocolate; slight spicy foliage. Upright vigorous bush with dark green foliage. Nearer a polyantha than a floribunda.

SALET. M. Medium pink, 8.9. (Lacharme, 1854.) One of the best of the moss roses. Flower large, flat when open, rosy pink; the bud is heavily mossed; some recurrent bloom.

SARABANDE. F. Orange red, 7.9*. AARS 1960. (Meilland; int. Conard-Pyle, 1959; Pat. 1761.) Large trusses of dazzling light scarlet-orange single flowers on a rather low bush; semiglossy foliage; free bloom. Good for mass effect where the color will not clash with other flowers.

SARATOGA. F. White, 7.5*. AARS 1964. (Boerner; int. Jackson & Perkins, 1963; Pat. 2299.) A delightful and important rose; medium ovoid buds opening to gardenia-like flowers, borne in clusters on strong stems; moderate fragrance; long-lasting; free blooming; fine dark leathery foliage on vigorous bush; to 3½ feet and nearly as broad.

SEA FOAM. S. Pol. White. (Schwartz; int. Conard-Pyle, 1964.) A shrub polyantha hybrid that can be used as a climber, ground cover, weeping over banks, or as a low shrub spreading to 6 or 8 feet. Everblooming in foamlike clusters of 2-inch, double flowers, pure white fading to cream, with slight fragrance. Almost disease free; requires little if any spraying.

SENECA QUEEN. HT. Pink blend. (Boerner; int. Jackson & Perkins, 1965.) Pink to apricot with tinge of yellow; good size and form. It reminds me of Mrs. Sam McGredy.

SHOW GIRL. HT. Medium pink, 7.6. (Lammerts; int. Armstrong Nurseries, 1946; Pat. 646, expired.) Still one of the best true pink roses for exhibition or cut flowers; upright bush, 3 to 4 feet.

SILVER MOON. LR. White, 8.0. (Van Fleet; int. P. Henderson, 1910.) A rampant grower, to 20 feet or more, with shiny almost evergreen foliage and profuse June bloom. The semidouble pure white flowers, 4½ inches in diameter, are reminiscent of the Cherokee parent but this rose is very hardy; blooms best in full sun. Try floating two or three blooms in a low green Chinese bowl. Given up by some nurseries; still offered by Roy Hennessey.

SILVER TIPS. Min. Pink blend, 7.6*. (Moore; int. Sequoia Nursery, 1961.) Deep pink bud; double flower with lavender pink petals tipped with silver, 1 inch across; small, feathery foliage; low plant.

SINCERA (Armistad Sincera). HT. White, 7.6*. (Camprubi; int. Conard-Pyle, 1963; Pat. 2055.) An excellent pure white rose from Spain; long lasting flowers of exhibition form, on long stems; rather free blooming; upright, hardy bush.

SNOW FAIRY. F. White, 7.7*. (Camprubi; int. Conard-Pyle, 1963; Pat. 2376.) Utterly delightful, perfectly named; a joy in the garden and wonderful for small arrangements. Small, pointed bud; clear white, high-centered flowers, 1½ to 2 inches, in clusters; excellent leathery, glossy, dark green foliage.

SOEUR THERESE. HT. Medium yellow, 7.5. (F. Gillot; int. Conard-Pyle, 1931.) An old reliable; tall but spreading; healthy bush, fine for the beginner. Long buds; large, golden to cadmium yellow flowers on long stems; free-blooming.

SONG OF PARIS. HT. Mauve. (Chabert; int. Armstrong, 1964.) Many visitors to my garden resent lavender in a rose but I have come to like it and this is the best yet, in my opinion. Substantial, double blooms, exhibition form, lasting well, formed singly or several together; leathery foliage; bush to 3 feet.

SOUTH SEAS. HT. Medium pink, 7.8*. (Morey; int. Jackson & Perkins, 1962; Pat. 2184.) A huge and gorgeous rose on a vigorous, tall bush. Large ovoid bud, coral pink to apricot, opens to very double "Tahitian pink" flowers, to 7 inches across; very long lasting, pleasing even in old age; large leathery foliage. An excellent rose for garden display or for cutting. I would rate it 9.0 or better.

SOUVENIR DE LA MALMAISON. B. Light pink. (Beluze, 1843.) Very large, double fragrant flowers, cream with rosy centers; plant bushy, tall in the South, dwarf in the North. A famous and influential rose, still available from J. J. Kern, Roy Hennessey.

SPARTAN. F. Orange red, 8.5. (Boerner; int. Jackson & Perkins; 1955; Pat. 1357.) One of the best roses ever, tolerant of cold, heat, drought, and pests, making a stunning display along a drive or for any location away from clear pinks. There are bursts of bloom which return very quickly if old flowers are promptly cut off. Orange-red to reddish coral flowers, to 3½ inches, hybrid tea form, high-centered at first but opening like a geranium, borne singly or in clusters; fine glossy foliage, reddish when young; rather tall bush. A climbing Spartan is now available.

SPECTACULAR. Cl. Orange red, 7.5. (Mallerin; int. Jackson & Perkins, 1956; Pat. 1416.) Double, cupped to flat, fragrant, scarlet-red, 4-inch flowers, in clusters; glossy bronze foliage; climber to 8 feet; hardy; repeats in autumn.

STARFIRE. Gr. Medium red, 8.0. AARS 1959. (Lammerts; int. Germain, 1958.) Large, to 5 inches, double flowers, currant-red, fragrant, in candelabra form on long stems; glossy foliage; vigorous tall bush. Listed by California, Ilgenfritz, and Inter-State Nurseries.

STARLET. F. Medium yellow, 7.4. (Swim; int. Armstrong Nurseries, 1957; Pat. 1604.) A hybrid tea in miniature with very double, clear yellow "stars," 2½ inches, on long stems, borne singly or few in a cluster. I like this rose.

STERLING SILVER. HT. Mauve, 7.0. (G. Fisher; int. Jackson & Perkins, 1957; Pat. 1433.) One of the first mauves, a rose to challenge all arrangers in the annual Sterling Bowl tournament. Pinkish lavender buds open to silvery, fragrant blooms, of perfect form. Better as a cut flower from the greenhouse than as a garden bush.

SUMMER SNOW. F. White, 7.4. (Perkins; int. Jackson & Perkins, 1938; Pat. 416.) Hardy, prolific bloomer, with great clusters of pure white flowers on low compact bush. Has been widely planted but being superseded by more modern whites.

SUMMER SUNSHINE. HT. Deep yellow, 7.6*. (Swim; int. Armstrong Nurseries, 1962; Pat. 2078.) Pure yellow, long stemmed flowers, 5 inches across, on low to medium bush.

SUSPENSE. HT. Red blend, 7.6*. (F. Meilland; int. Conard-Pyle, 1960; Pat. 1944.) Bicolor, turkey red with outside of petals yellow-ochre, 55 to 60 petals; dark green foliage.

SUTTER'S GOLD. HT. Orange blend, 8.1. AARS 1950. (Swim; int. Armstrong Nurseries, 1950; Pat. 885.) A fitting commemoration of the discovery of gold in California. Beautiful, pointed bud, yellow shaded with orange; golden, rather open flower, on a long graceful stem; bush vigorous and branching, to 4 feet; free bloom through the summer.

SUSAN LOUISE. S. Pink. (Adams; int. Stocking, 1929.) A disease-free, or nearly so, rose for the South and the West Coast, an everblooming bush form of Belle Portugaise, 4 or 5 feet high; long pointed deep pink buds and flesh-pink, semidouble flowers.

SWEET AFTON. HT. White. (David Armstrong and H. C. Swim; int. Armstrong Nurseries, 1964.) Very fragrant, pink to nearly white blooms, not too double, on tall, strong plant.

SWEET FAIRY. Min. Light pink, 8.3. (de Vink; int. Conard-Pyle, 1946; Pat. 748.) A very dependable miniature for garden or window sill.

Flowers small, 1-inch, double, cupped, appleblossom pink; fragrant enough to scent a room.

TEXAS CENTENNIAL. HT. Light red and deep pink, 7.8. (Watkins; int. Dixie Rose Nursery, 1935; Pat. 162, expired.) A sport of President Hoover and much like it with upright bush, long, strong stems; flowers red with some gold, turning deep pink with age.

THE DOCTOR. HT. Medium pink, 7.6. (F. H. Howard; int. Dreer, 1936.) Everyone loves the enormous flowers, occasionally reaching to 7 inches, satiny rose-pink, fragrant. Sometimes blooming rather sparsely, sometimes fairly abundant, always worth waiting for; medium low bush.

THE FAIRY. S. Light pink, 8.6. (Bentall, 1932; int. Conard-Pyle, 1941.) Introduced as a polyantha, now classed as a shrub, this fine rose is usually described as a *low* spreading bush. It is spreading all right, mine going out to 7 feet but in time they get 4 feet or more high. The glossy, hollylike foliage is covered with clusters of small, pink flowers, resembling Dorothy Perkins in miniature. Perfect for arrangements, it also provides continuous garden display from mid-June to Thanksgiving. Mildew on buds or foliage is extremely rare and this rose hates to be sprayed, so leave it alone to enjoy without work. Be sure to give it room to expand; plant it as a shrub or a hedge, or to accent an entrance.

THE FARMER'S WIFE. F. Light pink, 7.8*. (Boerner; int. Jackson & Perkins; Pat. 2196.) Medium tall floribunda with large, glowing, sunrise-pink flowers on long stems; long-lasting, somewhat fragrant. I use this as part of a pink hedge and love it but hear it is not so good in foggy areas.

TIFFANY. HT. Pink blend, 8.8. AARS 1955. (Lindquist; int. Howard Rose Co., 1954; Pat. 1304.) Long, pointed, deep pink buds, golden at base, open to warm rich pink flowers, produced singly but abundantly on long stems; fragrant; plant vigorous, upright; foliage dark green. A must rose for exhibition or garden.

TRAVIATA. HT. Red blend, 7.1*. (Alain Meilland; int. Conard-Pyle, 1963; Pat. 2283.) An excellent novelty; top half of petals raspberry red, lower half white; blooms large, double, of good form, borne singly and several together; dark green foliage.

TROPICANA (Superstar). HT. Orange red, 8.5*. (Tantau; int. Jackson & Perkins, 1962; Pat. 1969.) More orange than red, very brilliant, medium-sized flowers, very long-lasting, with slight fragrance; borne singly but freely. My bushes are tall but they are said to be medium to low in cool areas. Large glossy, dark green foliage. An excellent garden decorative, as well as cut flower but use this color with some caution about companions.

VANGUARD. S. Orange blend, 8.2. (Stevens; int. Jackson & Perkins, 1932.) A hybrid rugosa, very tall, practically a climber. My New Jersey bush covered half the side of the house, going up to the second story windows without support; my Springvale bush has made a good start. Flowers are large, salmon orange or pinkish, very fragrant. The decorative large, glossy, rugose foliage is seldom attacked by pests so I never spray Vanguard. There is profuse bloom for 3 weeks or more, starting in late May and a most attractive green bush the rest of the summer. Listed by Tillotson's.

VOGUE. F. Pink blend, 8.2. AARS 1952. (Boerner; int. Jackson & Perkins, 1951; Pat. 926.) Of hybrid tea form, dark cherry coral buds opening to flowers flushed with salmon, 3½ inches across; glossy foliage; tall bush; very hardy; very desirable.

WAR DANCE. Gr. Orange red, 7.4*. (Swim & Weeks; int. Conard-Pyle, 1962; Pat. 2017.) Medium to large, cupped, double, high-centered flowers, orange red with dark smoky overtones; long-lasting; often borne singly as a hybrid tea, sometimes in clusters. The bush has a spreading habit, large, leathery foliage.

WHITE BEAUTY. HT. White. (Texas Rose Research Foundation, 1965; Pat. 1825.) A white sport of The Doctor, with the same very large flower and fragrance on a good bush. The open bloom with yellow stamens is particularly attractive.

WHITE BOUQUET. F. White, 7.5. AARS 1957. (Boerner; int. Jackson &

Perkins, 1956; Pat. 1415.) Gardenia-like flower, large, with dark green foliage; bush spreading, of medium height.

WHITE DAWN. ClHT. White, 8.5. (Longley; int. University of Minnesota, 1949.) Double white flowers in clusters; recurrent bloom; vigorous climber with glossy foliage.

WHITE KNIGHT (Message). White, 7.2. AARS 1958. (Meilland; int. Conard-Pyle, 1957; Pat. 1359.) A very beautiful, exhibition flower, high-centered, pure white. Most of the bushes I have seen in gardens across the country appear less than vigorous.

WILLIAM R. SMITH (Blush Maman Cochet). T. Pink blend. Another southern favorite. Double flowers, center pale pink, outer petals creamy flesh, base citron yellow; long stems; rich green, leathery foliage.

WORLD'S FAIR. F. Dark red, 8.0. AARS 1940. (Kordes; int. Jackson & Perkins, 1939; Pat. 362, expired.) A cheerful bedding rose, attracting much attention at the former New York World's Fair and still highly desirable. Flowers cherry-red to dark red, velvety, 4 inches across, in clusters of 10 or more; vigorous bush of medium height. Not in my latest Jackson & Perkins catalogue but still listed by Ackerman and Tillotson's.

WORLD'S FAIR SALUTE. HT. Medium red. (Morey; int. Jackson & Perkins, 1964.) Beautiful high-centered red blooms of fine form, on long stems; moderate damask fragrance; large, leathery foliage; bush to 3½ to 4 feet. A worthy tribute to the 1964 World's Fair.

ZAMBRA. F. Orange. (Alain Meilland; int. Conard-Pyle, 1964; Pat. 2140.) A blazing, scorching orange, wonderful where the color will not clash. The open flowers are flat, semidouble (11 to 13 petals) 3 inches across, and they fade pleasingly to salmon-pink, Fashion being one of the parents. The bush is vigorous, of medium height; the foliage is a leathery pleasing green.

If this list were twice as long it might have included roses that are not yet my personal friends, more of the older roses that are still good and more new roses with their true worth yet to be proved. The old and new roses included here are *good* roses. There are some for every use and every part of the country and every rose lover, beginner or expert. If they have not succeeded with you, perhaps you had poor speciments to start with or maybe you coddle them too much. Please try again before you blame the variety. And grow a bush at least two years before you decide on its worth!

Naturally no one nursery handles all of these varieties. The firms listed here are selected to represent different parts of the country but most of them sell nationally. Remember that it makes little difference where your rose is grown provided you choose a variety right for your own location and can get it in good condition for your own best planting time.

As with the varieties, the nursery list is not all-inclusive. It is limited to firms from whom I have received recent catalogues and who have consented to being listed for retail sales. Many nurseries are wholesale only; some are wholesale but make retail sales to local patrons; some firms sell roses grown for them by others; some specialize in potted roses and these have to be for local sales for it costs too much to ship in containers and there may be quarantine problems involved in interstate shipment of soil.

NURSERIES SPECIALIZING IN ROSES
(and offering plants through retail catalogues)

ACKERMAN NURSERIES, Bridgman, Michigan.

ARMSTRONG NURSERIES, INC., Ontario, California.

ARP ROSES, INC., P.O. Box 3338, Tyler, Texas.

BREEDLOVE NURSERIES RETAIL, P.O. Box 450, Tyler, Texas.

BRIGHTRIDGE ROSE COMPANY, 125 Brightridge Avenue, East Providence 14, Rhode Island. Walter D. Brownell, Jr. offering Brownell roses.

C. L. BROWN & SON, Rose Growers, R.D. 5, Carlisle, Pennsylvania.

CALIFORNIA NURSERY COMPANY, Niles District, Fremont, California.

CARROLL GARDENS, P.O. Box 310, Westminster, Maryland.

THE CONARD-PYLE COMPANY (Star Roses), West Grove, Pennsylvania.

D & D ROSE GARDENS, 42 Monmouth Road, Eatontown, New Jersey.

FRED EDMUNDS ROSES, P.O. Box 68, Wilsonville, Oregon 97070.

ELMER ROSES COMPANY, 4273 Riverside Drive, Chino, California.

EMLONG NURSERIES, Stevensville, Michigan.

EARL FERRIS NURSERY, Hampton, Iowa 50441.

FRUITLAND NURSERIES, P.O. Box 3506, Augusta, Georgia 30904.

GOLDEN STATE NURSERIES OF GEORGIA, INC., P.O. Box 11670, Atlanta, Georgia 30305.

ROY HENNESSEY'S, Rt. 1, Box 288, Scappoose, Oregon 97056.

PAUL J. HOWARD'S CALIFORNIA FLOWERLAND, 11700 National Boulevard, Los Angeles 64, California.

ILGENFRITZ NURSERIES, P.O. Box 665, Monroe, Michigan 48161.

INTER-STATE NURSERIES, Hamburg, Iowa 51640.

JACKSON & PERKINS COMPANY, Newark, New York and 204 Rose Lane, Pleasanton, California.

FORREST KEELING NURSERY, Elsberry, Missouri.

KELLY BROS. NURSERIES, INC., Dansville, New York.

JOSEPH J. KERN NURSERY, Box 33, Mentor, Ohio 44060. Specializing in old roses; does custom budding.

E. V. KIMBREW, P.O. Wills Point, Texas 75169.

THE KRIDER NURSERIES, INC., Middlebury, Indiana.

KROH BROS. NURSERIES, P.O. Box 536, Loveland, Colorado.

LAMB NURSERIES, E. 101 Sharp Avenue, Spokane 2, Washington. Offers miniatures.

MARTIN'S ROSE NURSERY, P.O. Box 177, ARP, Texas 75750.

EARL MAY SEED AND NURSERY Co., Shenandoah, Iowa 51601.

McCONNELL NURSERY Co., LTD., Port Burwell, Ontario, Canada.

MINER'S ROSES, P.O. Box 341, Boynton Beach, Florida. Roses for Florida on Fortuniana understock.

MINI-ROSES, Sta. A, P.O. Box 4255, Dallas 8, Texas. Miniatures exclusively but a wide selection.

MOORE MINIATURE ROSES, Sequoia Nursery, 2519 Mineral King, Visalia, California. Miniatures only.

NEW LONDON ROSES, P.O. Box 386, Overton, Texas 75694.

ROSEDALE NURSERIES, Hawthorne, New York. Potted plants only.

ROSEWAY NURSERIES, 2935 S.W. 234th Avenue, Beaverton, Oregon 97005.

R. H. SHUMWAY, P.O. Box 777, Rockford, Illinois 61101.

SPRING HILL NURSERIES, Tipp City, Ohio.

STANEK'S, INC., E. 2929 27th Avenue, Spokane, Washington 99208.

STARK BROS. NURSERIES, Louisiana, Missouri. Lists some varieties not available elsewhere.

STOCKING ROSE NURSERY, 12505 North Capitol Avenue, San Jose 33, California.

P. O. TATE NURSERY, Route 3, Tyler, Texas.

THOMASVILLE NURSERIES, INC., Thomasville, Georgia. Good source of Tea roses.

WILL TILLOTSON'S ROSES, Brown's Valley Road, Watsonville, California. Old and new roses.

TY-TEX ROSE NURSERIES, P.O. Box 532, Tyler, Texas.

THE WAYSIDE GARDENS Co., Mentor, Ohio 44060.

RUSSELL WILSON NURSERIES, Winsboro, Texas.

PERCY H. WRIGHT, 407 109th Street, Saskatoon. Saskatchewan, Canada. Limited distribution of roses for severe winters.

MELVIN E. WYANT, ROSE SPECIALIST INC., Johnny Cake Ridge, Mentor, Ohio.

CHAPTER III

LIVING WITH ROSES

It used to be fashionable to stick the rose garden far away from the house, hidden behind the evergreens, on the theory that rose bushes were ugly most of the year. A few landscape architects cling to this notion but many now fit a few shrub and climbing roses into the landscape picture and some allow roses their rightful place in the outdoor living room. And in the new housing developments, now spreading from city to city, roses are appearing more and more in front yards for everyone to enjoy.

Admittedly a prejudiced rose nut, I think that roses are beautiful nine months of the year and tolerable the other three. Even in winter a neat bed of hybrid teas looks a lot better than perennial beds swaddled with salt hay or boxwood shrouded in burlap. The red or orange hips of many species and climbing roses are colorful most of the winter and the early spring foliage of some floribunda roses is utterly delightful.

The alphabetical list of rose varieties in the last chapter is intended to provide you with roses suited to your particular mode of living. But be-

fore we take up the possibilities for you I'd like to digress for a few pages
and talk about my own living with roses.

As a child, it was vicarious. We had a very few old roses in our yard
but mostly it was bouquets from kind neighbors that triggered my life-
long affection. When I went to Cornell for graduate work, Dr. L. M.
Massey was my senior adviser and since his research was with rose diseases that became my field also. I grew some roses myself, worked with
many more in the test plots and display plantings at the University.

There followed two years when I lived without roses, in a one-room
apartment in a not very beautiful city. The most vivid remembrance of
those two years is of a flaming row of Paul's Scarlet Climber that I
passed each morning on my way to work. I determined to duplicate it
which meant I had to have some land. And that need for land crystal-
lized my decision to start out on my own as a plant doctor.

When I hunted for a location I had only two requirements—something
within my lean pocketbook and enough room to grow roses. I had to buy
instead of rent so the roses could stay put and I had to make good at
plant doctoring to support the roses, even though they were to be guinea
pigs for testing sprays and dusts. The result was a tall, narrow, most un-
prepossessing house on a long narrow lot, about 320 by 54 feet, filled
with ancient trees, shrubs, and weeds.

A tall privet hedge edged the lot on one side and a driveway on the
other, while a huge cherry tree in front of an old barn cut it into work-
able proportions. The first year I concentrated on the area between the
back door and the barn, retrieving some sort of lawn under the cherry
tree and propping up the old grapevine that marked off this section into
a secluded drawing room, wonderful for tea except when aphids dripped
down out of young curled foliage or birds feasted on the fruit.

On the house side of the grapevines I stretched my row of Paul's Scarlet as background for a rose living room. I planted the climbers too close
together so I later moved one across the path, tying the branches together
to form an arch that stayed without support. I went back to Cornell and
yanked out of two years' growth of weeds some Dr. W. Van Fleet climbers that had been inoculated with various diseases during the course of
experiments and had recovered therefrom. These were set along the privet
hedge at the left of the lot. On the right side, along the drive, I planted

lilacs as background for a wide perennial border. In the beginning, floribundas were used as accent among the perennials but in the course of
time the roses took up most of the space.

In the very narrow bed along the path from the back door to the
grapevine I planted a pink hedge of Else Poulsen accented with Betty
Prior. This was the third wall of my outdoor living room (the fourth
was the house) and, strategically placed to be in full view whether I took
my solitary meals at the dining table or in the big chair by the radio or
out under the pear tree, it provided color eight months out of the year.
When the Kieffer pear was in full bloom and daffodils made a yellow
ribbon down the path Else put out the loveliest reddish foliage imaginable. Toward June came the pointed bright pink buds and the slightly
double pink flowers. For several years there was a row of blue iris at
Else's feet but there was never enough time for the constant dividing,
plus borer and soft rot control, that iris demands, so the pink and blue
color scheme was carried out with an edging of blue pansies, giving way
to ageratum, backed by blue eupatorium and pink snapdragons.

My rose living room was furnished with ten rose beds, five on each
side of a broad grass path. To facilitate spray tests the roses were mixed
as to color and variety in each bed but the same combination replicated
in the different beds. Most were hybrid teas but floribundas at the inner
edge of each bed kept a continuity of color. By a fortunate accident I
chose Kirsten Poulsen, sister to Else, and the single flowers on this tall
vigorous bush blended so perfectly with Paul's Scarlet in the background
it was hard to tell where one began and the other left off.

When the vegetables in the garden back of the garage gave way to
twenty-four small rose test beds polyantha Orange Triumph, repeated in
each bed, gave continuity of color. It crowded the hybrid teas but I kept
it for its gaiety and because the foliage reacted so distinctly to many
sprays and pests. In July and August, when red spiders abetted by DDT
had dropped most of the leaves, I wanted to disown the thing but when it
came back with fresh flowers and foliage in September I was again lost
in admiration.

Red spiders were the limiting factor in growing roses in the back garden. A tall hedge on one side, a wooded hillside in back, a row of shrubs
backed by a row of trees on the third side, a garage and an apple tree in

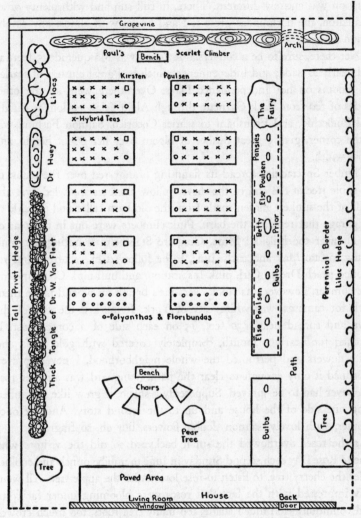

Grapevine

Paul's   Bench   Scarlet Climber   Arch

Kirsten   Paulsen

x-Hybrid Teas

Dr Huey

The Fairy

Pansies

Betty Prior   Else Poulsen

Else Poulsen   Bulbs

Tall Privet Hedge

Thick Tangle of Dr. W. Van Fleet

o-Polyanthas & Floribundas

Bench
Chairs

Pear Tree

Tree

Bulbs

Perennial Border   Lilac Hedge

Tree

Path

Paved Area

Living Room   House   Back
Window   Door

FIG. 11. My Rose Living Room (Scale: 1 inch = 10 feet).

front, plus all the weeds I never managed to eliminate, made this portion of the garden absolute heaven for spider mites. None of the dusts and sprays I tried was completely effective. Over next door, however, where my floribundas overflowed around my neighbor's vegetable patch, the situation was entirely different. There, in full sun and with plenty of air circulation, the floribundas grew tall and bushy with almost any combination pesticide keeping them free from trouble.

Over there, sure to be a conversation piece, was Masquerade, 5 feet tall and nearly as wide; and Independence which had great clusters of scarlet-red blooms on hot Independence Days. Over there were all the other shades of red from dark Garnette through Alain (alas, no longer listed). Red Pinocchio, and Frensham to scarlet Cocorico. Salmon Fashion was at the corner, giving great flushes of bloom over her 6-foot height and 5-foot width.

Climber Spectacular spread its flaunting orangy red over the trunk of the apple tree at the end of the drive, yellow climbers sprawled over the walls of the sunken garden made from the old barn cellar and the side of the garage that replaced the barn. Pink climbers were out in the rear of the lot near the hillside: Mme. Gregoire Staechelin flaunting her pink beauty in late May and early June, to be followed by recurrent but restrained peach Dream Girl, pink Inspiration, and buff-pink Clytemnestra. The climber, however, that took everyone's breath away, and made them reach for cameras, was white City of York. It marked the end of the drive and spread nearly 30 feet, 15 on each side of a corner post. It bloomed for nearly a month, completely covered with gold buds and white flowers and perfumed the whole neighborhood. I never sprayed it, pruned it only enough to clear the path. Vanguard was another rose that never had to be sprayed. Supposedly a shrub, it grew like a climber, along one side of the house and up to the second story. Another once bloomer, with lovely, salmon double flowers, but oh, so fragrant!

As the roses overflowed the small backyard so did the visitors who came to Rose Day each second Sunday in June to imbibe punch and cookies under the cherry tree, to listen to rose lore under the apple tree. All went away impressed with the fact that roses were blooming under far from ideal conditions—too much shade, too many tree roots, too much crowding, and a mistress who spent her time doctoring other people's roses and had little time for her own.

When the Garden Club of Montclair started a Garden Center and planned a "wheel of Life" garden, I was given the task of planting two pie-shaped sectors, on either side of a central fountain, to roses. The soil was almost impossible; every inch had to be pried out with a mattock and one side was so impervious there was no drainage. But we managed to improve the soil and have a constant display of color from late May to December. The garden always appeared to contain more than its 250 bushes because of the way the floribundas responded to open space and full sun. Starting next to the fountain in one sector we planted low pink Pinkie, then went up in steps through Pink Rosette, Pink Bountiful, and Ma Perkins to grandiflora Queen Elizabeth, accenting the corners with dark pink Cheerio.

The matching bed in the other sector started with dwarf orange Margo Koster, backed by orange-reds—Fusilier, Independence, Geranium Red and Cocorico. The other beds had hybrid teas but again accented with floribundas and there was a whole row of these to make the "rim" of each wedge of pie. One was red—Alain, Red Pinocchio, Donald Prior, World's Fair; the other had yellows and salmon—Fashion, Pinocchio, Goldilocks and King Boreas.

It was Spartan, however, that stole the show at the Montclair Garden Center. Before it was on the market we had a gift of fifty bushes from the originator, Eugene Boerner of Jackson & Perkins. The bushes were delivered in March to the warm building and it was a week before anyone told me they were there, during which time the canes developed long tender sprouts. The day after planting we had an icestorm and that summer the worst drought in our history. We had put those roses along the driveway, in poor soil, although we did incorporate organic matter in individual holes. Spartan had no mulch, though the rest of the roses had buckwheat hulls, and not one bit of artificial watering. The bushes grew tall, bloomed and bloomed, survived the winter with no protection and no losses and bloomed again, bringing visitors from far and wide to see "that rose."

To keep such a public garden, seen by hundreds every week, presentable means a constant cutting out of fading blooms. In June these roses were cleaned up nearly every day; the rest of the summer I went two or three times a week, collecting two or three bushels of dead flowers at every visit. Such constant cutting back to a good bud kept the new flowering shoots coming quickly and provided color through hot summers when roses often go into a decline.

For twenty-five years I sprayed other people's gardens from March to November—six days a week unless it rained or I had a lecture date. There came a time when such physical laboring was too much and I gave up the active part of plant doctoring and devoted more time to writing. That meant giving up my garden assistant. Instead of gaining leisure to enjoy my own roses I found myself trimming the hedge, mowing the lawn, edging the beds, trying to keep the shrubs in bounds. When the vastly increased tax bill arrived (August, 1961) it all seemed too much and I decided to try living without roses. I telephoned a realtor, telephoned Springvale and by night was committed to moving. My house, with its 600 roses, was sold in a month—to a landscape contractor—and I spent the intervening time burning up the accumulation of a lifetime, reducing furniture from eight rooms to two. Bringing with me only a dozen miniature roses and a rooted cutting of Kirsten Poulsen (because it is no longer commercially available) I started an entirely new mode of life.

Springvale is a new development for "senior citizens," retired and semiretired people. Thirty low buildings, averaging 17 apartments each, have been fitted onto the grounds of an old estate so carefully that almost all the trees have been saved, almost every apartment has a magnificent view of the Hudson River and the mountains on beyond. There are all sorts of facilities—an Inn which is a retirement hotel but with a restaurant for the rest of us to use, stores, a swimming pool. Most important of all, *every* apartment has space for a small garden near the doorstep and every space is filled with overflowing bloom.

I had steeled myself to be content with the miniatures and perhaps a half dozen hybrid teas in my personal plot but then I learned more land could be had for the asking and I didn't have to live without roses after all.

The miniatures were, of course, planted immediately, in the two-foot border running between my concrete terrace and the walk servicing our rear, groundfloor apartments. Everyone stops to talk about this narrow border and to wonder if the tiny roses are real. Bloom starts with snowdrops and blue and gold crocuses, then grape hyacinths and pink and white water-lily tulips, followed by an edging of alternating blue and white pansies. In May, pink geraniums go in back of the miniatures, sunk in their pots in a rug of blue ageratum, with taller blue eupatorium flowering in late summer.

Immediately after transplanting the miniatures and putting in the first bulbs, I had to leave for a two-month lecture trip. I came back to snow and rose catalogues. I kept filling out orders for more and more roses, old and new, I simply had to have. The nurseries wrote that they again wanted to send test roses. Adding these up I found that I was committed to planting almost two hundred roses, which would start to arrive almost immediately, with no beds prepared. I had expected to dig my own beds; I had not expected to go overboard quite so soon!

Rosedale Nurseries came to the rescue, providing labor, vast quantities of peat moss and other supplies. On paper, the job had figured to one day for two men. It actually took three men three days, due to the rocks and difficult terrain, and the cost was far more than my budget but the results have been worth it. It certainly does pay to give roses a good start in life. Nothing afterwards can make up for inadequate soil preparation. The beds for roses arriving in succeeding years were personally prepared, slowly and painfully. It took me a week this past spring to dig the soil for a bed only 3 by 15 feet, but I ended up with a real stone wall made with the boulders removed from that small area.

This is not a formal rose garden. It is a sprawling affair, fitted into the terrain, planned to avoid rock ledges. A driveway, winding down the hill on the side of our building, stops at the rear walk. Beside the drive, hiding the drain, are low shrub roses—Otto Linne and Frau Dagmar Hartopp. The main garden is northwest of the drive—two halves, about 6 feet wide, of a big horseshoe. Here are mostly hybrid teas—pinks, blends, and white on one side, reds, orange, and yellow on the other—but blended with other types. Both ends of the horseshoe are finished with floribunda Ivory Fashion, with blue lobelia and white alyssum at its feet. Golden Slippers, Fashion, and Fashionette edge both sides of the path through the center of the horseshoe, making a transition from the pastels in the left bed to the more brilliant colors in the right bed.

West of the horseshoe a split-rail fence marks the boundary of Springvale land and here there are climbers—Golden Showers, New Dawn, Blossomtime, Katie, Aloha, Clair Matin—to form a background. Going South the climbers give way to shrubs—Golden Wings, Frau Karl

Druschki, Agnes, Henry Nevard, Pink Grootendorst, Salet, Frühlings-morgen and Belinda. Duet and Pink Parfait, bordered with Mrs. R. M. Finch, form a focal point at the end of the driveway. The private owner of the land behind the rail fence has planted a row of arborvitae behind these shrubs, providing a lovely background although possibly stealing some of the moisture needed by the roses. Shallow stone steps go from the drive into the shrub area, flanked by lovely white Snow Fairy on either side and then some of the new test roses, most of which now have names—Candy Stripe, Traviata, Song of Paris and many more.

South of the shrubs, and paralleling the whole length of the building is a pink hedge, with a sea of dogwoods in its rear. It starts with my favorites, continuously blooming Else Poulsen and Betty Prior, and goes on through The Farmers' Wife, Queenie, Robin Hood, many plants of County Fair, and ends with The Fairy. Scattered through are Queen Elizabeth and various pink hybrid teas and a couple of perpetuals. I *love* my pink hedge. I eat my lunch on the terrace and gloat over it. Lighted at night from the top of the building it is the last thing I see before bed.

Gayer, mostly new roses continue the line of the hedge out to the bluff above the road and just beyond the end of the apartments. More roses have filled in all the bare spots in the neighbors' personal plots by their doorways. There is no room left within view of my terrace, so I have no idea where next year's test roses, or the roses I can't keep myself from ordering, are to go. But I'll probably be doing more digging somewhere.

This retirement garden is strictly a display garden. I try out new roses but I don't use untested chemicals that might be toxic to roses. Rose Days have been continued (June, 1965, marked the 25th) but every day is vis-iting day. The roses respond lavishly to all the love and admiration be-stowed upon them by residents, guests of residents, prospective tenants, and strangers curious to see what Springvale is like. Those who are troubled in mind or body come to sit on the bench in the sun amid the roses, or come there to cool off while they watch the sunset.

I have always said that roses respond to love and the Springvale roses prove it. Of course, if you want to be literal, there is an explanation. Just as I clean house when I expect visitors indoors, so I clean the roses for visitors outdoors. And since company comes every day, so every day, or almost, the old blooms get cut off. The roses also get watered more often than my New Jersey roses that had visitors mostly once a year and it is this copious watering, plus constant removal of fading flowers, that keeps roses producing without going into summer doldrums.

Now let's come back to *your* roses and *your* mode of life. If you go away for all summer and have no one with whom to trust your hybrid teas, then keep that class small, with foolproof varieties like Red Radiance and subzeros like Pink Princess and Curly Pink that are so tolerant of blackspot that they will provide fall bloom even if unsprayed all summer. Place your emphasis on spring-flowering shrub roses or large-flowered climbers that have a fine June display and disease-resistant foliage the rest of the season, and on such floribundas as are relatively disease-free and will provide masses of color all fall. If you live in the South, go in heavily for tea roses that do not require a continual fight against blackspot. Try Louis Philippe and Susan Louise; enjoy the old climbers—Marechal Niel, Cherokee, and white or yellow Banksia. If you live in the far North, your easiest roses are species native to the prairies or roses like Patricia Macoun bred for cold climates, or hybrid rugosas or subzero hybrid teas. But if you live in the temperate zone, are at home to enjoy your roses most of the year and don't begrudge them an hour or so a week of regular attention, then you can have many types and varieties with your choice limited solely by what will make a harmonious whole.

HYBRID TEAS

I have no favorite rose. Whenever I am asked to name one I say that it is the rose I am looking at at that moment. I used to try to choose a dozen hybrid teas but I can no longer. For every rose that might be mentioned there are a dozen more to dispute its place. Many nurseries offer a special collection for beginners and this may not be a bad way to start. They choose non-temperamental varieties of which they have a large supply, so you get good stock. Out of the dozen there will probably be one or two for which you feel no special affinity but you have only paid the price of nine or ten roses purchased separately.

After that first dozen I doubt if you will allow anyone else the fun of choosing your roses. You will buy singly, or perhaps three of a variety, and spend half the winter planning and replanning your garden, wondering what you can move in the garden to have room for one more rose bed and what you can do without to have the price of one more rose. And each year, when the brand new roses appear in the catalogues, you'll have to try one or two to see if they really are lovelier than those you already have.

HYBRID TEA ROSES BY COLOR

Red—Christian Dior, Christopher Stone, Chrysler Imperial, Crimson Duke, Crimson Glory, Etoile de Hollande, Grand Duchess Charlotte, Helene Schoen, Indiana, Karl Herbst, Lotte Gunthart, Mirandy, Mr. Lincoln, New Yorker, Nocturne, Poinsettia, Queen o' the Lakes, World's Fair Salute.

Red blend—Banzai, Hector Deane, Mme. Henri Guillot, Rose Gaujard, Suspense, Traviata.

Orange red—Aztec, Hawaii, Orange Flame, Tropicana.

Light red and deep pink—American Beauty, Charlotte Armstrong, Red Radiance, Rubaiyat, Texas Centennial.

Pink—Blithe Spirit, Columbus Queen, Curly Pink, Dainty Bess (single), Duet, Editor McFarland, Emily, First Love, Katherine T. Marshall, Lulu, Mrs. Charles Bell, Pink Duchess, Pink Favorite, Pink Peace, Pink Princess, Radiance, Royal Highness, Show Girl, Sweet Afton, The Doctor.

Pink blend—Candy Stripe, Comtesse Vandal, Chicago Peace, Confidence, Gail Borden, Good News, Granada, Grand Opera, Helen Traubel, Kordes Perfecta, Mission Bells, Mme. Cochet-Cochet, President Herbert Hoover, Tiffany.

Apricot and orange blends—Angels Mateu, Cape Coral, Condesa de Sastago, Duquesa de Penaranda, Lucky Piece, McGredy's Sunset, Mojave, Mrs. Sam McGredy, Seneca Queen, South Seas (pinker than this ARS classification indicates).

Yellow and yellow blend—American Heritage, Burnaby, Cecil, Eclipse, Garden Party, Helen Hayes, Lily Pons, Lady Elgin, Lowell Thomas, King's Ransom, McGredy's Yellow, Mrs. Pierre S. du Pont, Peace, Soeur Therese, Summer Sunshine, Sutter's Gold.

White—Blanche Mallerin, John F. Kennedy, Kaiserin Auguste
Viktoria, Matterhorn, Memoriam, Neige Parfum, Pedralbes,
Sincera, White Beauty, White Knight.
Mauve—Song of Paris, Sterling Silver.

The list above is limited to the varieties described in Chapter II. There
are many other fine hybrid teas with which you can paint pictures in
your garden. Some rose lovers prefer to separate colors, the pinks in one
bed, red in another, yellows in a third. This works best for the large
public rose garden where a whole bed is devoted to a single variety. For
backyard planting I like to see the colors mixed in each bed but with
some one color repeated enough in the garden to give a pleasing over-all
effect. Even with mixed colors, varieties cannot be placed in indiscriminate
juxtaposition. Most of the new orange reds, like Tropicana, are horrible
next to the bright clear pink of an Editor McFarland or Show Girl. But
orange tones can work in with the coppery pink of Mme. Cochet-Cochet
or with a brilliant bicolor like Condesa de Sastago or Suspense. If you
want to work from clear pinks to yellows you can make a transition with
Peace or Lucky Piece or Chicago Peace which have both pink and
yellow in their petals. Most of the true reds, and especially the dark reds,
are good neighbors with light pink, peach or salmon, and white roses can
always be sandwiched in to prevent clashes.

Mixing colors in beds has more than esthetic value; it is a very
definite aid in disease control. Most of the yellow roses, and the blends,
have Pernetiana blood in their veins that makes them particularly susceptible to blackspot. If one or two susceptible roses are next to rather
resistant roses the disease does not make as much headway as when all
the susceptibles are grouped together. I liken it to the common cold. If
you sneeze in a crowded room and the people nearest you are the kind
that take cold at the drop of a hat, then they, too, will go sneezing around
and pretty soon there will be such an epidemic of colds that even the
hardiest will succumb.

When it rains, blackspot spores are splashed to the rose leaves near
by. If the spores land on Radiance, or Etoile de Hollande, there may be
one or two black spots formed but there is no great increase in the amount

of inoculum (meaning the spores of the infective agent). If, on the other hand, that sneezing yellow or apricot rose is surrounded by a lot more yellow roses there may be hundreds of black spots formed on their leaves, in which thousands of little black fruiting bodies and millions of spores are produced. Soon there is such a vast amount of inoculum being splashed around by rain or spread by you as you work among the roses when they are wet that even the pink and red varieties that ordinarily shake off the disease succumb to it and drop their leaves.

Whenever you buy new roses there is the possibility of bringing in blackspot via lesions on the canes. If you buy a dozen plants of one variety from the same nursery and if that nursery had bad luck with its control program that year, that block of roses may be defoliated in your garden the first season despite your own protective program. I have seen this happen more than once. Usually you can get the disease under control by the next season but I am a great believer in diversified planting. The Elmwood Avenues in towns stricken by the Dutch elm disease are mute testimony to the danger of putting all your eggs in one basket. It works that way with roses, too.

In planting hybrid teas and other bedding roses, make the beds narrow enough so you can care for the plants without having to get into the beds and all scratched up. I can't tell you how much future cussing a little forethought will prevent. I cared for one garden where a large semicircle of evergreens was filled solidly with roses. It looked beautiful but it was awful to work in. I seldom came away without ruining a pair of stockings and usually, in getting between the roses to spray or cut off dead bloom, I managed to step on a bush or break off a branch. If you don't have narrow beds always provide paths through the jungle.

A good width for a rose bed is 5½ feet. This provides for three rows 24 inches apart and 9 inches from each edge. In the South, where bushes grow larger, such a bed might take only two rows. If you are still an advocate of hard pruning and seldom let your roses reach normal size, you may want to plant a bit closer. Roses should be spaced so that when in full foliage they almost touch, thus keeping the ground shaded, but far enough apart so that one rose does not compete with another for food and light.

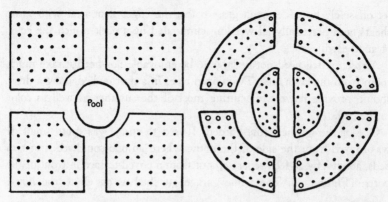

FIG. 12. Left, 132 hybrid teas in square beds around a pool, a popular plan but more difficult to maintain than the circular garden at Right, where 130 hybrid teas plus 28 floribundas are planted in narrow beds covering smaller total area.

Rose beds curved around a pool are lovely but if you have a pool you need fish to keep away the mosquitoes and if you have fish you cannot dust the roses without covering the pool. You may, however, spray fairly close to a pool by directing the spray rod away from the water and watching the wind.

Don't border rose beds with mint or lettuce or strawberries or other edibles. Think of the poisons you'll be using on the roses every week!

Don't border rose beds with boxwood, if you want to save time. Boxwood is beautiful but it takes many more hours to keep it healthy and sheared than the roses themselves require.

Although it is better not to plant annuals between rose bushes they can often be used on the outside of a bed. I am partial to pansies, lobelia, ageratum and sweet alyssum used in this way. Here at Springvale I have alternating pink and white petunias at the feet of the floribundas making up the pink hedge.

Over the years I have observed rose beds edged with wooden or metal bands, bricks at every angle, paving blocks, as well as the boxwood mentioned above. I have worked on paths made of white stone, gravel, brick, concrete and flagstone. It seems to me that the simplest arrangement, requiring the least maintenance, is the most beautiful—rose beds set off solely by wide green grass paths, the edges kept neat with grass shears, and practically all weeding eliminated by a dark mulch the color of good earth.

A rose garden need not be large to be enjoyable nor need it take much room from the lawn area. Two dozen roses in a narrow bed along a drive should provide flowers for cutting most of the summer as well as color in the bed.

One of the loveliest rose gardens I used to spray was quite small. It was moved from the side of the house where no one could see it to two beds, about 5 by 20 feet, separated out from a paved terrace in front of the porch (Figure 13). The white garage attached as an ell to the house

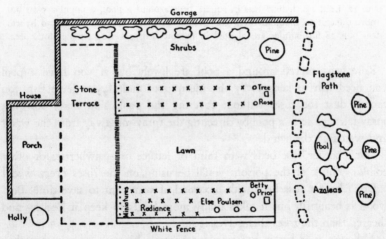

FIG. 13. A small rose garden planned for maximum enjoyment from porch and terrace.

formed a background on one side and was matched by a white fence on the other. At one end of the grass area there was a small pool, really a birdbath, in front of evergreens. Frau Karl Druschki was used as a tree rose at the far end of each bed but her standard was hidden by Betty Prior, while Else Poulsen, Radiance and Mrs. Charles Bell were put along the fence. The hybrid teas numbered less than fifty and, except for pink along the fence, colors were mixed, with two or three plants of each variety. The beds were deeply prepared with plenty of organic matter and the flowers were cut with loving care to keep the bushes strong and tall. Parties on the terrace celebrated the beauty of the roses in June but they were almost as lovely in July when the family was away and the maid took over watering and cutting, for she also loved the roses and kept them blooming in hot weather.

I know I am harping on this subject of love but my rounds took me from that small garden where the roses were patently happy to another where they were obviously unhappy. In that second garden the several hundred roses were hidden far away from the house and visited chiefly by the butler who was expected to bring in quantities of long-stemmed flowers every day. The bushes never were allowed to grow for garden display, almost never were seen by visitors.

FLORIBUNDAS

The small polyantha roses have mostly given place in our gardens to floribundas (hybrid polyanthas) which can be depended upon to give continuous color from June to Thanksgiving. The two classes together (and most lists now include polyanthas among the floribundas) can provide every height, from 12 inches to 12 feet, for every imaginable purpose —low edging, bedding and mass display, medium or tall hedges, specimen shrubs, or accent in the perennial border. They are particularly well adapted to the ranch homes in new developments and are often used in place of evergreens for foundation plantings and along the front fence or path. Our suburbs, seen as we drive along the streets, are far more colorful than in past years. Life would be desolate indeed without floribundas.

Floribunda Roses by Color

Red—Crimson Rosette, Donald Prior, Frensham, Garnette, Red Pinocchio, Nadine, World's Fair.

Red blend—Masquerade, Orange Triumph, Rumba.

Orange red—Capri, Cocorico, Crown Jewel, Fire King, Floradora, Fusilier, Geranium Red, Ginger, Heat Wave, Independence, Sarabande, Spartan.

Pink—Betsy McCall, Betty Prior (very tall), Cecile Brunner,

County Fair, Else Poulsen, Frolic, Gruss an Aachen, Mrs. R. M. Finch, Pink Bountiful, Pink Chiffon, Pinkie (low), Polka, Rosenelf, The Farmer's Wife.

Pink blend—Fashion, Fashionette, Ma Perkins, Margo Koster (dwarf and more orange than pink), Peach Glow, Pinocchio, Vogue.

Yellow—Gold Cup, Golden Fleece, Goldilocks, King Boreas, Starlet.

Orange and yellow blends—Apricot Nectar, Circus, Golden Slippers, Jiminy Cricket, Little Darling, Zambra.

White—Ivory Fashion, Moonsprite, Saratoga, Snow Fairy, Summer Snow, White Bouquet.

Mauve—Lavender Girl, Lavender Princess, Lilac Dawn, Pigmy Lavender.

Many of the new orange red floribundas, especially the dazzling ones like Sarabande, have to be placed rather carefully but some, like Spartan, have enough pinkish tints so that they fit in easily with many other roses. Dwarf polyantha Margo Koster is mostly a difficult orange and I don't see how it got classed as a pink blend. But I love this little rose where the color is right. One of my clients used it around a terrace with dwarf blue ageratum with excellent effect.

It used to be argued that floribundas had no fragrance but that has changed. Saratoga (AARS 1964) has a delightful scent as well as fine flowers freely produced on a vigorous bush. Ivory Fashion may be less fragrant but it is tops for performance, continuous through the summer, and for beauty.

Floribundas are considered hardier than hybrid teas. They mostly winter well, they do provide more continuous color but most of them are just as subject to disease and most have to be sprayed along with hybrid teas. Betty Prior is an exception. She is quite free from mildew and other problems even when grown next to Else Poulsen who always has to be sprayed. When you are spraying a whole garden anyway it does not make much difference which bush is more disease-free but if you want a bush around a birdbath or in some other location where pesticides are undesirable I highly recommend Betty Prior.

GRANDIFLORAS

Grandiflora roses form a somewhat nebulous class between floribundas and hybrid teas. The first rose to be so designated, in 1954, was Queen Elizabeth, a luscious pink on a tall and sturdy bush, with large flowers on long stems, borne singly or several together. This is still rated highest of the thirty-one grandifloras listed in the 1964 *Guide for Buying Roses* of the American Rose Society. I personally rate John S. Armstrong equally high. The very dark velvety red flowers are produced continuously on a sturdy bush that is both tall and spreading. Both Queen Elizabeth and John Armstrong need more room than the average hybrid tea but some grandifloras, such as salmon-orange Montezuma and dusky scarlet War Dance, have the habit of hybrid teas and can be readily grown with them. Yellow Buccaneer is so tall and willowy it may need support; Golden Girl is a better bush. Grandiflora Pink Parfait is usually more restrained than hybrid tea Duet but both are fairly tall in my garden and are good companions. June Bride is a medium tall, rather good white but it is surpassed by Mount Shasta with its large, perfect, hybrid-tea form flowers. New for 1965 is two-toned pink Garden State, as tall as Queen Elizabeth.

MINIATURES

Miniature roses were not one of my early addictions. I would see them at the edge of clients' hybrid tea beds and think them pretty much lost. Then one spring I had to prepare an exhibit on rose culture for our state Flower Show in mid-May. There would be few if any garden roses then and I did not want the hothouse variety so I ordered, in March, some dormant miniatures, 3 Red Imp, 3 Sweet Fairy, 3 Tinker Bell. I potted them up in a mixture of compost, peat moss, sand and soil and put them by the living-room windows. By show time they were all blooming merrily and I placed them in three small window boxes, sunk in peat moss, and with white violets from the back hill between the pots. In no wise discouraged by several show days without sun, the miniatures came back to my garden. I planted some directly, sunk the rest in the beds in their pots. In January each year I brought them into the house and, despite my neglect of their crying need for humidity indoors, some survived years of this in-and-out performance, still in the same pots. Red spiders go with indoor potted roses like fleas on a dog. Unless the roses are washed daily and the humidity kept high, the mites gradually win out. My intentions are good but by the time the little roses go back in the garden they have lost most of their leaves. Meanwhile they have been a lot of comfort as I have slaved at the typewriter. You really have to see miniatures indoors to appreciate their perfect form, the jauntiness of a Red Imp, the very sweet fragrance of Sweet Fairy.

Despite their small size, and true miniatures are not supposed to be over a foot high, these baby roses are perfectly hardy. Mine had no winter protection in Glen Ridge, receive none here in New York, and some of those first acquisitions are among those brought along to Springvale. Red Imp stays only 6 inches high but I also transported some taller favorites—Baby Masquerade, Pixie Gold and Pixie Rose. The two latter were brought to me one winter by Louisa Lunceford, miniature enthusiast and blue-ribbon winner. I was home recuperating from an operation and Louisa had journeyed to Pennsylvania to purchase them and had them repotted in her own magic mixture. One of the most delightful gifts I ever had, it is still enchanting hundreds of people, who always stop to exclaim over the two Pixies as they walk by my terrace.

Other tiny roses have joined the originals. Some have been ordered by mail, more brought home from the New York Flower Show in March, enjoyed for a few weeks on the windowsill, then moved to the terrace border. I have only scratched the surface with varieties—darling Baby Betsy McCall, Opal Jewel, Silver Tips, Eleanor, Dian, Pink Heather, a few others. If you really want to know all about miniatures read Margaret E. Pinney's *The Miniature Rose Book*. Mrs. Pinney grows more than 150 baby roses and has described every one down to its sepals, hypanthium, prickles, parents, and chromosomes. I don't know them that well; I merely love them.

CLIMBERS AND SHRUBS

Climbing roses belong, of course, on houses and porches and garages, over arbors, and along fences; but how about letting them be the walls of your outdoor living room, or at least the flowered wallpaper if you have a green hedge, or a row of evergreens, or a brick wall, or wooden fence to start with? Red climbers are lovely against a green background or a white house or next to white Silver Moon or City of York, or flesh-colored New Dawn or Dr. Van Fleet. They don't belong on a red brick house or next to bright pink roses. Blaze is probably the most popular red climber, seen everywhere in the suburbs, and the improved types now available produce almost as abundantly in June as once-bloomer Paul's Scarlet Climber and continue quite satisfactorily through the summer. Don Juan is a lovely fragrant dark red, of hybrid tea form, very long-lasting. Climbing hybrid teas are not always satisfactory in the North but Cl. Crimson Glory performs well.

Golden Showers is probably tops as a yellow climber but it is more a pillar rose, growing upright in somewhat vase form, with hundreds of large golden blooms produced successively among lustrous foliage. Mrs. Arthur Curtiss James (Golden Climber) is a once-bloomer and usually takes two or three years to come into good production. If the old canes are trained horizontally there will eventually be abundant bloom—hybrid-tea flowers produced mostly singly on long stems.

There are many desirable climbers in the pink tones, most of them with large flowers that repeat through the summer, some with a single abundant flowering in spring. I particularly like Mme. Gregoire Staechelin, partly because it starts the season, a week or two ahead of most varieties, and because it has such beautiful fruits at the end of the season. Mary Wallace, with its masses of rich pink June flowers, is hardy into Maine. New Dawn is a foolproof climber that seldom needs to be sprayed and is a lovely delicate pink. It is more rampant than Blossomtime, which has dainty two-toned pink double flowers repeated frequently, and Katie, also a two-toned pink. Dr. J. H. Nicolas and Aloha have flowers of hybrid-tea form and size. Both are excellent where conditions are right, meaning full sun and a chance to stretch out their arms.

Silver Moon is a very beautiful white climber that has gone out of favor because it grows too rampantly and flowers but once. White Dawn is slightly more restrained and repeats quite well through the summer. City of York is the best white climber I have ever seen, although it, too, usually blooms only once and is also rather rampant. But what bloom! Masses and masses of it, so fragrant, so very, very beautiful. See page 52 for more enthusiasm on this rose.

Most climbers can be used as trailing roses on banks. City of York as used here at Springvale is a good example. Half of the bush is used to cover an iron railing above a bank, the other half has been pegged down over the slope, providing an excellent ground cover after its blooming season. This rose, with its dark, shiny foliage, almost never requires spraying. Some roses are used solely as creepers. Among these is the old white Memorial Rose (*Rosa wichuraiana*) with glossy, almost evergreen foliage and Max Graf, a single bright pink hybrid rugosa that blooms in partial shade.

In planting roses on banks you don't just stick the bush into the side of the slope. You cut into the hill enough to make a level shelf, about a yard square, and then prepare the soil deeply as you would any rose bed. After the bush is placed securely the edge of this shelf is built up with stones to keep soil from washing away from the roots.

CLIMBING ROSES BY COLOR

Red—Blaze, Paul's Scarlet Climber, Don Juan, Spectacular.

Pink—Aloha, Belle Portugaise and Pink Cherokee for the South, Blossomtime, Clair Matin, Clytemnestra, Dr. J. H. Nicolas, Dr. W. Van Fleet, Dream Girl, Inspiration, Katie, Mary Wallace, Mme. Gregoire Staechelin, Max Graf (creeper), New Dawn.

Yellow—Golden Showers, High Noon, Lady Banksia, Marechal Niel and Mermaid for warm climates, Mrs. Arthur Curtiss James.

White—City of York, white Cherokee and white Banksia for the South, Patricia Macoun for the North, Pax, White Dawn.

Shrub roses advance the rose season a full six weeks if you start with very early *Rosa primula* and the single yellow *R. hugonis*. The latter is often called Father Hugo's rose. I never did get it to live in New Jersey because it was always too near other roses that were being fertilized. Hugonis dislikes pampering. It blooms here at Springvale because I planted it in unimproved soil near a rock ledge, some distance from beds with normal feeding programs. A little later in the season we have *R. xanthina* and Persian Yellow, both with double, yellow flowers. The latter blooms at the same time as brilliant scarlet and orange Austrian Copper and both shrubs are somewhat subject to blackspot.

Tall Agnes, with amber-gold buds and very large, very double creamy yellow flowers is a joy in late May and early June. The fragrant blooms are fine for cutting and scarcely missed from the bush. I tie the longest canes over to the split-rail fence, which keeps Agnes from getting too tall and encourages flowering all the along the prickly stems.

Vanguard is the other hybrid rugosa I could not live without and the plant here at Springvale gives promise of matching my Glen Ridge friend. It is never sprayed, seldom fed, and the foliage remains handsome after the display of large, fragrant salmon flowers is over. Now I have a new favorite in one of Kordes' shrubs. Frühlingsmorgen is such an early bloomer it did not have time to flower the first spring after planting. The next year I moved the bush and it did not recover fast enough after a severe winter. This past season first flowers came on May 15th and I could scarcely tear myself away to go to the garden club convention. When I returned, nearly a week later, the bush was indescribably beautiful with a multitude of large, single soft pink flowers, with yellow and lavender tints. As I write this, after weeks of drought, the soft green, locust-like foliage is still good and the round dark red crabapple hips are most decorative.

Frau Karl Druschki and Golden Wings are classified as hybrid teas but they are both definitely shrubs in vigor and size. Both give repeat bloom, Golden Wings continually producing its single cream-colored flowers, Frau Karl bursting with hundreds of flowers in June, presenting a few at a time the rest of the season.

Hybrid Perpetuals should be planted as shrubs; they are too tall and have not enough summer flowering for use in beds. If you place them in the background, or as you would any other bush that has a single period of bloom, you can enjoy the June explosion and not worry about later sparseness. With most hybrid perpetuals, however, you do get some bloom through the summer and handsome, dark red, so fragrant Henry Nevard performs well in this regard.

Salet is my only sample of a moss rose but there are other good varieties. I have Salet next to Pink Grootendorst with its clusters of flowers like tiny pink carnations, and at the corner there is hybrid musk Belinda with its great clusters of small rosy-pink blooms. If you have no place at all for shrubs or old roses I'd advise you never to look at Tillotson's catalogue with its mouth-watering descriptions and not to read Richard Thomson's *Old Roses for Modern Gardens*.

I have left until last any discussion of The Fairy, a shrub polyantha I almost always use to start people growing roses. Here is truly a no-work rose, good in any poor location, asking never to be sprayed. The Fairy starts out sprawling, then fills in the center and in a couple of years you have a bush two yards wide and a yard or so tall. Bloom starts in mid-June and continues to Thanksgiving. The delicate pink flowers, resembling a miniature Dorothy Perkins, are in tight clusters above shiny, small dark green leaves. The color fades a bit in the heat of summer but comes back with reasonable temperatures. The Fairy is fine on a bank, or flanking a garden entrance, or in a hedge or just as a specimen shrub. Anyone who has once grown The Fairy (and I give it as a door prize at garden club meetings) is a sucker for more roses. This rose plays a most important role in the making of a rosarian.

And now The Fairy has a rival. I met Sea Foam when it was introduced at Conard-Pyle's Red Rose Rent Day (September, 1964) and I brought home a huge pot covered with foamy white clusters. Also a shrub polyantha, Sea Foam is said to be as versatile and as pest-free as The Fairy, another inducement for starting roses.

USING ROSES

There are many ways to enjoy roses in the house without having them in quantity or with such long stems they rob the plant of leaves needed to make food for the next crop of flowers. I have squat little pottery jars for short-stemmed roses and glass bowls, like fish bowls, for new roses cut with almost no stem. A short-stemmed rose can be used as the focal point of an arrangement in a shell or the center of a tussy mussy in a metal lace container, perhaps with The Fairy and blue ageratum completing the nosegay. I keep ivy growing in Oasis in low containers in my apartment and when company is expected stick in a short-stemmed rose for accent.

And I put roses with longer stems singly along the window sill. Empty Creme-de-Menthe bottles make most attractive single vases, once the label is scrubbed off.

Small arrangements making use of short-stemmed hybrid teas or floribundas are good for bedside tables in the hospital. I use Oasis in small aluminum pans left from frozen foods or else in orange-juice or nut cans sprayed green with an aerosol enamel paint. Such small delights, so readily discarded when the flowers fade, sometimes bring more cheer than a fancy arrangement from a florist.

A gala centerpiece for a tea party, particularly good in these diet-conscious days, is a sponge or angel cake "frosted" with an enormous full-blown rose, perhaps The Doctor, or South Seas, with its short stem hidden in a tiny vial of water in the hole in the cake.

The old idea that roses are too elegant to be put in anything but glass or silver is nonsense. I love delicate Betty Prior or County Fair in the Steuben crystal bouquet vase and I also like aristocratic Royal Highness in the Paul Revere silver bowl but for every-day living I have The Fairy in a little brown pottery jug, perhaps three stages of a red rose in a low, oblong piece of brown pottery or three pink roses in a white pottery crescent lined with pink.

Roses are not too aristocratic to be used with "coarse" zinnias and marigolds. Surely brilliant Condesa de Sastago or Suspense or some of the orange reds like Tropicana or Aztec are right at home with Mexican pottery and bright annuals.

When I had time to make a buxom bouquet for my Glen Ridge living room I started with a blue pottery bowl and Red Radiance, then blue eupatorium, pink phlox, rose snapdragon and zinnias, and more roses, ranging from shell pink to red. Here at Springvale, for a living room with white walls and rose draperies and cushions, I start with a big white plastic bowl and Chicago Peace, then other blends, rose and pink, sometimes accented with dark red John S. Armstrong, and all mixed with pastel zinnias, snapdragon, cleome, perhaps some white eupatorium. There should be no rules for using roses except that the result must satisfy you. If you can live with your arrangement with joy, then it is right no matter what the combination of flowers used or whether the container is cheap or costly.

Scientific evidence has been accumulating recently showing that cut flowers, and especially roses, do last longer in one of the solutions such as Floralife. It helps to take a pitcher of this to the garden and to place the roses directly into it, at relatively warm temperature. Later the roses can harden in the refrigerator. See the next chapter, Showing Roses, for more hints on conditioning.

I have never tried drying roses in a mixture of borax and sand or cornmeal or the newer silica gel (sold as Dryrox and under other trade names) so that they look fresh in the middle of winter. Nor have I gathered fragrant petals to make potpourri or jam and hips for soup, cookies, or conserve. I have not even done much with corsages; when I want to wear a rose it is simpler to stick it into a lapel vase. But if you have inclinations along these lines there are books that go into exact detail. I can recommend, from reading, if not emulation: *Dried Flowers with a Fresh Look* by Eleanor Reed Bolton; *Rose Recipes* by Jean Gordon; and *Corsage Craft* by Glad Reusch and Mary Noble.

Roses make fine Christmas presents. You can order your pet variety, or two or three, and send a card saying they will be along in time for spring planting, or you can send a gift certificate and a catalogue. Sometimes you can order miniature roses for Christmas, complete with tray, pots, pebbles, and soil for indoor enjoyment. One winter I collected three roses in a Georgia nursery to take as a visiting gift to a friend in Alabama. They were teas so as not to require much attention and I planted them myself so my hostess had nothing to do but enjoy them. I have gone so far as to give pruning shears and a rose order for a wedding present and my gift for the first baby is likely to be a floribunda rather than an embroidered robe.

And roses can be a memorial! Less than a week after the first draft of this book was started, light-hearted, gay Johnny Westcott gave his life in Korea. As I planted gay roses (not white, but yellows and blends and reds) for his parents to share with the neighbors who loved Johnny from babyhood, I thought of the words Liberty Hyde Bailey wrote when Dr. J. Horace McFarland retired from editing the American Rose Annual.

"My dear McFarland,

You and I are growing old. We have seen the years go by and we look toward the sunset. Friends and associates have dropped away. Now you tell me you are to quit the editorship of the Rose Annual. I understand; but the roses will be as prime and fresh as ever. They will bloom in every returning spring, whatever may be the sorrows and sins of men. Every season will see the resurrection. Always they will be young and better ones will come."

CHAPTER IV

SHOWING ROSES

I HAVE never gone in for exhibiting or judging roses. My excuse has been lack of time but after reading the American Rose Society requirements for an accredited rose judge I decided it was mental as well as physical laziness. When, however, I helped start the North Jersey Rose Society and we started putting on Rose Shows, I had to bone up a bit.

Too many of us are afraid to exhibit our roses. We are sure we have nothing worth entering and then, when we see the entries of braver folk, think, "Why, my Crimson Glory is just as good as that!" The only way to win ribbons is to start showing. It is still possible to have beginner's luck and win out over a veteran. Then we go on to learn techniques which are not too difficult. As an aid in learning these techniques I suggest studying *"Roses—Growing for Exhibiting"* by Harold H. Allen, a veteran trophy and ribbon winner.

1. *Choose varieties of exhibition type.*

Before buying new roses check the reports in the American Rose Magazine of winners in shows over the country. Glance through the

descriptions of rose varieties in Chapter II of this book and note which
have exhibition type blooms. Check the fine lists given by Mr. Allen in
his book. Order several plants each of a few varieties rather than a
single bush of many different kinds.

2. *Prune with the date of the show in mind.*

The number of days from the time a stem is cut until the topmost bud
produces a specimen bloom depends on the variety, time of year, the
locality and the type of pruning. Roses grown for exhibition are usually
pruned a little harder than those for garden display but people differ
in how much they take off. Fred S. Glaes, a Director of the American
Rose Society, veteran rose exhibitor and judge, says that in his Pennsylvania garden roses pruned hard in spring take 60 days to flower while
moderate pruning brings them along in 53 days. James A. Gallagher on
the West Coast averaged 42 days for a September Show and 50 if blooms
were wanted in October when days are shorter. Harold Allen, of Ohio,
says that in the North Central States the time varies from about 39 to
53 days, or an average of about 46 days plus two days for hardening in
the refrigerator. This is for a fall show. Clarence H. Lewis, now president of the American Rose Society, former chairman of the Committee
on Training and Accrediting Judges, figures 49 to 56 days in late
summer. The cool climate of England apparently delays bloom. According to Bertram Park's *Roses,* it takes 70 to 100 days from spring
pruning.

Some of our North Jersey Rose Society blue ribbon winners kept
detailed records in the first years of our shows. Jack Lissemore pruned his
roses 42 to 50 days before an early fall show. Margaret Moles found that
her roses, in a somewhat more shaded location, averaged 45 to 53 days to
produce an exhibition bloom from the time a firm healthy cane was
cut back just above a sound bud in a leaf axil. Both exhibitors reported
that Peace and Rubaiyat were slow compared to Tallyho, Chrysler
Imperial, New Yorker, and Nocturne. One season Taffeta bloomed for
Jack in only 35 days. Most floribundas took about 53 days for Margaret
in a normal season.

Seasons, however, are seldom "normal." One year our members pruned
roses back at the recommended time for a late September show and we

had the gloomiest August on record, scarcely any sun. The best roses came in a week after the show. In 1959 an unusually hot, sunny August brought roses to full bloom a week or two ahead of the September show date. If you are a serious rose exhibitor you will want to keep your own records on varieties for several seasons. If, as suggested, you have several plants of one variety you can cut them back to a good bud on a stout cane at varying intervals.

In his book on exhibiting Harold Allen suggests that if August 1 is an average pruning date for a September 18 show you start pruning about July 27 and prune some every day until August 6 to allow for variances in the weather. If you have any doubt about timing cut early rather than late. You can hold roses for a week or so in the refrigerator if you have to but there is no way to speed up bloom if Nature does not cooperate. Remember to add an extra day to condition the rose after it reaches its peak of perfection.

Some recommend rubbing off all buds below the new shoot; others feel that this may weaken the bush and that it is possible to get exhibition bloom on two or more shoots developed from the same cane. Disbudding the side flower buds is absolutely obligatory for specimen roses in hybrid tea and hybrid perpetual classes except for *single* roses which *must* be shown naturally without disbudding. The earlier you disbud the better. If the bud is gently pinched out between thumb and finger while still very tiny there will be no visible scar tissue and all the strength of the cane will go into exhibition bloom. If you wait until the bud is half-grown some food will have been diverted and you may be penalized half the score for stems for evidence of recent disbudding.

The rule for grandifloras has been that they must not be disbudded whether shown on a single stem or in a spray. In 1964 the American Rose Society modified this to allow grandifloras to be disbudded as well as grown naturally. Most shows will still have two classes, one for single stem specimens, one for sprays or clusters.

With floribundas there is often a question as to what constitutes a spray. According to C. H. Lewis a spray may be defined as "one cane showing two or more five-leaflet leaves at the base, above which many bud eyes on the cane should produce growth terminating in a cluster or clusters of bloom." Sometimes there is secondary growth branching from part of the spray; this can be pinched out or not depending on symmetry and whether there will be evidence of recent removal. A desirable spray has fresh, full-bloom blossoms, several buds, and some between stages, with no spent bloom. This is hard to achieve because the center flower is often fading before the others are ready. Sometimes the center can be skillfully removed without leaving a noticeable void in the spray; sometimes it is best to leave the fading flower in place.

3. *Fertilize sufficiently; water copiously.*

Liquid feeding every ten to fourteen days may supplement the usual applications of a balanced fertilizer. Some use the old-fashioned "tea" made by suspending a bag of manure in a barrel of water; some make a last application of an organic rose food; some rely on foliar feeding. Some are devotees of liquid fish fertilizers; some are trying preparations from seaweed. Whatever the food, watering is essential, at least weekly, and *very* thoroughly, for large size, good color and substance in flowers. Rose bushes fed and watered late in the season for a fall show are not always long-lived; they may develop frost cracks and subsequent cankers in the unripened wood. Forego this extra-late feeding on bushes not expected to produce exhibition blooms.

4. *Maintain a rigid schedule of disease and pest control.*

Evidences of disease and insect injury are serious defects. You may have to spray every few days late in the season to prevent powdery mildew from deforming buds and blooms. Near show time discontinue use of any spray which may discolor petals. Before conditioning show roses be sure to wipe off all residue from leaves with an old nylon stocking, bit of cotton or other soft material. Harold Allen suggests adding a few drops of liquid detergent to the washing water. The American Rose Society does not permit polishing oil of any sort on the foliage but some have found sweet milk a good cleaning agent that cannot be detected by the judges.

5. *Cut specimens at the right time; condition properly.*

Roses are best cut in late afternoon, with early morning next choice. Some exhibitors cut morning, noon, and night, starting five or six days before the show to get each variety in the best condition. Roses with comparatively few petals, like Crimson Glory, are cut when they are quite tight; roses with many petals, such as Peace, should be slightly more open. Floribundas are cut just before the cluster reaches maximum beauty.

Under conventional procedure roses are placed in water as they are gathered. Most suggest that the stem be cut on a slant so that it does not rest squarely on the bottom of the container; some say this does not matter. Warm water is preferred to cold; it allows the water to rise faster in the stem. A few inches of water at the base of the stems is sufficient. If flowers are not placed in water immediately, they should have the stems cut again when brought indoors and then be placed in warm water. If they have wilted, a drastic procedure may bring them back to life. Hold the cut end of the stem in water that is almost boiling while you count to ten. Immerse only the cut end in this very hot water; do not submerge the stem; and be sure to hold the blooms away from the hot steam.

Experiments with greenhouse roses indicate that the vase life of cut roses can be doubled if they are taken at the proper stage of maturity and immediately placed in containers of warm (100° to 110°F.) preservative (such as Floralife or Roselife).

During conditioning, keep containers in a cool dark place without drafts. For more than overnight, this place should be a refrigerator, kept at around 35°F.; never under 33° nor over 40°. Veteran trophy winners either have an old refrigerator used just for roses or else go out for meals for several days before the Show. Roses and some foods don't mix well. Apples, particularly, give off a gas inimical to roses. Each bloom should be protected with a plastic bag or a cap of waxed paper, fastened so that it does not touch the petals. Relatively new are clear plastic containers, sold as Rose Keepers, for storing and transporting exhibition roses.

Another method of taking care of roses that come into bloom a week or two ahead of show date has been used successfully by some rosarians although the topnotch winners don't rely on it. The procedure was described by Ruth H. Brand in "Preparing Your Roses for Show," in the September, 1953, *American Rose Magazine*. Roses are cut when the buds soften but before they actually start opening. They are labeled and cleaned (rubbing both leaf surfaces with soft flannel or sheepskin, removing damaged leaves or crippled petals) as they are cut. *Without placing in water,* they are stored in clear plastic film (Saran-Wrap). Excess moisture is removed from foliage and bloom, soft florist wax paper is wound spirally around the stem to cover thorns and the single specimen is laid on a piece of plastic cut 3 to 5 inches longer than the stem. The two lengthwise edges are brought together and folded over about ¾ inch, and the folding repeated until the wrapping comes as close as possible to the rose without injury. The ends are fastened with freezer tape to make an airtight package. Roses so prepared in separate packages can be stored (flat to save space) 10 to 14 days if the temperature can be held at 33° to 35°F. Remove from the refrigerator four to five hours before the show, open at the stem end, cut off 1 to 1½ inches and place in a container with 3 or 4 inches of warm water (110° to 120°F.). Place in a cool place for three or four hours, then take to the show in the same container without removing wrappings. Take these off on arrival, recut stems, and place in water-filled exhibition vases. If the roses must be transported a long distance they are left in the refrigerator until the last minute, and the stems cut and placed in warm water at the show.

6. *Attach variety name to every specimen.*

Most general flower shows and a few rose shows have a catch-all class for varieties unknown to the exhibitor and unrecognized by the classification committee but to compete in most classes you must know the variety. This means labeling every rose as you cut it in the garden, for you are sure to get mixed up afterwards. Print the name in indelible pencil on a strip of heavy wrapping paper or a string tag and fasten this around the neck of each rose before cutting. You must first, of course, make sure that the wooden, plastic or metal labels are already correctly placed in the garden and this goes back to planting time. Did you make a map and mark the exact position of each variety? And did you remember to change the map every time you replaced a bush or added another? Garden labels are not the inanimate objects they seem. They turn up in the most unlikely places. Gardeners cultivating or pruning, children wandering through, windstorms and other causes mean that the label in front of your bush as you cut for the show is not to be trusted too far. If in doubt, check back to the map.

Every rose enthusiast has a pet system of labeling. I have always used the metal "Rose Markers" from the Everlasting Label Co. (new address, Box 13A, Delta, Ohio). They are inexpensive (100 for $5.50) stay in place well, and last for several years.

7. *Transport carefully.*

Do not take your roses to the show in an open container exposed to the wind. Wrap each specimen separately in soft florist waxed paper and lay them in lined cardboard boxes with a roll of newspaper for a neck pillow. Pliofilm bags filled with ice cubes and fastened tightly can be placed at the base of stems. Dr. O. M. Harper, who has transported roses long distances to shows, used to place the stems in orchid tubes which had been sterilized, filled with boiled water, and kept in the refrigerator until packing time. If you take exhibiting very seriously you will probably have special metal containers or refrigerators for transportation but if you have gotten that far you know far more about it than I do so we'll stop here.

8. *Make out entry cards correctly.*

Fill out one entry card for each specimen, group, or arrangement to be exhibited. Print your name and address, the variety name, class number, and section letter on both portions of the entry card. In most rose shows there are separate named classes for the more popular varieties and then classes to cover the sixteen basic color groups of the American Rose Society (see page 31). To place a variety in the right color class look it up in the current American Rose Society *Guide for Buying Roses.* In small shows roses may be classified merely as white, yellow, pink, red, and blends. To make sure of the right type, hybrid tea or hybrid perpetual, rambler or climber, floribunda or grandiflora etc. check your variety in *Modern Roses 6,* a copy of which should be near the entry desk of every rose show.

An exhibitor may enter a variety only once in a show but as many varieties as he desires in a given class. A rose variety may be exhibited

in all competitive classes for any American Rose Society award when
it is available through domestic outlets or is a non-patented foreign rose,
provided it has been described in the section "New Roses of the World"
of the American Rose Annual and has been accepted by the American
Rose Society Rose Registration Committee.

JUDGING STANDARDS

Roses are judged according to the American Rose Society Scale of
points. Specimen roses are judged according to variety and not one kind
against another.

Form—25 points

The flower should be in its most perfect phase, usually, but not always,
when the bloom is half to three-quarters open; it should have a well-
formed center, and a circular outline. Roses with many petals usually
score higher than those with few.

Color—25 points

Color is affected by locality, soil, altitude, general climate as well as
seasonal variations of temperature and moisture, but it should be true to
variety, pure, fresh and brilliant. The petals should not be stained with
chemicals or weather, faded, washed out or blued with age. Judges
should know what color can be expected of a variety at any given time
and place.

Substance—20 points

This means the petals should be thick, firm, crisp, with a vigorous
healthy look. Points will be taken off if petals are flabby, soft or thin
or have abnormal texture.

Stem and Foliage—20 points

The stem should be in proportion to the flower, neither too long nor
too short, strong enough to support the bloom and showing some five
leaflet leaves. A tea, hybrid tea (except a single) or hybrid perpetual
that has not been disbudded is disqualified and a rose showing signs of

recent disbudding is penalized. Foliage that is diseased, damaged by insects or handling, or shows spray residue, counts heavily against the score. Leaves should be abundant, well placed, rich healthy green. Of course, some varieties are naturally a light, soft green, others are dark and leathery.

Size—10 points

Mere size counts little unless the rose is nearly perfect in other respects. It should be somewhat larger than average for the variety. Floribunda, polyantha and climbing roses that have flowers in clusters are judged for the attractiveness of the cluster on the stem with loss of points if too few blooms are open, if they are faded, or if there are too few buds.

ROSE ARRANGEMENTS

Most general flower shows do not require the material shown in artistic arrangements to be grown by the exhibitor. Rose shows under auspices of rose societies require at least three classes of arranger-grown roses. No American Rose Society medal or certificate may be given except in such classes.

Points considered in judging flower arrangements in rose shows are:

	Points
1. Design (Balance, Dominance, Contrast, Rhythm, Proportion, Scale	25
2. Interpretation and Suitability	20
3. Color	15
4. Distinction and Originality	15
5. Relation to Container	15
6. Condition	10

ROSE JUDGES

The American Rose Society provides a training school for judges at its district meetings or at other times. Any person applying for a certificate as an apprentice judge must pass the judging school test and have been a member of the Society for two years. He must have personally grown roses or be engaged in their scientific culture; must know intimately the characteristics and range of variability of at least 100 varieties and be able to verify labeling; must know and be disposed to follow American Rose Society rules and technical requirements concerning disbudding, bud vs. bloom, ideal form, substance, color, size, etc. of individual varieties; must be observant and careful in all details; must be a person of high integrity, able to subjugate all personal likes, dislikes and biases; must be able to substantiate decisions with concrete and specific reasons; must be diplomatic, constructive, definite and understandingly assertive in adhering to rules and passing judgment. He must have exhibited for at least three years and in five shows and have worked as a clerk or novice in three rose shows.

To be accredited as a rose judge the applicant must hold an apprentice judge certificate and must have satisfactorily judged at least five rose shows, or flower shows where roses predominated, preferably working with a rose judge accredited by the American Rose Society. And even an accredited judge faces the possibility of losing his or her certificate unless five or more rose show judgings are reported in a four-year period.

So, with all these restrictions, you may confidently enter your roses in a show knowing they will be judged as fairly as is humanly possible. If at first you don't capture ribbons, by all means try again.

CHAPTER V

PROPAGATING ROSES

Aʟᴛʜᴏᴜɢʜ growing roses from "slips" is an old, old custom it is one that I myself have seldom practiced. I have had enough trouble finding room to test new varieties from nurseries and time enough for their care. There has been, however, renewed interest in propagating for fun and some of it may be necessary if we are to continue to enjoy older roses that nurserymen have discarded because the highly publicized novelties sell better. I am not speaking now about the true "old roses." Thanks to Richard Thomson and other advocates many of these are coming back in the catalogues. The roses I mourn are some of the fine introductions of the past few decades, already lost to commerce because the volume of sales was not high enough. These include roses listed in the third edition of this treatise and regretfully omitted from this fourth revision because they are not readily available. To get such "lost" roses you must beg cuttings from a friend and start your own bushes. Technically, you are not allowed to propagate patented roses but many patents have now expired and many excellent roses have never been patented.

The various methods of propagating roses are well detailed in *The Rockwells' Complete Book of Roses* and in other rose books. The September, 1958, American Rose Magazine had a special section on various methods of propagation and a directory of equipment. In that issue Elmer S. Siuda of Chicago outlined the following system:

Take cuttings any time after first June bloom until the first bloom-killing frost, late July being a good time. Select from the strongest blooming lateral stems just after petals of the open bloom have begun to fall. Make a straight cut ¼ inch below the second or third set of five leaflets. Remove the lower leaf, cut off the spent bloom and you have a cutting 7 to 9 inches long. Immerse in water, then dip the bottom inch of stem in rooting powder (Rootone or Hormodin). Place cutting in a prepared hole filled with about 3 inches of moist sand; water until the sand is saturated, then cover with a glass jar. Every second or third day remove jar and water enough to keep sand damp but not flooded. The base of the cutting should callus in about 3 weeks and root growth be well started in 4 to 6 weeks. At that time transplant into regular garden soil in a location that receives morning sun. Keep covered with jar; water occasionally, not too often. Hill up jar with soil before ground freezes solid; remove jar temporarily on warm days in spring to let the plant harden off; remove jar permanently when all danger of frost is over. When moving such rooted plants to another location dig with a ball of soil.

Mist propagation is a popular and successful short-cut method. Louis C. Gross, former president of the North Jersey Rose Society, currently Director of the Penn-Jersey District of the American Rose Society, has written out for me his method of rooting hybrid tea soft wood cuttings with mist. I quote Lou's words verbatim:

"Propagating roses under mist is so easy, quick, and sure, it's a propagator's dream come true. In my case the rooting medium is vermiculite but it can be perlite, sand or any medium that is sterile. The cutting (or slip) is the stem of any rose that has just finished blooming, but it can be removed from the plant a week before or later, and still root effectively. The shorter the stem, the faster the rooting. The longer the stem, the bigger an early plant. Eventual size of all plants of course depends upon the variety. Rooting is done any time the plants are in bloom and up to six weeks before freezing.

"From the stem are removed the bloom and the bottom leaves. The cutting is then dipped in Rootone and set in the vermiculite. With cuttings placed as close together as possible, eighty can be accommodated in an overall area of 2 by 4 feet. The location must be in full sun for quick results, and the cuttings are covered with a 2 by 4 plastic tent (cost $4.95), but it can easily be homemade.

"In pioneering the method I used a fog-producing nozzle that had to be turned on for several seconds every hour during the day. This works fine but it requires manual attention. Results that are just as good can be secured with a mist-producing nozzle ($2.50) that can be turned on at 8 A.M., left on all day using very little water, and turned off at 5 P.M. Any garden hose will do, and so will any pressure. The cuttings thrive under the constant mist and full sun.

"In one week rooting begins if every day is sunny. In another week the 'eyes' break and swell. In the third week the new growth can be 1 inch or more. Extra time has to be added to this schedule, of course, if there are cloudy days.

"After the third week, 'hardening' must begin. This means turning on the mister later in the morning and shutting it off earlier in the afternoon, as the days go by. In the fifth week there should be many tiny buds in the tent and in six weeks the whole bed should be in full bloom. There is no more exciting sight in the world! After the tent is removed, misting can be continued as needed, or until one is certain the full exposure to sun will not burn off the young plants.

"During this entire process there is no possibility of disease or insects. Of course, once the misting is discontinued, or cut down appreciably, the young foliage must be protected. A spray solution is likely to burn. Light dusting is best."

A complete Constant Mist Propagation System is offered in the advertising pages of the American Rose Magazine (by Mist Methods Co., Winchester, Tennessee) but the price is more than that of the nozzle plus tent quoted by Mr. Gross.

Layering is perhaps the easiest way to propagate climbers and other roses with long flexible canes. Simply bend down a branch so that part of it (not the tip) can be covered with soil, first cutting into the bark slightly. Put a stone on the soil to hold the branch in place and when roots are developed separate the new plant from the parent.

Air layering is another way to start new plants from old. Remove leaves from a section of a young cane or lateral, make a deep slanting cut half to two-thirds through the cane and place sphagnum moss in the cut to hold it open. Tie a generous wad of moist moss around the cane, wrap in plastic film, tied at the sides and ends; cut off the stem when roots have formed in the sphagnum. A variation of this, reported by Mrs. Moe Ruvensky, uses a material called "Jet Magic Root Wrap" (sold by Garden Miracles, P.O. Box 57, Gladstone, Oregon). Choose a cane on a strong plant and when flowers begin to fade remove thorns in an area 6 inches long. Make two horizontal cuts, 1 inch apart, completely encircling cane, and remove bark and cambium layer from beneath cuts. Cut a piece of Root Wrap one-half longer than needed to encircle cane. Remove polyethylene backing and place tape around cane to cover exposed wood and overlap the bark. A callus is formed in 2 or 3 weeks and when the swelling protrudes well beyond the bark remove the new plant from the parent, trimming off any wood below the callus and all soft wood and foliage. Plant the callus about 5 inches below ground level, in full sun, pack soil firmly around it and water well. Feeding roots develop quickly from the callus.

Roses grown commercially are budded rather than own-root cuttings and sometimes amateurs try their hand at this. Grow your own understock or purchase seedlings, setting as high as possible 10 to 12 inches apart in rows 2 to 2½ feet apart. For a bud stick choose the plump stem of a rose that has just shattered, cut off the top of the stick, just below the first 5-leaflet leaf, and snip off the rest of the foliage, leaving the basal half inch of each stem to serve as a handle in inserting the bud. Clean the understock near ground level. With a budding knife, make a horizontal cut, ½ to ¾ inch, through the bark but not deep enough to enter the wood. Now make a perpendicular cut, about 1 inch long, from the center of the first cut, thus making a T-shaped incision, and very carefully lift up the right-angled corners. Now cut a vigorous bud from the bud stick with an oval piece of bark and the leaf stem attached; remove the wood without injuring the bud and slip the shield bearing the

bud into the incision on the understock. Tie in place with raffia or a rubber band. Budding is done in June or July. The next spring cut off the
top of the understock plant half an inch above the bud. When the latter
has grown about 10 inches pinch out the top to make a bushy plant. If
you don't have room to grow understock you can bud directly into the
cane of a climbing rose, such as Dr. Huey, and then, after the wood has
fully matured, cut the cane and root as you would any other cutting.

If you have experienced all the other joys of rose growing and showing
you may want to try your luck at hybridizing, making a new variety.
The Rockwells have an excellent chapter in their book called "Creating
Your Own New Roses." Assemble tweezers, small pointed scissors, mag-
nifying glass, and plastic bags or envelopes. Choose a bud on the female
parent ready to open but still closed; remove all petals, starting with the
outside row; then remove all stamens with tweezers, to prevent self-fer-
tilization, and tie on plastic bag. When the stigmas are slightly sticky and
a bit darker they are ready to receive pollen from the male parent which
has already been selected and tagged. Remove petals from the latter, remove the bag from the female, and brush the stamens back and forth
over the pistil. Replace the bag; tie it tight; leave it for a week or so, then
remove. If the cross has taken, the hip will stay green and grow, ripening in about 3 months. Seed may be sown at once, spaced individually
in flats, in rows 1 inch apart and ¼ inch deep, or may be saved for later
planting.

In the October, 1958, *American Rose Magazine,* C. H. Lewis reports
his method of growing roses from seed. He fills a flat, preferably made
of untreated cypress, with 2 inches of sterile soil tipped with a 1-inch
layer of vermiculite. This is moistened with rain water and placed in a
window with northerly exposure, temperature not over 70°F. Rows are
marked 2 inches apart, ¾ inch deep, and seeds are poured from an enve-
lope rather than planted individually. They are obtained by hitting the
pods or hips with a rubber mallet. The flat is covered with ½-inch mesh
wire on a light frame and the soil kept moist at all times. Now all you
need is patience. Some seeds germinate in two months, others in two
years.

The August, 1964, *American Rose Magazine* contains two brief articles
on seed propagation by amateur rosarians. One, Fred M. Battle, refriger-

ated his roses at 46°F. after planting in trays. The other, Dale W. Mein-
zinger, found he got nearly twice as much germination in the attic at
38° to 60° as in the refrigerator at 40°.

We come to the usual conclusion. There is no one best way for any
part of rose culture. Do join the American Rose Society and read the
Magazine and the Annual, including the advertising pages, to see how
many ways there are to have fun with roses.

CHAPTER VI

ROSE ENEMIES

POSSIBLE enemies of the rose are legion. There are at least five hundred insect pests and perhaps half as many bacteria, fungi, and viruses causing disease. Rodents are often a menace and pets occasionally. There are troubles due to weather and physiological disturbances connected with deficiency or excess of nutrients, too much or too little water. Through the ages, partly by Nature's process of survival of the fittest, partly through breeding and selection, good roses have developed a tolerance of their enemies, thriving with a little protection, existing even if neglected. Unfortunately, the rose is sometimes defenseless against man, who so often defies the law of Nature. The specimens that are sent to me for diagnosis continue to show spray injury more often than pest injury. People keep on dosing their roses with more and more "cures" when their crying need is for a little intelligent neglect.

Despite many pages given here to a consideration of rose enemies and their control, most roses require a minimum of upkeep. Don't be discouraged by this listing but also don't rely on it as being all-inclusive; it is merely a tabulation of the more common problems with a few occasional pests. Ignore this section, if you wish, until you need information about some specific pest bothering your roses.

To make things a little easier in finding the answer to your problem of the moment, the next few pages chart out rose enemies according to the plant part affected—Root and Crown, Cane and Shoot, Leaf, Bud and Flower; the chief diagnostic signs or symptoms; and the heading in the alphabetical list that follows under which you can find a more complete description and control measures.

Starting on page 184 there is a brief discussion of the spraying and dusting equipment used in applying control measures, an alphabetical list of chemicals, and a list of some of the combination pesticides currently available. These combinations make it possible to ward off most rose enemies in one operation, taking only a few minutes a week. Please do not let this chapter deter you from the fun of living with roses.

ROOT and CROWN PROBLEMS		
Chief Sign or Symptom	*Probable Pest or Disease*	*Described Under*
Rough, roundish bump at crown or on larger roots.	Crown Gall (Fig. 14)	GALLS
Roots in witches' broom effect.	Infectious Hairy Root	GALLS
Large swelling on root.	Rose Root Gall	GALLS
Small, nodular swellings in roots.	Root Knot (Fig. 15)	NEMATODES
Roots killed back from tip.	Meadow Nematodes	NEMATODES
Roots eaten by whitish grubs.	Larvae of June, Asiatic, Japanese, Goldsmith, or Fuller Rose Beetles, or Rose Chafers	BEETLES
Roots disturbed, plants dying.	Pine Mice	RODENTS
As above; ridges in soil.	Moles	RODENTS
Soil granular near bush.	Ant Nest	ANTS
Bush dying, reddish sclerotia like mustard seed at base.	Southern Blight	BLIGHTS
Rot at root crown; fan-shaped white mycelium, sometimes honey toadstools; in California.	Armillaria Root Rot	ROTS
Similar rot; in Florida.	Clitocybe Root Rot	ROTS
Bush wilting in summer; buff mycelium on ground; Southwest.	Texas Root Rot	ROTS

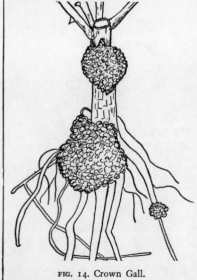

FIG. 14. Crown Gall.

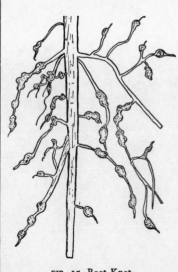

FIG. 15. Root Knot.

CANE and SHOOT PROBLEMS

Chief Sign or Symptom	Probable Pest or Disease	Described Under
Round, white encrustations.	Rose Scale (Fig. 16)	SCALE INSECTS
Large, fluted white sacs.	Cottony-cushion Scale	SCALE INSECTS
Large, hemispherical, brown scale.	European Fruit Lecanium	SCALE INSECTS
Small, hemispherical scale.	Black Scale	SCALE INSECTS
Circular, reddish brown scale.	California and Florida Red Scales	SCALE INSECTS
Oyster-shaped scale.	Oystershell Scale	SCALE INSECTS
Flat, white powdery insects massed at leaf axils.	Mealybugs	MEALYBUGS
Hole in pith; canes dying back.	Pith Borers—sawfly larvae, bees etc. (Fig. 17)	BORERS
Tips of shoots dying back to double row of punctures.	Raspberry Cane Borer	BORERS
Tips of shoots wilting; California.	Raspberry Horntail	BORERS
Raised spirals in stem of *Rosa rugosa* or *R. Hugonis*.	Rose Stem Girdler	BORERS
Gouty gall in stem.	Red-necked Cane Borer	BORERS
Mossy gall.	Mossy Rose Gall	GALLS
Canes gnawed at base.	Field Mice; Rabbits	RODENTS
Curved slits in bark.	Buffalo Treehopper	TREEHOPPER
Dark sooty areas near wounds.	Stem Canker (Fig. 18)	CANKERS

FIG. 16. Rose Scale on cane; detail of round female and thin male.

FIG. 17. Pith Borer; cane split to show larvae of carpenter bee.

FIG. 18. Stem Canker, following frost cracks, left, and pruning wound, right.

CANE and SHOOT PROBLEMS

Chief Sign or Symptom	Probable Pest or Disease	Described Under
Similar canker, but tiny slits in bark, sometimes gall above girdled portion; not common.	Brand Canker	CANKERS
Small white spots with purple to red margins grouped on canes; large buff areas in spring, with yellow spore tendrils.	Brown Canker (Fig. 19)	CANKERS
Dark, glistening spore pustules in cankered area.	Coryneum Canker	CANKERS
Cane girdled with punky region at crown; greenhouse roses.	Crown Canker	CANKERS
Dieback of greenhouse roses.	Graft Canker	CANKERS
Blackening of graft or bud with death of scion.	Black Mold	MOLDS
Depressed light spots on canes with raised brownish margins.	Spot Anthracnose	ANTHRACNOSE
Dieback, wilting, sometimes basal canker.	Cane Blight	BLIGHTS
White, powdery or felty growth on shoots and canes.	Powdery Mildew	POWDERY MILDEW
Pink and green lice on new shoots.	Rose, Potato, and other Aphids (Fig. 33)	APHIDS
Branches webbed together at ends.	Fall Webworm	CATERPILLARS
Orange tendrils between branches.	Dodder	DODDER

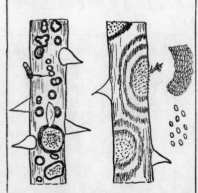

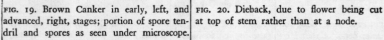

FIG. 19. Brown Canker in early, left, and advanced, right, stages; portion of spore tendril and spores as seen under microscope.

FIG. 20. Dieback, due to flower being cut at top of stem rather than at a node.

FOLIAGE PROBLEMS

Chief Sign or Symptom	Probable Pest or Disease	Described Under
Leaves skeletonized (with windows).	Rose-slug (Fig. 21) and Curled Rose Sawfly	SAWFLIES
Circles, ovals cut from leaf edge.	Leaf-cutter Bee (Fig. 22)	LEAF-CUTTER BEE
Leaves notched in from margin.	Fuller Rose Beetle (South); Imported Long-horned Weevil (Northeast)	BEETLES
Leaves chewed to lace.	Japanese Beetle (Fig. 23)	BEETLES
Leaves rolled, sometimes tied with webs.	Greenhouse Leaf Tier; Oblique and Red-banded Leaf Rollers Rose Budworm (Fig. 37)	CATERPILLARS
Leaves ravaged but not rolled.	Tent Caterpillars Brown-tail Moth (New England)	CATERPILLARS
Leaves devoured.	Grasshoppers	GRASSHOPPERS
Leaves stippled white.	Rose and other Leafhoppers (Fig. 24)	LEAFHOPPERS
Leaves yellowish or reddish or with reddish margins or with brown areas; mealy on underside.	Spider Mites (Fig. 25)	RED SPIDERS
Black spots with fringed margins; sometimes leaf yellowing, dropping.	Black Spot (Fig. 26)	BLACK SPOT
Circular white spots with raised reddish margins.	Spot Anthracnose (Fig. 27)	ANTHRACNOSE

  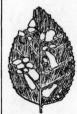 

FIG. 21. Skeletonized by Rose-slugs.

FIG. 22. Work of Leaf-cutter Bee.

FIG. 23. Japanese Beetle; foliage injury; adult, enlarged.

FOLIAGE PROBLEMS

Chief Sign or Symptom	Probable Pest or Disease	Described Under
Light brown spots with purplish borders.	Cercospora Leaf Spot	LEAF SPOTS
Gray spots, with small black dots.	Septoria Leaf Spot	LEAF SPOTS
Leaves with white wefts, edges curling.	Powdery Mildew (Fig. 29)	POWDERY MILDEW
Grayish down on underside of leaf, greenhouse roses.	Downy Mildew	DOWNY MILDEW
Orange or black pustules on underside of leaf.	Rose Rust (Fig. 30)	RUST
Leaves with mottled yellow pattern.	Mosaic (Fig. 32)	VIRUS DISEASES
Leaves with more or less uniform yellowing.	Deficiency of iron, nitrogen or other elements.	CHLOROSIS
Reddish spots on leaves.	Copper Injury (Fig. 28)	CHEMICAL INJURY
Browning of tips of margins, or brown spots.	Sulfur or Arsenical Burn	CHEMICAL INJURY
Leaves, stunted, twisted.	2,4-D Injury (Fig. 31)	CHEMICAL INJURY

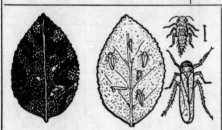

FIG. 24. Leafhopper injury; stippled upper surface of leaf, left; hoppers at work on underside, right; nymph and adult, enlarged.

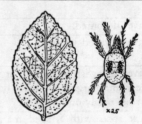

FIG. 25. Red Spiders and their webs on underside of leaf; single mite, enlarged.

FIG. 26. Black Spot, showing fimbriate margins to spots; section through spot with spores as seen under microscope.

FIG. 27. Spot Anthracnose.

FIG. 28. Chemical Injury: copper spray.

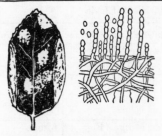

FIG. 29. Powdery Mildew on leaf; mycelium and spores as seen under microscope.

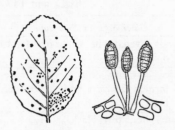

FIG. 30. Rose Rust, with detail of spores.

FIG. 31. Chemical Injury from 2,4-D; normal leaf at lower left, others stunted and deformed.

FIG. 32. Yellow Mosaic, a virus disease.

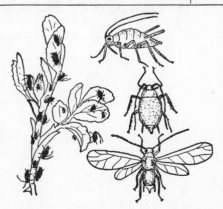

FIG. 33. Aphids on young shoot and bud.

FIG. 34. Powdery Mildew on buds.

BUD and FLOWER PROBLEMS

Chief Sign or Symptom	Probable Pest or Disease	Described Under
Buds covered with white felt; fail to open.	Powdery Mildew (Fig. 34)	POWDERY MILDEW
Lice covering buds or inside deformed flowers; white streak on petals.	Aphids (Fig. 33)	APHIDS
Small buds turn black.	Rose Midge (Fig. 35)	MIDGE
Large buds with color stay closed or open part way; brown edges to petals.	Flower Thrips (Fig. 36)	THRIPS
Flowers streaked.	Onion Thrips	THRIPS
Gray mold, often after thrips.	Blossom Blight	BLIGHTS
Small holes in bud; red and black beetle.	Rose Curculio (Fig. 37)	BEETLES
Shot-holes in bud and flower; small greenish beetle.	Rose Leaf Beetle	BEETLES
Shot-holes; small bronze beetle.	Strawberry Rootworm	BEETLES
Flowers devoured by oval, metallic coppery green beetles.	Japanese Beetle (Fig. 40)	BEETLES
Feeding by tan, long-legged "bugs."	Rose Chafer (Fig. 39)	BEETLES
Green, black-spotted beetles.	Spotted Cucumber Beetle (Fig. 40)	BEETLES
Night feeding by gray-brown weevil; South or greenhouse.	Fuller Rose Beetle	BEETLES
Hard, brown insects with "pincers."	European Earwig	EARWIGS
Large holes eaten into bud.	Rose Budworm (Fig. 37)	CATERPILLARS

FIG. 35. Rose Midge; injured bud and petiole; maggot and adult greatly enlarged.

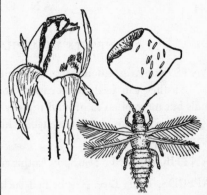

FIG. 36. Thrips injury to opening bud; petal removed to show insects inside; adult greatly enlarged.

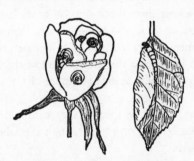

FIG. 37. Rose Budworm, feeding on bud and inside rolled leaf.

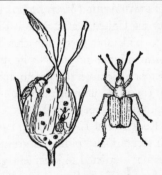

FIG. 38. Rose Curculio injuring bud.

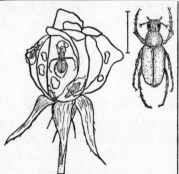

FIG. 39. Rose Chafer (rose bug) on flower.

FIG. 40. Japanese Beetles and Spotted Cucumber beetles feeding on flower; detail of cucumber beetle.

ENEMIES IN ALPHABETICAL ORDER

ANTS. Primarily troublesome for their nursing of mealybugs or aphids
    so they can feed in the insect honeydew. Sometimes seen on rose
buds but more often in ground nests which may disturb rose roots. Insert
⅛ teaspoon of 50 per cent wettable chlordane into nest and water well;
or use chlordane dust.

ANTHRACNOSE. See Spot Anthracnose.

APHIDS. Plant Lice. Soft-bodied sucking insects feeding on buds and
    succulent new shoots and leaves. Flowers are sometimes misshapen
and petals streaked by lice hiding between the petals and almost too small
to see.

POTATO APHID (*Macrosiphum euphorbiae*). Commonly present throughout the United States. Rose is the winter host. Black eggs on canes hatch
into pink and green lice that feed on new shoots and buds. Winged
forms migrate to potatoes in summer, return to roses in September and
October. Because the potato aphid is perhaps the most common species
on roses the summer migration explains why aphids are more of a problem on roses spring and fall.

ROSE APHID (*Macrosiphum rosae*). A large species, very common in
all sections, also pink and green, but feeding on roses through the whole
season; restricted to succulent growth.

SMALL GREEN ROSE APHID (*Myzaphis rosarum*). Green, without pink
forms, smaller than the rose aphid; not restricted to succulent growth.

GREEN PEACH APHID (*Myzus persicae*). Greenish yellow aphids with
three dark lines on the back; more important on spinach, potatoes and
peaches than on roses.

MELON APHID (*Aphis gossypii*). Small, green to black, common on
many plants, called the cotton aphid in the South, citrus aphids in California.

There are other aphids occasional on rose: the Black and Red Rose
Aphid (*Macrosiphum nigromaculosum*) rarely infesting leaves and stems;
the Hairy Rose Aphid (*Lachnus rosae*), dark, with hairs, on stems of
wild roses; the Rose and Bearberry Aphid, (*Amphorophora nervata*),
usually green, on leaves and twigs of cultivated roses and bearberry; the

Rose Grass Aphid (*Acyrthosiphon dirhodum*), yellow to pale green, wintering on twigs and leaves of rose, summering on grains and grasses; Yellow Rose Aphid (*Myzus porosus*, a pale species on wild and cultivated rose and on strawberry; the Strawberry Aphid (*Pentatrichopus fragarae-folii*), pale green, migrating from wild rose to strawberry; and the Cres-cent-marked Lily Aphid (*Neomyzus circumflexus*), yellow and black.

Any contact spray applied with pressure will control aphids: lindane, malathion, pyrethrum or rotenone. One of these is almost sure to be included in a combination rose pesticide but for a specific aphicide the old nicotine sulfate, 1 to 1½ teaspoons plus 1 tablespoon of soap flakes, is still effective. DDT kills aphids but also their parasites and predators so that its use often builds up aphid populations. Phosphates are also effective. Most are too poisonous for amateur use but dimethoate is com-paratively safe. Although used as a spray it has some systemic action, being transferred within the plant. Ground treatment with a systemic will control aphids for a month or so. Again, most of these are phosphates, very poisonous to handle; one (Scope, 2 per cent Di-Syston granules) is sold in a plastic container meant to minimize the hazards.

A stream of water from a hose can be temporarily effective against aphids and the washing action of a spray makes it more effective than a dust.

BAGWORMS. Pests of evergreens through much of the country, occa-sional on rose, with only one species (*Thyridopteryx ephemerae-formis*) commonly reported. Black and white caterpillars feed from spin-dle-shaped bags, 1 to 2 inches long. On roses it should be sufficient to cut off the bags before larvae hatch in late spring; spraying with Sevin, lead arsenate, chlordane or malathion is effective.

BEETLES. Forming the largest order of insects, injurious both as grubs, the larval state, and as adults. Beetles have chewing mouthparts and their first pair of wings is modified into hard horny sheaths (elytra) that meet in a straight line down the back. Beetles with a snout and with elytra fastened down so they cannot fly are known as weevils. A beetle with a long snout, often curved, is sometimes called a curculio.

ASIATIC GARDEN BEETLE (*Maladera castanea*). Serious along the Atlantic seaboard from Massachusetts to South Carolina, reported also from Ohio and West Virginia. The beetle is cinnamon brown, ½ inch long, same size and shape as a Japanese beetle. It appears in late June, hides in the soil during the day, comes out to feed at night. It is not as destructive to roses as to asters and other low plants. Eggs are laid in sod or weeds and grubs feed on roots. Treat lawns with chlordane or dieldrin as for Japanese beetles. Include Sevin, DDT or methoxychlor in the foliage spray.

BLISTER BEETLES (*Epicauta* spp.). Long, slender, rather elegant in appearance, gray, black, brown, or striped; named for their ability to cause a blister when crushed on the skin. Chiefly prevalent in late summer and more often on asters and Japanese anemone than on roses. Use DDT or methoxychlor spray or dust.

CHINESE ROSE BEETLE (*Adoretus sinicus*). A Hawaiian pest, often intercepted in shipments of flowers, cuttings etc. bound for California. A warning not to smuggle in plant material.

DIABROTICA BEETLES (western spotted cucumber beetle, *Diabrotica undecimpunctata,* and spotted cucumber beetle, *D. undecimpunctata howardi*). Of particular importance to roses in the South and West; feeding on flowers all season; of minor importance in eastern gardens in late summer and fall. The small green-yellow beetles have six black spots on each wing cover. Spray with DDT, Sevin or methoxychlor.

FULLER ROSE BEETLE (*Pantomorus godmani*) a grayish-brown weevil, with a white diagonal stripe on each side, ⅓ inch long, with a short snout. It eats notches in from margins of leaves, feeds on buds and flowers but only at night; the larvae feed on roots. This is a greenhouse pest in the North but common outdoors in the South and on the Pacific Coast. The beetles are active on many ornamentals; if larvae are abundant on roots, foliage may turn yellow. Dust plants and soil with chlordane, malathion or lindane.

GOLDSMITH BEETLE (*Cotalpa lanigera*). Related to June beetles, most injurious in the Southwest where it defoliates cottonwoods. The larvae feed on roots of roses and other ornamentals. The beetle is about 1 inch long, hairy, lemon-yellow on top, bronze underneath; the larva resembles a white grub; the life cycle takes two or three years.

GRAPE COLASPIS (*Colaspis flavida*). Clover rootworm, most important in larval state on corn roots from eastern states to Arizona. Very small brown beetles, covered with rows of punctures, make long curved feeding marks in leaves of apple, sometimes other plants, including roses.

GRAPEVINE HOPLIA (*Hoplia oregona*). Reddish brown scarab beetles, silvery underneath, ⅓ inch long, feeding on blossoms of roses and other plants. They are a problem on the West Coast and seem to prefer white flowers. The grubs feed on roots of roses and lawn grasses. Lindane dust has been used for control.

IMPORTED LONG-HORNED WEEVIL (*Calomycterus setarius*). First noted in New York in 1929, now present from Vermont to Maryland and in Illinois and Iowa, a general feeder on many plants and sometimes a house pest. Black beetles, ⅜ inch long, covered with grayish scales and with a metallic cast, feed chiefly on foliage, eating irregular areas in from the margin, but sometimes eat rose flowers. There is one brood and eggs are laid in sod. Use the same control measures as for Japanese beetles.

JAPANESE BEETLE (*Popillia japonica*). First found in 1916 near Philadelphia. The area of continuous infestation extends from Maine to South Carolina and west to Ohio. But the beetles have also established a beachhead in Michigan, Indiana, Illinois, Iowa, and Missouri. An infestation in California, starting in 1961, has apparently been eradicated. More than 275 trees and shrubs are attacked but the rose is a prime favorite. Gangs of beetles, up to twenty or thirty at a time, demolish a flower and chew foliage to lace.

The beetles are a beautiful metallic green and copper, oval, ½ inch long, with six small patches of white hairs extending from under the edge of each wing cover at the side and rear. Adults appear in late June, build to a peak in July (in the vicinity of New York City) start to diminish in August, mostly disappear in September with a few stray individuals left for October. Each female lives from thirty to forty-five days, laying her eggs at grass roots in lawns. The grubs hatch in ten to twelve days, feed on the roots until cold weather, burrow deeper in the soil to avoid freezing in winter, then return near the surface in spring, pupating in late May. The grubs are dirty white with brown heads, soft and hairy, ¾ to 1 inch long when grown, usually found in a curved position.

Rose leaves can be adequately protected by spraying weekly, often enough to keep new growth covered. Sevin, a relatively new broad-spectrum insecticide is particularly effective against Japanese beetles but, like DDT, it kills some beneficial insects that keep mites in check and so a miticide should be included in the spray. DDT, methoxychlor, malathion and lead arsenate are other possibilities. I still use, mostly, a combination spray (Tri-ogen) containing lead arsenate, since this presents no threat to insect friends. Contact sprays of pyrethrum and rotenone are fairly satisfactory. It is difficult to protect flowers that open between spray applications. Some recommend a daily light dusting but this may be harmful to the rose. I think it wiser to continue to spray weekly and to cut roses for the house each morning during the peak of the beetle season. Since this comes between the June display and the fine autumn roses there is no need to get too upset by beetles in midsummer. I heartily disagree with anyone who suggests cutting back roses in summer or pinching out buds as a beetle control measure.

Traps will capture a great many beetles but don't put them near the rose garden. The bait draws beetles from all neighboring gardens, only a fraction of which get into the trap. The rest feast on your roses when they might just as well have been left to dine next door. Handpicking beetles into a jar of kerosene is all right if you have the time, and don't spill kerosene on the roses, or work while the bushes are wet and spread blackspot.

To reduce the general beetle population lawns can be treated with dieldrin, 4¼ pounds of a 1½ percent dust, or 5 pounds of 2½ percent granules per 1000 square feet; or with chlordane, 5 pounds of a 5 percent dust or ½ pound of 50 percent wettable powder applied as a spray. For long-term control, milky disease spore dust, sold as Doom or Japidemic, is prepared from grubs inoculated with the bacterial disease. A teaspoon of dust is spotted in lawns at 3- to 5-foot intervals. It takes about three years for this natural control to make much headway.

JUNE BEETLES (*Phyllophaga* spp.). Large, reddish brown or black beetles, also known as May beetles or June bugs; large grubs known as white grubs. There are many species and they are of more consequence in the Middle West and the South than in the East. The life cycle takes three years in cold climates, one or two in warm climates. During most of this period the grubs feed on roots of roses and other cultivated plants as well as on grass roots. During the year of their spring flight the beetles feed, at night, on foliage of trees and shrubs and on rose blooms. Treat sod as for Japanese beetles; spray foliage with Sevin when adults are active; some hand picking may be necessary for roses on spring evenings.

ORIENTAL BEETLE (*Anomala orientalis*). Also called Asiatic beetle and a close relative of Asiatic garden and Japanese beetles; found in New York, New Jersey, Rhode Island, Pennsylvania, and North Carolina. It is the size and shape of a Japanese beetle but is straw-colored with varying dark markings. It is occasionally found feeding on flowers but is relatively unimportant.

ROSE CHAFER (*Macrodactylus subspinosus*). Usually known as Rose Bug, a slender tan beetle, about ½ inch long with long, spiny legs. It feeds on buds and blossoms in late May and June, chiefly peonies and roses, but in some sections is serious on foliage of grapes, elms, and other plants. It is general through the eastern states and as far west as Colorado and Texas but it is much more serious in upstate New York and New England than near New York City. The population seems to decrease as Japanese beetles increase. There is one brood a year, lasting three or four weeks. Control with 5 percent DDT dust, applied about every four days as blossoms open, or DDT spray, using 2 tablespoons 50 percent wettable powder to a gallon of water. Sevin or methoxychlor can be substituted for DDT. Some gardeners protect their roses with a temporary cheesecloth fence, stretching somewhat higher than the bushes. Even if it is open on top, the beetles seem not to fly over the barrier.

The GREEN ROSE CHAFER (*Dichelonyx backi*) is recorded on roses but is chiefly a pest of conifers.

RHABDOPTERUS BEETLES (*Rhabdopterus* spp.). Small, oval, blackish-brown shining beetles, feeding at night on buds and new leaves in Florida, Texas, other warm states. More important on camellias than on roses.

ROSE CURCULIO (*Rhynchites bicolor*). This rose snout beetle has several forms; the eastern is red with a black undersurface and black curved beak, about ¼ inch long; western forms vary from black and red to black with a greenish luster. All drill holes in buds of both wild and cultivated roses, the buds either not opening or producing petals riddled with holes. Small white larvae develop from eggs laid in rose hips but drop to the ground for pupation and hibernation. The rose curculio is particularly destructive in North Dakota and other cold regions, breeding in wild roses and swarming to cultivated roses in such numbers as to prevent almost all bloom. Spray or dust with DDT.

Rose Leaf Beetle (*Nodonota puncticollis*). A small, shiny green to blue beetle, not much bigger than a flea beetle, distributed from New England south and west to Arizona and Montana. I rarely see it in New York and New Jersey gardens, meet it occasionally in Pennsylvania.

Strawberry Flea Beetle (*Altica ignita*). Metallic green, golden bronze or purple, 3/16 inch long, on strawberry, rose, and many other plants. The foliage is riddled with small round holes and leaves may turn brown around the holes. Most damage is early in the season; DDT could be used on rose.

Strawberry Rootworm (*Paria fragariae*). On strawberry, rose, other ornamentals, and fruits. Rose leaves, in greenhouses or outdoors, have numerous small shot-holes; bark of new shoots may be gnawed off and buds eaten out by very small bronze beetles. The brown and white spotted grubs feed on strawberry roots. In California there are two generations on outdoor roses, several in greenhouses. Dust with chlordane or lindane. A parathion aerosol can be used by commercial greenhouse operators.

BLACKSPOT (*Diplocarpon rosae*). By far the most serious rose disease through most of the United States but not reported from Arizona, Nevada and Wyoming and not often serious in California and semiarid sections with low summer rainfall.

The leaves have one or more black spots distinguished by a fimbriate (fringed) margin and minute black spore pustules in the center. In very susceptible varieties the leaves turn yellow and drop rather quickly; in tolerant varieties there is little yellowing or defoliation. No variety is entirely immune but some, like Pink Princess, are very resistant and some, like Radiance, are very tolerant. Some years ago we learned that there are many different strains of the fungus so that a variety resistant to the disease in one state may not be in another. Yellow, copper, and orange roses with Pernetiana parentage are particularly susceptible. Repeated defoliation from blackspot makes roses more inclined to winter injury and dieback.

Primary infection comes from spores formed in old leaves on the ground and, probably more often, from fresh spore pustules formed in

small dark lesions wintered on the canes. The germinating spore penetrates directly through the cuticle on either the upper or lower leaf surface
and does *not* enter through an open stoma. Penetration is accomplished
with a minimum of six hours of continuous moisture. After that the
fungus is inside the leaf where it is unharmed by protectant sprays.
Theoretically it is possible to burn it out with eradicant sprays but these
are usually injurious to the leaf.

The spores are splashed by rain, or the hose, and are not spread to
any extent by air currents, although wind-blown rains in hurricanes can
carry them quite a distance. In gardens where foliage is kept dry by
watering with a Waterwand or Bubbler or with a soil-soaker hose there
is little blackspot except in rainy periods or when there is dew heavy
enough to drip. In gardens where an overhead sprinkler is run in the late
afternoon or all night there is almost certain to be blackspot. A good
mulch, in place early in the season, provides a mechanical barrier between
infective material on the ground and developing foliage overhead and
also prevents splashing, thereby reducing the distance spores can be
spread from the canes.

Sanitation has been somewhat overemphasized as a control for blackspot. It is certainly helpful to remove the first spotted leaves if you work
when the plants are dry but if the disease has gained a head start, removal
of all spotted leaves may reduce the food manufacturing areas so much
it will be more harmful than gradual defoliation by the fungus. It is also
helpful to rake up fallen leaves in the fall but this will not eliminate the
danger from cane lesions, either on established bushes or those newly
purchased and planted. Although some of us think that a dormant spray
of 1 to 8 lime sulfur immediately after pruning reduces somewhat the
danger from cane lesions there is no experimental evidence to prove this.
There is evidence showing that pruning back canes on infected bushes
to almost ground level in spring greatly reduces early season infection.
But this is a drastic step I would not take unless the winter forced me
to it.

There is no substitute for protective spraying. Carried on religiously,
every week from the time bushes come into full leaf until after hard
frost, such a program can keep a garden entirely free from blackspot
year after year, even though infective material arrives on new bushes.

With lapses in a program so that roses go into a rainy period without a thin coating of chemical over the leaves there is almost sure to be black-spot. There are many chemicals that are satisfactory when properly used, which means applying often enough to be sure the plant is protected before each rain. This does not mean rushing out to put on another spray or dust right after a rain. Modern fungicides are formulated so they do not readily wash off; they merely wear off as the plant grows. An average of every seven days is often enough, though in spring this may mean every six days and the time can be stretched to eight or nine days when growth slows up in a dry summer.

Over forty years ago, at Cornell, I obtained complete control of black-spot on very susceptible Persian Yellow roses with good old Massey dust, 90 parts fine sulfur, 10 parts arsenate of lead, while the untreated bushes adjacent were completely defoliated. You can't get Massey dust any more, although some dust mixtures include a small amount of sulfur. The chief objection to sulfur is that it burns at high temperatures.

Also at Cornell I learned that a strong copper spray, as in bordeaux mix-ture, could, in cool, cloudy weather, almost defoliate roses. Later, when I went into business as a plant doctor, I found that a weak ammoniacal copper, as included in the three-way spray, Tri-ogen, also gave complete control of blackspot if applied regularly enough and was safe in hot New Jersey summers, although injurious to some rose varieties if applied when the temperature was below 55°F. It is worth noting, however, that both Massey dust and Tri-ogen contain lead arsenate and this does have some fungicidal properties even though considered primarily as an insecticide.

Black ferbam, an iron compound, was the first of the organic fungicides that came on the rose scene after World War II and is still included, usually with some sulfur, in some combination rose pesticides. It is rela-tively inconspicuous on foliage but it does badly discolor blooms. Maneb, sold as Manzate or Dithane M-22, zineb, sold as Dithane 78 or Parzate, and captan, Orthocide, have all become standard for blackspot control. All leave a slight whitish residue on foliage and all are ineffective against powdery mildew. The newer folpet, better known under the trade name of Phaltan, is outstanding for blackspot control and aids in the control of mildew although not entirely satisfactory for this. The white residue is rather noticeable but bearable in view of the benefits obtained. From the standpoint of appearance I still prefer Tri-ogen but a Phaltan mixture may be somewhat more potent if blackspot has already started in a garden. Phaltan should not be used too strong—about 1 to 1¼ tablespoons of the 75 percent wettable powder (Ortho Phaltan Rose & Garden Fungicide) to 1 gallon of water. Do not add a sticker-spreader; some increase injury to the plant from Phaltan. The fungicide can be used with Isotox (a combination insecticide-miticide, containing DDT, lindane, malathion, Tedion and a spreader that is compatible with Phaltan).

Other fungicides control blackspot but sometimes and in some formulations may be injurious: dichlone (Phygon); dodine (Cyprex); glyodin; and Dyrene. Dichlone is now used mostly in aerosol bombs where it seems to be reasonably safe.

As I write these words *The Exchange* arrives with a note about Polyram as a control for blackspot. This fungicide, introduced in 1963 for fruit and vegetable applications, has just received U.S. Department of Agriculture registration for use on ornamentals. Directions call for 6 teaspoons per gallon of water of Polyram 80 percent wettable powder.

BLIGHTS. The word blight is used to designate a disease whose chief symptom is the sudden death of leaves, shoots, or flowers. Not many rose troubles come in this category, although a dieback similar to a blight may accompany canker diseases.

BOTRYTIS BLIGHT (*Botrytis cinerea*). This weakly parasitic cosmopolitan fungus appears as a gray mold on buds and flowers in wet weather, often causing balling. The same gray mold is sometimes found on canes of packaged roses kept too moist but the disease is most important on roses stored over winter for spring sales. Satisfactory storage control has been obtained by a 20 percent PCNB dust (Terraclor) or spraying with captan or Vancide 51. In the garden keep fading flowers cut off promptly; if necessary, spray with captan or zineb.

CANE BLIGHT (*Botryosphaeria ribis* var. *chromogena*). Also called dieback and canker, reported on roses from Alabama, Maryland, Texas, and Virginia but identical with a generally distributed disease of currants. Leaves wilt, gradually turn brown but stay attached to the cane which may have a basal canker. Prune out diseased canes.

Other fungi are sometimes reported as causing cane blights but are rarely important.

SOUTHERN BLIGHT (*Pellicularia rolfsii*). Not common on roses but reported from Florida, Kansas and Texas; very common on most annuals and perennials. The fungus, with its reddish tan sclerotia resembling mustard seed and white mycelial threads, attacks the crown, causing general blighting and death. Remove plants and all surrounding soil, making sure that none of the very small sclerotia are left behind.

SHOOT BLIGHT (*Pseudomonas syringae*). A bacterial disease of lilacs, a blast, reported on roses in Arkansas.

THREAD BLIGHT (*Pellicularia koleroga*). A southern disease, from North Carolina to Texas, on many different plants, including roses, with leaves matted together by brown fungus threads like spider webs. Prune out infected portions.

BLIND WOOD. Sometimes a shoot that should produce a flower bud at the tip simply fails to do so. There are many theories but no real explanation. Some varieties produce more blind wood than others and some do it soon after planting, but after a few weeks start to bloom normally. It helps to cut back such a shoot immediately, forcing a lower bud to start which usually produces a normal flower. See also Rose Midge for one cause of failure to bloom.

BORERS. Larvae of bees, wasps, sawflies and beetles may work in rose canes or twigs causing dieback. Presence of the borer may be indicated by a hole in the pith or by sawdust extruded from holes in the stem.

CURLED ROSE SAWFLY (*Allantus cinctus*). The larva bores into the pith of pruned rose canes, after feeding on leaves. See also under Sawflies.

FLATHEADED APPLE TREE BORER (*Chrysobothris femorata*). More common in trees, occasional in rose stems. The larva is a yellow-white grub, 1¼ inches long, with a broad, flat enlargement just behind the head. The beetle is a metallic dark gray to brown, with the head end blunt, the rear tapering. The Pacific Flatheaded Borer (*C. mali*) is a similar species distributed through western states.

RASPBERRY CANE BORER (*Oberea bimaculata*). A long-horned beetle, pest of raspberry and blackberry from Kansas eastward, occasional on rose. Adults are slender, cylindrical beetles, ½ inch long, black with yellow stripes, yellow thorax with two black spots. The female in egglaying makes a double row of punctures around the stem a few inches from the tip, causing dying back of the soft succulent terminal shoot to that point. The grubs work down through the pith, pupating near the crown. Cut and burn wilted tips as soon as noticed, pruning 6 inches below the punctured area.

RASPBERRY CANE MAGGOT (*Pegomya rubivora*). Found from coast to coast on brambles and rose. Tips of new shoots wilt, sometimes with a purplish discoloration at the base of the wilted part, or are broken off clean as though cut by a knife. Galls may be formed in the canes. White maggots, ⅓ inch long, tunnel down in the canes and pupate there. The flies, half the size of houseflies, emerge in spring to lay eggs in leaf axils or tender shoots. Cut off infested tips several inches below wilted portions.

RASPBERRY HORNTAIL (*Hartigia cressoni*). A yellow and black wasplike insect with a horn at the rear, on blackberry, raspberry, loganberry and rose in western states. Eggs are inserted under epidermis of tender tips and larvae spirally girdle these, causing wilting and death. Cut below affected portions.

ROSE STEM SAWFLY (*Hartigia trimaculata*). An eastern horntail, appearing in early summer and laying eggs in punctures made in rose canes. Whitish larvae bore through the canes, one to a cane, causing shoots to wilt, stunt or die back.

ROSE STEM GIRDLER (*Agrilus rubicola*). Primarily a rose pest, sometimes found in raspberry. Small greenish bronze beetles lay eggs under bark, preferably *Rosa rugosa* or *R. hugonis*. The grubs make one or two spiral mines around the canes which swell at such points and sometimes split. Cut out canes with swellings early in the spring. Another species (*A. ruficollis*) called the Red-necked Cane Borer, makes gouty galls on blackberry, raspberry and occasionally on rose.

SMALL CARPENTER BEE (*Ceratina* spp.). When you see a hole in the cut end of a rose stem and then split that stem longitudinally, you may see a row of five or six yellowish, curved maggots lined up in separate cavities or small, less than ½ inch, dark, bluish-green bees that look more like flies. Watching for holes in canes and cutting back to sound wood is usually sufficient control. Some recommend painting all pruning cuts to prevent entrance. Some tree paints are safe; others may be injurious; orange shellac is inconspicuous and non-injurious. Avoid pruning back roses in autumn, when the wood does not callus quickly.

BUDWORMS. Small caterpillars feeding in or on opening buds. See
    Rose Budworm, Green Fruitworm, Greenhouse Leaf Tier and
Oblique-banded and Red-banded Leaf Rollers under Caterpillars.

BUGS. True Bugs are sucking insects with wings folded flat over the
    abdomen. They are not common problems on rose.
    FOUR-LINED PLANT BUG (*Poecilocapsus lineatus*). Bright red nymphs
with black dots and green adults with four black stripes cause, by their
sucking, round, depressed spots in leaves. Rare on roses, common on
other ornamentals in the East.
    HARLEQUIN BUG (*Murgantia histrionica*). Flat black bugs with bright
red markings. More important in the South but not common on rose.
Stink Bugs, Leaf-Rooted Bugs, and Lygus Bugs may also feed on southern
rose blooms.
    TARNISHED PLANT BUG (*Lygus lineolaris*). Small, flat, oval mottled bugs
blacken terminal shoots and buds. Much more important on dahlias than
on roses.

CANKERS. A canker is a localized lesion or diseased area on a woody
    structure. On a rose cane it is a spot of dead tissue which may enlarge
until it girdles the cane, destroying the water-conducting system and
resulting in dying back from the tip. The two canker diseases most frequently found on roses are brown canker and stem canker. The latter,
often called common canker, usually starts in wounds; the former is
truly parasitic.
    BRAND CANKER (*Coniothyrium wernsdorffiae*). Rather rare in the
United States and probably confined to northern states, being confused
with stem canker in the South. Initial symptoms are small, reddish spots,
often starting around treehopper and other wounds. The spots enlarge,
the centers turn brown or tan and have little longitudinal slits over black
fruiting bodies (pycnidia) which bear small olive-brown spores. The
margin of the lesion is usually reddish purple but the canker may enlarge
until the cane is girdled, with a swelling or gall formed above the girdled
part and the cane dying back to it. The disease has been serious in this
country chiefly on climbers that are protected for winter with moisture-
retentive materials. Control lies in eliminating winter protection, merely
taking canes down from supports and holding them near the ground

with crossed stakes. There is apparently no natural infection in summer so protective spraying has no value.

BROWN CANKER (*Cryptosporella umbrina*). A widespread, serious disease, present in most sections where roses are grown. Very small purplish spots on canes soon acquire a white center and reddish purple margin. Many small round spots may be grouped on a single cane, but during the winter, and especially on portions covered with earth or other moist material, the spots coalesce to large cankers, often several inches long, with tan centers and purplish borders. Such cankers, in moist weather in spring, are covered with yellow spore tendrils. If the cankers girdle the canes there is subsequent dieback.

Although spots are most common on canes, they may occur on leaves and flowers. Leaf spots are purple or buff, or white bordered with purple; flower spots are cinnamon-buff. Infection takes place either through wounds, especially in soft wood injured by frost, or through uninjured bark.

Control by cutting out diseased canes at spring pruning, followed by a dormant lime-sulfur spray. Summer spraying for blackspot, especially with copper or sulfur, keeps brown canker under fair control. Avoid winter mulches that will keep canes too warm and moist; cankers are often more serious in spring if the canes have been swaddled in salt hay or straw or leaves.

CORYNEUM CANKER (*Griphosphaeria corticola*). Small, dark glistening spore pustules appear in cankers at the base of canes and sometimes a gall, resembling crown gall, forms above a canker which has girdled a cane. Cut out such infected canes.

CROWN CANKER (*Cylindrocladium scoparium*). Usually confined to greenhouse roses but also reported from the field. The bark darkens into a water-soaked punky region at the crown, sometimes girdling the cane but seldom causing death; bloom may be reduced. The fungus lives in the soil and enters through pruning and other wounds under conditions of abundant moisture. The soil should be changed or sterilized and the benches washed with formaldehyde before refilling.

GRAFT CANKER (*Coniothyrium rosarum*). A greenhouse disease starting at the graft, encouraged by the warm, moist propagating frame and producing a large amount of dead wood when plants are moved to the greenhouse bench. The fungus is thought by some to be identical with that causing stem canker.

STEM CANKER (*Leptosphaeria coniothyrium*). Also called common canker and present in almost every rose garden. The fungus is a rather weak wound parasite, entering through stubs left in pruning, insect wounds, scratches or thorn scars, frost cracks, or the jagged edges left when stems are broken instead of cut. The canker may or may not have a definite margin but it is distinguished by the sooty masses of dark olive spores just under the epidermis. The bark does not have the little longitudinal slits characteristic of brand canker but there is often a similar dieback if the cane is girdled.

Control by eliminating cultivating wounds, by always cutting *close* to a bud or leaf axil so no stub is left, and by pruning below diseased portions. Avoid overfeeding and watering late in the season. This promotes the succulent growth likely to be split by frost at the first sudden drop in temperature.

There are various other fungi associated with cankers and dieback on rose but they are relatively unimportant.

CATERPILLARS. Caterpillars are wormlike larvae of moths and butterflies. Those that sometimes appear on roses go by many other names.

BROWN-TAIL MOTH (*Nygmia phaeorrhoea*). Present in New England, feeding on roses as well as trees. The caterpillars are 1½ inches long, reddish-brown to nearly black, with a white broken stripe along each side, red tubercles on rear segments. They are covered with long brown hairs which are poisonous and cause a rash if touched. White moths with brown "tails" lay eggs in globular yellow hair clusters and young caterpillars winter in webbed nests. Cut off and burn winter webs. Spray roses with lead arsenate, DDT, or methoxychlor as for other chewing insects.

CANKERWORMS (Spring, *Paleacrita vernata;* Fall, *Alsophila pometaria*). When roses are near shade trees or apple or other fruit trees their leaves may be eaten by looping caterpillars, inchworms, that are green or brown with white and fellow stripes along the body, about 1 inch long. The usual spray schedule, which should contain some sort of stomach poison, will take care of these occasional May visitors. Sevin is effective, nonpoisonous for the operator.

CORN EARWORM (*Heliothis zea*). Also known as the tomato fruitworm, sometimes feeding on rose buds or flowers. The caterpillars are 1½ inches long when full grown, reddish brown to green with brown, black or green stripes.

FALL WEBWORM (*Hyphantria cunea*). Branches are webbed together at the tips, rather than at crotches as with tent caterpillars. Common on trees in late summer, the pale caterpillars, with long silky gray hairs arising from black and yellow tubercles, may feed in the flower garden when other food is scarce. Cut off and burn the webs wherever noticed.

FRUIT-TREE LEAF ROLLER (*Archips argyrospila*). Present from coast to coast, often serious on apple, feeding also on other fruits and ornamentals. Green worms with brown heads may feed in rose buds, tie and web leaves together.

GREEN FRUITWORM (*Lithophane antennata*). Pale green larvae with white stripes, fat, 1 to 1½ inches long, sometimes feed on rose buds but primarily on young apples. The adult is a grayish moth. Spray with DDT or lead arsenate.

GREENHOUSE LEAF TIER, Celery Leaf Tier (*Udea rubigalis*). Present throughout North America, feeding on many greenhouse and garden flowers and vegetables. Yellowish green caterpillars, ¾ inch long, with a white stripe and dark green line down the center of the back, roll, fold and tie together leaves and terminal shoots. Cut off infested parts. Spray with DDT, or with pyrethrum, repeating in half an hour.

OBLIQUE-BANDED LEAF ROLLER, Rose Leaf Tier (*Archips rosaceanus*). Pale green, black-headed larvae feed in rose buds, then work inside rolled leaves, often tying several together. They also feed on many other ornamentals, fruits and vegetables. The moth is red-brown with irregular dark lines on the fore wings. There are two generations: spring and late summer. Remove rolled leaves; dust bushes with DDT or Sevin.

OMNIVOROUS LEAF ROLLER (*Platynotus stultana*). A citrus pest but also feeding on many other plants, including rose in greenhouses. The larva is yellowish or greenish brown with a ragged stripe down the back.

RED-BANDED LEAF ROLLER (*Argyrotaenia velutinana*). Similar to the oblique-banded roller but with red bands across wings of the moth. There may be three generations. Spray with lead arsenate or Sevin.

ROSE BUDWORM (*Pyrrhia umbra*). Larvae of the bordered sallow moth eat into buds of roses, snapdragon and other garden flowers. There are two forms. One caterpillar is greenish, spotted with black tubercles and has prominent dark, longitudinal stripes; the other has light orange markings on the back. Remove infested buds as noticed.

TENT CATERPILLARS. The Eastern Tent Caterpillar (*Malacosoma americana*) is the familiar one making its ugly nest in branch crotches of wild cherry and other trees. After leaving the webs the full-grown caterpillars, 2 inches long, dark, hairy, with white, brown, and yellow lines and blue spots, often feed on roses as they get ready to spin their dirty white cocoons on tree trunks or buildings. The Western Tent Caterpillar (*M. pluviale*) is common in the Pacific Northwest, living in small, compact nests. The larvae, tawny with blue and orange spots, feed on fruits and on rose. The Forest Tent Caterpillar (*M. disstria*) does not make a real tent but lives in large colonies like armyworms. It is bluish or black with white spots and yellow stripes. Any stomach poison used for other chewing insects should protect roses from tent caterpillars.

Other caterpillars are occasionally reported on rose. The Orange Tortrix (*Argyrotaenia citrana*) is a pest in California and in greenhouses. The larvae, dirty white with brown heads, rolls leaves of many types of plants. The Red-humped Caterpillar (*Schizura concinna*) has a red head and a red hump on its yellow-brown body. It is distributed over most of the country, feeds on many fruits and ornamentals. The Yellow Woollybear (*Diacrisia virginica*) is the very hairy yellow, black-striped larva of the Virginia Tiger Moth. It is a general feeder on many vegetables and flowers.

CHEMICAL INJURY. Most chemicals used in sprays and dusts are phytotoxic under certain conditions. There is a narrow margin between the amount required for pest control and that which is injurious to plants. Exact dosage is always important. This must never exceed the amount stated on the label and in many cases this amount must be reduced to prevent injury under certain conditions. Temperature and humidity influence phytotoxicity. Some chemicals are incompatible and should not be used in combination or closely following each other. Although many directions call for adding a sticker or spreader this, too, may be unwise. Some additives increase injury, probably by increasing penetration, and some decrease efficiency, probably by increasing run-off.

ARSENICAL INJURY. In too strong doses lead arsenate will cause marginal burning, dead spots in leaves, or dead areas between veins.

COPPER INJURY. Small red spots on leaves, often followed by yellowing and defoliation; most pronounced early in the season or in cool, cloudy or rainy weather.

DDT INJURY. An orange or yellowish cast to foliage.

FERTILIZER BURN. If leaves are moist at the time of application and are accidentally hit by fertilizer they will have burned spots. Burning may follow feeding in very hot weather even if the foliage is not touched. Never allow concentrated fertilizer to get on the canes; do not use too much at once; spread evenly over the area; water well. In applying foliar fertilizers do not exceed recommended dosage.

INCOMPATIBILITY. Sulfur is incompatible with oil sprays; some insecticides, including malathion and Sevin, may not be used with bordeaux mixture, lime sulfur or other alkaline compounds containing lime; lead arsenate is incompatible with soap, and so on. Proprietary combinations will be of compatible chemicals; be cautious in making your own combinations.

MERCURY TOXICITY. Roses are extremely sensitive to mercury vapor and have been seriously injured when paints containing mercury were used to paint sash bars in greenhouses. Covering the paint with a paste of dry lime sulfur mixed with lime, flour and water has reduced the amount of toxic vapor. Do not treat soil with mercuric chloride near roses.

SOLVENT INJURY. Sprays prepared as emulsions usually have some petroleum product as a solvent and this so-called "inactive" ingredient has caused injury in too strong doses or in too hot weather even though the pesticide chemical itself is safe. Bombs should be held at least 18 inches from plants to allow the propellant to evaporate; otherwise it burns (more literally freezes) the tissue.

SULFUR INJURY. Browning or scorching of tips and margins of leaves, sometimes followed by yellowing and defoliation; bleaching of some flower colors, especially red. Use sulfur and sulfur compounds cautiously when the temperature approaches 80°F. and omit above 85°F.

SMOG AND SMOKE INJURY. Roses may be severely injured by sulfur dioxide from industrial processes with the only control at the source. Smog, from unsaturated hydrocarbons and ozone in the atmosphere, causes losses in roses and many plants in California. Spraying or dusting with zineb reduces the injury in some cases. Greenhouses can install activated carbon filters.

WEED-KILLER INJURY. Any sprayer used for applying a weed-killer should be thoroughly rinsed before being used for roses. If the sprayer has had 2,4-D it is almost impossible to clean it sufficiently for rose protection. Mark that sprayer with red paint and use it solely for plant destruction. If 2,4-D is used on lawns its volatile properties may injure roses some distance away. New shoots are curled and twisted; new leaves are very small. Usually the bushes gradually recover.

CHLOROSIS. The yellowing of normally green tissue due to the partial failure of chlorophyll to develop or its destruction after development. Often due to unavailability of iron and more common where soils are naturally alkaline, chlorosis may also be caused by a deficiency of nitrogen, manganese, or magnesium, or a lack of oxygen for the roots.

With iron deficiency, or lime-induced chlorosis, the yellowing usually starts on the youngest leaves and progresses downward. Such a condition is common in the arid Southwest where the land has a high calcium carbonate content. Control by soil treatments, adding sulfur or iron sulfate at not more than 1 to 2 pounds per 100 square feet for a single application, followed by a mulch. For an immediate effect, spray foliage with iron sulfate, 1 ounce to 3 gallons of water. Chelated iron, sold as Sequestrene and under other trade names, may be applied to the soil to give a quick effect. Use on foliage with great caution, following directions for dilution. Avoid excessive irrigation with highly alkaline water. The choice of understock may be important in alkaline regions. Scions on Multiflora are said to be more prone to chlorosis than those on Ragged Robin.

Chlorosis from magnesium deficiency occurs chiefly on light sandy soils subject to leaching in high annual rainfall or excessive irrigation. Yellowing starts on lower leaves and progresses upward. Such soils are usually acid in reaction and can be corrected by using dolomitic limestone.

When the manganese-iron ratio is disturbed the chlorosis is often remedied by spraying with manganese sulfate.

Yellowing and dropping of foliage indicates poor drainage, with roots getting insufficient oxygen in a water-logged soil.

When leaves on a whole cane are yellow but do not drop, the cause may be nitrogen deficiency, which can be remedied by a high-nitrogen fertilizer.

DEER INJURY. Increasingly, even in crowded suburbs, deer come into the garden in spring and browse on tender new rose shoots. One repellent is a carbamate, sold as Z.I.P. in most garden centers, and is meant for spraying on foliage. Another, bone tar oil, sold as Magic Circle Deer Repellent by State College Laboratories, State College, Pa., is meant to be applied in a circle around plants or garden bed.

DEFICIENCY DISEASES. Besides the chlorosis discussed already we have marginal browning, bronzing or scorching due to lack of potassium. This appears first on lower leaves and advances upward; leaves may be crinkled, whole plant stunted. Use a complete fertilizer containing 5 to 10 percent potash. Wood ashes also help to supply potassium.

In phosphorus deficiency there may be a general grayish cast to foliage with old leaves mottled light and dark green, reddish or purplish pigments on stems, general stunting and slow growth. Most commercial fertilizers have an adequate proportion of phosphorus but it may be added separately as superphosphate. Bonemeal provides phosphorus but it is very slow-acting.

In greenhouses leaf scorch may be due to boron or calcium deficiency. Boron deficiency may also cause blindness but very often blind wood develops without any proven cause.

DIEBACK. This is not a specific disease but a symptom. Dying back of the cane or shoot from the tip occurs with many diseases. It is a symptom of cane blight, a frequent aftermath of defoliation by blackspot. It occurs when cankers girdle canes at the base or when they are split by frost, or when roots have been subjected to wet soil over a long period. More than a dozen fungi, aside from those causing canker diseases, have been isolated from canes showing dieback but one, *Diplodia* sp. is most commonly associated with such a condition. This is a weak parasite and apparently grows in tissue dying from other causes. When flowers are cut off at the top of a stem instead of back at the leaf axil there is usually dieback to the node (see Figure 20). Diplodia dieback commonly occurs in Florida after pruning, unless cut surfaces are painted with orange shellac.

DODDER (*Cuscuta* spp.). One of the few flowering plants that are
parasitic. Dodder is not especially common on roses but in some
localities the orange tendrils and white flowers envelop almost every
flower and shrub in the vicinity. Infested portions must be cut out and
burned because even a small portion of a tendril attached by suckers to the
stems will start growth over again.

DOWNY MILDEW (*Peronospora sparsa*). Fairly common on roses
under glass, seldom found on outdoor roses. Yellowish blotches
appear on upper leaf surfaces and a grayish down on the underside.
Leaves may drop and blooming is delayed but the plants are not killed.
Proper ventilation to reduce humidity is helpful, as is spraying with a
weak copper or zineb.

EARWIGS. The European earwig (*Forficula auricularia*) was discov-
ered at Newport R.I. in 1911 and in Seattle, Washington, in 1915.
Long a garden and household pest in New England and the Pacific
Northwest it is now a problem along the Atlantic seaboard from Maine to
Delaware and Pennsylvania and in Colorado and California as well as the
Northwest. Earwigs are hard, dark brown, up to ⅘ inch long, slender,
with a pair of pincers or forceps at the tip of the abdomen, larger and
more curved in the male. The front wings are very short and the hind
wings are folded up under them. Earwigs seldom fly; they run. Eggs are
laid on soil; young nymphs feed on leaves, older earwigs eat blossoms of
roses and many other plants. Chlordane, Sevin, or lindane dust or spray
can be used on plants and around hiding places. If used with caution,
dieldrin can be sprayed around infested areas but not on plants.

GALLS. A gall is an outgrowth or swelling, more or less spherical, of
unorganized plant cells. Galls are caused by bacteria, fungi, insects,
and sometimes by a virus. What appears to be a gall is often merely callus
formation around a wound. Crown gall is most important on roses.

CROWN GALL (*Agrobacterium tumefaciens*). A bacterial disease common on roses, brambles, some other woody and herbaceous plants, characterized by somewhat rounded tumors with rough, irregular surfaces.
When dead or dying roses are excavated they are sometimes found to
have a large gall near the crown and smaller galls on the roots. The bacteria live in the soil and are capable of surviving at least two years in the

absence of any suitable host. They enter the rose through wounds made in cultivating or budding, or by rodents or insects, very likely by nematodes. Soil infestation comes from infected plants or with irrigation water.

Control by exclusion so far as possible, refusing any new plant showing gall formation when it comes from the nursery. Avoid cultivating and other wounds. When a diseased plant is removed, dig out all surrounding soil and replace it with new. Commercial growers may fumigate the old soil with methyl bromide, as for nematodes, but this is too poisonous for the average amateur. Two years' growth of cowpeas, oats, or crotalaria between rose crops will starve the bacteria out of the soil. There has been promising work with antibiotics but not yet very practical results. The disease is unpredictable. Cuttings or seedlings can be placed in infested soil and remain healthy or a diseased plant can be moved to a new location and recover so that it is difficult to test efficacy of treatments. The disease remains a problem, taking a definite but uncertain toll of rose bushes; keep it out of your garden if you can.

INFECTIOUS HAIRY ROOT (*Agrobacterium rhizogenes*). This disease was long considered another manifestation of crown gall but the causative organism is now recorded as a distinct species. A great number of hairy roots protrude directly from stems or localized hard swellings at the bud union. The effect is that of a witch's broom. Hairy root is not as common as crown gall; the precautions are the same.

MOSSY ROSE GALL (caused by *Diplolepis rosae*). A globular mass of mosslike filaments surrounds a cluster of hard cells, each of which contains the larva of a gall wasp. The galls appear in June and July with the larvae remaining in the cells until spring. This phenomenon is more common on species roses, especially *Rosa rugosa;* I have never met mossy gall on a hybrid tea. There is no control except cutting out infested stems.

ROSE ROOT GALL (caused by *Diplolepis radicum*). Another species of wasp causes a large conspicuous swelling, 1 to 2 inches across, very infrequently on roots of cultivated roses. Cut off such galls.

GRASSHOPPERS. May migrate from vacant lots or grassy fields to the rose garden, eating foliage, especially tender new shoots, and flowers. Use chlordane, lindane or DDT spray or dust.

LEAF-CUTTER BEES (*Megachile* spp.). In nearly all parts of the country rose leaves are seen with ovals and circles cut out of the margin. This is the work of a medium-sized, black, brown or metallic bee which cuts out these precisely tailored portions to make nests in wood or in the pith of rose, dahlia and other stems. The ovals line the walls of a cell and after an egg is laid in it, the circle forms a cap. There is no real way to control the leaf damage; because the cut-out portions are not eaten by the bee a stomach poison does little good. Nor do we really want to kill leaf-cutter bees because they are primarily beneficial, being important pollinators. Cut out wilted or dying shoots that have been used as nests.

LEAFHOPPERS. Sucking insects which, by their withdrawal of sap from the underside of a leaf, produce a stippled white pattern on the upper surface. The adults are slender, elongated, with rooflike wings that meet in a straight line. The nymphs are similar but wingless. There are several species on roses but all act the same, working from underneath and hopping away quickly when disturbed.

APPLE LEAFHOPPER (*Empoasca maligna*). Common on apple and rose east of the Rocky Mountains and in the Northwest. In late summer and fall foliage turns pale, the upper surface flecked with many small white spots, the underside covered with dark bits of excrement and white cast skins. The leafhoppers are greenish white, have only one generation a year.

POTATO LEAFHOPPER (*Empoasca fabae*). A wedge-shaped green leafhopper not primarily a pest of roses but probably responsible for some of the browning of leaf margins in August. It breeds in the South, swarms north to feed on apple foliage, then goes to beans, potatoes, and dahlias causing hopperburn, marginal browning.

RED-BANDED LEAFHOPPER (*Graphocephala coccinea*). Common and conspicuous on roses and other flowers but apparently not very injurious. The front wings are gaudily decorated with alternate bands of magenta and green or blue.

ROSE LEAFHOPPER (*Edwardsiana rosae*). A pest of apple and rose, producing the characteristic stippling of leaves and sometimes a slight yellowing and curling. Eggs winter under the bark and nymphs hatch soon after first leaves are formed. Adults are creamy white to light yellow. Eggs for a second generation, which may be active until late autumn, are laid in leaf veins in midsummer. The spring brood is usually well-enough controlled with any contact insecticide, nicotine, rotenone or malathion, but the disastrous fall brood, which often sucks leaves nearly white, usually requires DDT, 1 to 2 tablespoons of 50 percent wettable powder to 1 gallon of water or combination spray. Dimethoate is sometimes suggested.

WHITE APPLE LEAFHOPPER (*Typhlocyba pomaria*). Generations in May and September, October blanch apple leaves white and then move over to roses. The foliage shows a rather coarse stippling and the undersurface is covered with shining black dots of fecal deposits. Use DDT in October.

LEAF SPOTS. Diseases so designated are characterized by rather definitely delimited lesions on leaves, often a brown or tan center with a darker margin. Blackspot and spot anthracnose are discussed under those headings.

CERCOSPORA LEAF SPOT (*Mycosphaerella rosicola* = *Cercospora rosicola*). Confined to rose and rather general but much more serious in the South. In Florida and Texas Cercospora leaf spot may be even more serious than blackspot. Spots start as small, yellow-green dots, then change to small, light-brown areas with purplish borders, or the centers may be grayish with brown borders. The tissue sometimes falls out, leaving a shot-hole effect. Perithecia, winter fruiting bodies of the fungus, are formed in fallen leaves to provide spring infection. *Mycosphaerella rosigena* is sometimes listed as a separate species but is doubtfully distinct from *M. rosicola*. A southern species, *Cercospora puderi,* is known only by its imperfect state. The spots are very small, dingy gray with reddish-brown margins. The disease is most serious on poorly grown plants. Maneb is recommended for control, or Dithane M-45, a combination of zinc iron with maneb.

SEPTERIA LEAF SPOT (*Septoria rosae*). Reported from Mississippi, New Jersey, and South Carolina. Spots with gray centers, speckled with dark fruiting bodies, have dark margins.

The few other fungi connected with rose leaf spots are of minor importance, with infections probably secondary. Protective measures in use for blackspot should be adequate for other leaf spots.

MEALYBUGS (*Pseudococcus* spp.). Soft, oval sucking insects covered with a white powdery wax extending in short filaments around the body; usually found clustered by leaf axils. Mealybugs are not common on roses but may appear on neglected bushes in the South. They are fostered by ants after their honeydew so the ants should be controlled with chlordane in the nests. Spray the roses with malathion or dimethoate.

MIDGE (*Dasyneura rhodophaga*). Originally a greenhouse pest, the rose midge has become an occasional but very serious problem of outdoor roses. It is confined to rose. A very minute, yellow-brown fly lays eggs in flower and leaf buds. Feeding by small, whitish to orange maggots causes blackening and death or twisting and distortion of buds. Older buds develop a sharp crook in the pedicel. By the time shoots and buds have turned black and crisp the maggots have dropped to the ground to pupate. A fresh crop of flies appears in a week, the whole life cycle taking only two or three weeks in warm weather. Usually the roses bloom fairly well in June but the midge increases by midsummer so there is no bloom at all, even in a large garden where the bushes themselves look green and thriving.

To control, spray ground and bushes thoroughly with DDT, 2 tablespoons of 50 percent wettable powder to 1 gallon of water; repeat twice at ten-day intervals. Cut off and burn infested shoots.

MILDEW. See Powdery Mildew, Downy Mildew.

MOLD. A word used to denote profuse fungus growth on the surface of plant tissue. Gray mold is common on fading flowers and sometimes appears on canes. See Botrytis Blight under Blights.

BLACK MOLD OF ROSE GRAFT (*Chalaropsis thielavioides*). Usually on grafted roses, occasionally on budded roses in nursery fields. The dark fungus grows over and blackens the cut surface of stock and scion, preventing union and killing the scion. When outdoor roses are budded on Manetti understock the bud may turn black and die. Odorata understock is likewise susceptible, Multiflora moderately so, but Ragged Robin is immune. Infection takes place only through wounds. Control by using healthy understock or disinfect it two hours with formaldehyde, 1 to 320 dilution. Soak cuttings one hour in Ceresan before setting in field. Spray greenhouse benches, tools, etc., with copper sulfate; prevent spread of spores by workmen on hands, clothing, and budding knife.

LEAF MOLD (*Cladosporium* spp.). Olive-brown spores form a dark velvety coating in high humidity; seldom a problem on roses.

NEMATODES. Almost microscopic, filiform animals, also called eel-
worms, living in soil and responsible for many plant diseases and
decline in vigor. Formerly the root-knot nematode, which turned out to
be not one but several species, was considered the only one of great
importance but now it is taking a rather minor place among the nematodes that are either endoparasites, living inside plants, or ectoparasites,
living in the soil and feeding on plant roots from the outside. Because of
the wounds made by nematodes in the feeding process there is often a
link with diseases caused by soil fungi.

The danger of nematodes to garden roses was studied under a grant
from the American Rose Foundation. From collections of soil samples
from twenty-seven states we learned that at least fourteen genera of
parasitic nematodes are associated with roses showing signs of ill health.
We do not know that all of these cause specific diseases in roses but some
do and probably all cause loss of vigor, stunting, possibly death if present
in large enough amounts.

DAGGER NEMATODES (*Xiphinema* spp.). Very common migratory ectoparasites with long stylets. The American Dagger Nematode (*X. ameri-
canum*) is associated with decline of many cultivated plants, including
roses, over the country. The European Dagger Nematode (*X. diversicau-
datum*) is a proven pathogen of roses, causing chlorosis and elongated
swellings and curling near tips of roots. It is more important in greenhouse roses. Control means disposal of all plants in a bed, careful steriliza-
tion of soil and bed, and replanting with clean stock. The California
Dagger Nematode (*X. index*) causes terminal swelling and angling of
main roots, death of lateral roots of grape, fig and rose.

LANCE NEMATODES (*Hoplolaimus* spp.). Stout, cylindrical, rather large,
somewhat migratory, found around some ornamentals, including roses.

LEAF AND STEM NEMATODES (*Aphelenchoides* spp.). Male and female
adults both elongate, wormlike; ecto- and endoparasites, found in buds,
leaves and stems of strawberries, chrysanthemums, ferns, and other ornamentals; represented in 15 percent of samples of soil from rose roots.

MEADOW OR ROOT LESION NEMATODES (*Pratylenchus* spp.). The Walnut
Meadow Nematode (*P. vulnus*) and Scribner's Meadow (*P. scribneri*)
are known parasites of roses. Cobb's Meadow (*P. penetrans*) and De
Man's Meadow (*P. pratensis*) are associated with decline in roses among

many other plants. The nematodes are widely distributed endoparasites, males and females wormlike, with a blunt end in the female. First symptoms are usually yellow, black, or brown lesions on feeder roots. As the roots are killed, new surface roots may be produced in a witch's broom effect. Bushes show dieback symptoms, are stunted, may die. In one California nursery chemical treatment of soil infested with *P. vulnus* increased Number 1 grade roses by 400 percent.

PIN NEMATODES (*Paratylenchus* spp.). Very small, common ectoparasites. Males are rare; the female has a long stylet, curved body.

RING NEMATODES (*Criconemoides* spp.). Short, thick-bodied ectoparasites with a wide host range.

ROOT-KNOT NEMATODES (*Meloidogyne hapla*). The Northern Root-knot Nematode is the common species on roses. The females are white, pear-shaped, can be just seen with the naked eye; the males are slender, wormlike. Nodule-like swellings are formed in roots, mostly the fibrous roots in roses. The galls are ⅛ to ¼ inch in diameter, up to ½ inch long, and form an integral part of the root. This distinguishes them from incipient cases of crown gall where the nodule can be broken off. Yellowing of foliage, stunting and early death are above-ground symptoms.

The young larva migrates through the soil to a root tip, moves in to the axial cylinder of the root and becomes sedentary. It injects a secretion which stimulates the formation of three to five giant cells and food is absorbed through these host cells. The female deposits eggs in an extruded brownish jelly, from 400 to 2000. The larvae develop inside the eggs and become free in the soil only when the host root cracks or decays. They may attack the same root in another place or a new root. At 80°F. a generation takes only twenty-seven days; at 67°F. the cycle averages eighty-seven days; below 55° activity ceases.

SHEATH NEMATODES (*Hemicycliophora* spp.). Ectoparasites that retain molting skins as extra protection to bodies that remain attached to roots.

SPIRAL NEMATODES (*Helicotylenchus* spp.). Ectoparasites, inserting the head into a root but with the body remaining outside in a ventrically curved spiral. They are found in many soil samples from rose roots with Steiner's Spiral (*H. nannus*) common in the Southeast.

STUBBY-ROOT NEMATODES (*Trichodorus* spp.). Thick-bodied, migratory ectoparasites causing abnormal short stubby roots; on a great many hosts.

STYLET NEMATODES (*Tylenchorhynchus* spp.). Causing stunting of many ornamentals, occurring in over half of the rose soil samples.

Occurring only once each in fifty-two samples were a sting nematode (*Belonolaimus* sp.); needle nematode (*Longidorus* sp.); and a stem and bulb nematode (*Ditylenchus* sp.).

Aside from inspecting roses before planting, making sure they do not have telltale root knots, the best control for nematodes is soil treatment, preferably before planting, although some nematocides are reasonably safe around living plants.

Fallow soil can be treated with D-D Mixture, injecting 4 to 5 cc. 6 inches deep at 12-inch intervals, or with Garden Dowfume (ethylene dibromide), 5 to 6 cc. per injection at 12-inch intervals. Wait two to four weeks before planting. Commercial growers use the more toxic methyl bromide gas (Dowfume MC 2), a liquid in pressurized containers that is injected under a special plastic tent sold by the manufacturer. This must be done at least four weeks before planting, with all safety precautions followed exactly.

DBCP granules (sold as Nemagon or Fumazone) can be worked into the soil at time of planting—5 ounces per 25 square feet of soil surface. DBCP liquid may be used around established plants, figuring 3 teaspoonfuls of the 50 percent concentrate, per 35 square feet, and applying with water in a sprinkling can. V-C 13 Nemacide can also be used once a year after planting, using 5 teaspoons per 25 square feet, applied in water with the sprinkling can. Only one pesticide and only one application is safe during a single year.

The efficacy of soil drenches depends on the soil type. Nemagon is effective in some soils, gives poor control in others.

Most state experiment stations now have a nematologist on the staff. If you suspect your soil trouble is due to nematodes take a sample of soil and roots from an ailing rose bush, wrap in plastic, and mail immediately with all pertinent information.

PETS. Dogs sometimes disturb roses by burying bones too near roots but in general rose thorns provide adequate self protection. Cats don't mind the thorns and find the soft earth of rose beds much to their liking; if you add a buckwheat hull mulch they think it especially for their benefit. I have never, however, seen any real harm to roses from cats using their beds.

POWDERY MILDEW OF ROSE (*Sphaerotheca pannosa rosae*). One of the most important rose diseases, ranking ahead of blackspot in California and the Southwest and probably second in importance elsewhere. Small-flowered rambler roses are extremely susceptible but large-flowered ramblers and climbers with glossy foliage denoting Wichuraiana parentage are quite resistant. Floribunda roses vary in susceptibility. Most hybrid teas will mildew if located where there is little air circulation. The disease appears in the South and in California as soon as there is new succulent foliage. Around New York City it starts on ramblers and polyanthas in mid-May or earlier and is sometimes serious on hybrid teas in June but it is more devastating in late summer when cool nights following warm days increase humidity. For some reason many red varieties are particularly susceptible.

Mildew starts on young leaves in somewhat raised, blisterlike areas covered with a delicate white weft, under which the leaf turns reddish purple or occasionally black. Often the first symptom on a young leaf is a slight rolling of the margin. Soon the whole new shoot, including flower buds, is coated with a white powder on a felty base. Buds cease to develop or the flowers are deformed; the whole bush may be stunted.

The white felt is fungus mycelium, a tangled mass of threads that stays *on the surface,* obtaining food by sending little suckers (haustoria) into the plant cells. Chains of spores grow out at right angles from the mycelium and these give the powdery effect. Spores are dislodged from the top of the chain and are wafted by air currents to other rose bushes. If the air is dry they soon die but if, on reaching a new leaf surface, the humidity is high (and it often is at the leaf even if not in the general atmosphere) the spore germinates, penetrates the epidermal cell enough to form a haustorium and establish food relations with the rose, then produces other germ tubes to form the felty tangles on the outside of the leaf. Spore chains are formed and ready to start a new cycle in forty-eight hours. Contrary to most other fungi, powdery mildew spores do not germinate if submerged in an actual drop of water. Optimum humidity for rose mildew is high, 97 to 99 percent at the leaf surface; optimum temperature runs between 64° and 75°F.

As the season advances, felt is formed on some of the older canes and here winter fruiting bodies, perithecia, may be formed. On rare occasions they are formed in leaves. Perithecia are less common in rose mildew than in other powdery mildews and overwintering is by means of mycelium in dormant buds. In this way mildew usually can be brought into a garden on plants from a nursery just as blackspot comes in on cane lesions.

Although mildew flourishes on the succulent growth encouraged by high nitrogen fertilizers there is little likelihood of controlling it by soil chemicals beyond providing a *balanced* fertilizer. Thorough syringing with the hose discourages mildew temporarily. When syringing for red-spider control was practiced in greenhouses mildew was scarce; now that mites are taken care of by aerosols, powdery mildew is quite a problem.

Mildew on outdoor roses can be controlled with sulfur, copper, Karathane, folpet (Phaltan), and Acti-dione PM. The last is an antibiotic with a special spreader-safener that has become standard for mildew eradication, using 2 level tablespoons to 1 gallon of water. Karathane is also very effective but the safe dosage is low, ½ to 1 teaspoon per gallon, and it should not be used at high temperatures. Phaltan does a fair job of controlling mildew along with its excellent protection against blackspot but it is not sufficient for severe cases. The ammoniacal copper in Triogen and the copper oleate in Mildew King give routine control of mildew, may not be sufficient for eradication. Natriphene has been successfully used by some rosarians, has been less efficient for others. A new compound by Eli Lilly and Co. has been most promising in tests and has now been released under the name Pipron.

RED SPIDERS. Several species of mites are known as red spiders. They are not true insects but belong to the spider groups, having four pairs of legs at maturity instead of three. They are very small. A mite has been aptly called a speck of paprika on a cobweb, but even this is not quite true for the mite is often pinkish when young and yellow or green when adult. The species most common on roses is the Two-spotted Spider Mite (*Tetranychus telarius*), which has two black spots on its minute body.

Also reported on rose are the Southern Red Mite (*Oligonychus ilicis*) which has red nymphs and males, nearly black females; the European Red Mite (*Panonychus ulmi*), female red with curved spines; and the Four-spotted Spider Mite (*Tetranychus canadensis*) which, of course, has four spots.

Red spiders pierce the foliage, mostly from the underside, and suck out the sap. Leaves turn gray or yellow or reddish or have a reddish margin or burned bands. They usually have mealy cobwebs on the under surface with myriads of mites moving on the webs. A large infestation of mites usually causes heavy leaf drop and sometimes death of canes. Some roses are nearly defoliated by mites by midsummer. Mites winter on weeds around the garden and flourish in crowded situations without much air, so that general sanitary measures are helpful. Mites used to be held in check fairly well by natural enemies, parasites and predators, but large-scale use of DDT has killed many helpful insects.

Phosphate sprays, such as TEPP and parathion, are potent miticides but far too dangerous for general use in rose gardens. There are also systemic phosphates, such as demeton, phorate (Thimet) and Di-Syston that can be applied to the soil to render the rose uninviting to mites for some weeks. These also require too many precautions for the casual gardener although Di-Syston is now available in 2 percent granules (sold as Scope) in a container planned for reasonably safe application. Malathion is a very safe phosphate and was originally recommended for mites but it is no longer effective. Dimethoate (Cygon) is a fairly safe systemic phosphate that can be used as a spray. Dimite and ovex are effective miticides but sometimes injurious to roses. Trithion is a new recommendation.

Safe on roses, safe for the operator, and very effective are Aramite, Kelthane, and tetradifon (Tedion). Aramite is included in many combination sprays and dusts but is somewhat difficult to purchase separately because it is not allowed on food plants. Kelthane is available for fruits, vegetables and ornamentals. It is included in some combination pesticides, or can be used separately at 1½ tablespoons to 1 gallon. Tedion is included in Isotox, a useful insecticide, miticide combination.

RODENTS. Rabbits and mice gnaw rose canes, moles disturb the roots.

PINE MICE (*Pitymys* spp.). Distributed through eastern states from the Great Lakes to the Gulf of Mexico, from the Atlantic Coast to Kansas.

The pine mouse is about the size of a house mouse, with dark brown fur and a very short tail. It harms roses and other ornamentals, nursery stock, orchard trees, by cutting off the roots. It works entirely in the ground, burrowing from a few inches to several feet below the surface. Small exit holes indicate such burrows. The runs can also be located by poking around a rose bush with a stick or watering the ground and watching for too speedy disappearance of the water.

Pine mice can be trapped with wooden base snap traps, set with the trigger crosswise in an opened tunnel and a sprinkle of oat flakes for bait. Poison bait may be zinc phosphide on cubes of apple, sweetpotato or carrot; or peanuts, poisoned with ⅛ ounce strychnine dissolved with ⅛ ounce baking soda in ½ cup of water and poured over 2 quarts of nuts. Drop the bait into runs and cover with squares of roofing paper to protect birds and pets.

FIELD MICE (various species) make runs on the surface of the ground, under cover of salt hay, leaves or burlap and girdle canes by gnawing the bark. Avoid all this unnecessary material in winter protection if you can; if you must have it, delay application until the ground is frozen hard and the mice have found quarters elsewhere.

MOLES are really difficult to control and when their runs go under a rosebush they disturb the roots enough so that the plant dies or is very unhealthy. You can usually see the ridges marking mole tunnels before too much damage is done and can firm the ground back into place with your feet. Poison bait, thallium sulfate on peanuts, is sold under such trade names as Tat Mo-Go and Mole-Nots but mole traps set according to directions are said to be more effective. Moles are really partially beneficial in that they dine on beetle grubs but if you want to send the moles elsewhere treat lawns with chlordane or dieldrin.

Rabbits gnaw rose canes when snow covers other vegetation but if the bushes have been mounded with earth the canes beneath the soil mounds are safe. Nests of baby rabbits are often found in rose beds surrounded by boxwood or other hedges or covered with salt hay for winter. If rabbits should chew rose foliage during the growing season, which is not likely with other food at hand, there are repellents such as Rabbit Tox and No-Nib'l. Moth balls around a rose bed offer some protection.

ROTS. There are three root rots important on roses in three different sections of the country.

MUSHROOM ROOT ROT (*Armillaria mellea*). Also called oak root rot and Armillaria root rot, a decay of the root and root-crown prevalent in California. Sheets of tough, fan-shaped mycelium are found between bark and wood, the latter becoming soft and watery in texture. Oaks are very susceptible and the disease is most important on land recently cleared of oaks; many ornamentals may be attacked. At the base of rotten trees there sometimes appear clumps of honey-colored mushrooms that give the rot its name. They are 2 to 4 inches across the cap, on a stalk 4 to 6 inches high. Spores can start the rot only in trees already dead but the fungus spreads out from these in the form of black shoestrings (Rhizomorphs) that can enter healthy roots and work up to girdle the root crown. Roses may be injured when too much soil covers the roots and when they are kept too moist, often by watering the nearby lawn.

Remove diseased plants. Infested soil can be treated with carbon disulfite, 1⅗ ounces per hole injected 18 inches apart, but this treatment must be at some distance from all living plants and the ground not replanted for at least sixty days. Avoid overwatering and mounding soil over crowns.

MUSHROOM ROOT ROT (*Clitocybe tabescens*). A similar root rot that may be as serious in Florida as the Armillaria rot is in California. It is most prevalent on land recently cleared of oak and other hardwoods. Control measures are the same.

TEXAS ROOT ROT (*Phymatotrichum omnivorum*). The fungus is truly omnivorous, attacking 1700 species, but only in the Southwest, most of Texas, parts of Oklahoma, Arizona, Arkansas, California, Louisiana, Nevada, and Utah. Known also as the cotton root rot and very damaging to that crop, the disease is most destructive in neutral to alkaline soils and is not common in the commercial rose fields of East Texas where the soil is prevailingly sandy and somewhat acid. The rot is prevalent in wet seasons, from July to frost. Roses suddenly turn yellow, wilt, and die in a short time. Plants are killed in more or less circular areas. Mats of buff-colored mycelium grow out over the ground around a wilted bush but the fungus spreads chiefly by means of rhizomorphs through the soil.

Abundant organic matter in the soil reduces the rot by favoring antagonistic soil parasites. Even in root-rot soils it is often possible to grow roses for a few years. It is best not to plant them in continuous rows but in small groups separated by lawn areas, so the rhizomorphs cannot grow from root to root.

RUST. There are many rusts that attack various rose species but only one is common on cultivated roses. The name is given both to the fungus and to the disease it causes.

LEAF RUST OF ROSE (*Phragmidium mucronatum = P. disciflorum*). Not much of a problem in the East, though sometimes found in New York, New England, and, rarely, further south, but serious in the Southwest and along the West Coast and recently reported as a problem in Louisiana. This rust has four spore stages in its life cycle. The first two, in spring, cause very small orange spots on the underside of leaves. These appear light yellow when viewed from the upper surface. They are sometimes surrounded by a light green zone and the whole may make a cuplike depression in the leaf surface. Long narrow spots may be formed on young canes.

In the summer stage, powdery reddish-orange masses of spores are formed on the lower side of the leaf, the same area on the upper surface appearing as angular dead spots surrounded by a narrow green or reddish zone. Leaves may wilt and drop within five days of the appearance of the summer spores and this summer stage may be repeated every two weeks or so.

Toward fall, black spores appear in the summer lesions, gradually replacing the orange summer spores. In cool climates the summer cycle may keep repeating without any black spore stage.

It takes four hours of liquid water (not merely high humidity as with powdery mildew) and a favorable temperature (optimum 64° to 70°F.) for the rust spore to germinate and enter a leaf. In southern California the temperature is favorable for rust all season and rainfull is usually adequate from October to April. In the dry months dew or fog may provide sufficient moisture. In the East cold winters and hot summers keep rust at a minimum.

Sulfur dust was long the standard remedy for rust and later 10 percent ferbam was added to the sulfur. Zineb is quite effective for rust control;

Maneb, captan and Orthorix, a polysulfide spray, have been recommended. Coppers are unsatisfactory. Sanitation is generally advised; remove all old leaves harboring rust at spring pruning.

SAWFLIES. There are three species which work as larvae on rose foliage. See under Borers for the Rose Stem Sawfly. These false caterpillars are usually called slugs but the seldom noticed adults are small wasplike insects that deposit eggs in slits "sawed" in the leaves.

BRISTLY ROSE-SLUG (*Cladius isomerus*). The larva, ½ inch long, is yellowish green with a dark green stripe down the back and stiff hairs. When young it skeletonizes the leaf from the underside but later it eats large holes through the leaves, taking everything but the larger veins. There may be as many as six generations a year. The winter is spent in pale brown papery cocoons in garden trash.

CURLED ROSE SAWFLY (*Allantus cinctus*). The greenish larva, with sides and legs grayish white, eats the entire leaf tissue, usually feeding from a coiled position along the leaf edge. There are two generations, the resting stage being spent in the pith of soft, decayed wood. The larva enters rose canes through pruning cuts; see under Borers.

ROSE-SLUG (*Endelomyia aethiops*). Also called European rose-slug. The leaves are skeletonized, that is, everything is eaten but the epidermis and veins. The entomologists say that this velvety green worm that looks something like a tadpole works on the upper leaf surface but I am quite sure this is the species I find most often in gardens and the larvae feed mostly on the underside, making little windows in leaves. This species has but one brood, most damage being done in spring soon after the roses come into full leaf. Climbing roses and hybrid teas are both attacked. Skeletonizing that appears in late summer and fall is probably due to the bristly rose-slug.

All injury from rose-slugs can be readily prevented by spraying or dusting *early* with almost any stomach or even contact poison—lead arsenate, DDT, methoxychlor, Sevin, malathion, or rotenone. I have seen rose-slugs at work in Florida in January and in New Jersey the first of May. It pays to spray soon after the roses come into full leaf and to repeat weekly, for once the leaves are skeletonized the bush is defaced for the rest of the season.

SCALE INSECTS. There are many scales that attack roses in different
   parts of the country; the rose scale is rather general.

ROSE SCALE (*Aulacaspis rosae*). Widely distributed wherever roses and
brambles (raspberries, blackberries, etc.) are grown. Canes may be thickly
encrusted with roundish white females and long, narrow, snow-white
males. Climbers that are not pruned annually are more subject to scale,
but even hybrid teas may have the lower portion of a cane so heavily
infested it looks as if it had been whitewashed.

As with other scales, the female does the sucking, inserting her beak
and staying in one place for life after a brief crawling stage. Her dirty
white shield covers an orange or pinkish body and red eggs. In New
Jersey there are two generations a year, with eggs hatching in May or June
and again in August.

After thickly encrusted canes are cut out at spring pruning the best
control is a dormant spray of 1 to 9 lime sulfur (1 pint of the commercial
liquid to 1 gallon of water) but this cannot be used for roses on painted
trellises, houses or garages because it will stain paint. Likewise, it may
be injurious to buds that have broken more than ¼ inch and to southern
roses that do not go truly dormant. Malathion or dimethoate can be
substituted for lime sulfur, applied for the crawling stages. Oil sprays
are not very satisfactory for rose scale.

The Oystershell Scale (*Lepidosaphes ulmi*) with its gray or brown
oyster-shaped females is generally distributed across the country and is
sometimes found on rose canes, as is San Jose Scale (*Aspidiotus pernici-
osus*), small, gray, circular, and the European Fruit Lecanium (*Lecanium
corni*), a large, hemispherical, shiny brown scale.

Scale insects common on roses in the South and California include the
Cottony-cushion Scale (*Icerya purchasi*), noticeable for its large white
fluted cottony mass, covering red eggs, extending from a small brown
shield. A colony of Australian lady beetles may be more helpful than a
spray for this species. Other warm climate scales are: Black Scale (*Sais-
setia oleae*), a small dark brown to black hemispherical scale with ridges
on the back forming a letter H; Brown Soft Scale (*Coccus hesperidum*),
oval, flat, greenish; California Red Scale (*Aonidiella aurantii*), very small,
¹⁄₁₂ inch, round, reddish brown, found on leaves or canes; Florida Red

Scale (*Chrysomphalus aonidum*), circular, reddish brown to black. There are at least a dozen more scales also recorded on roses but control measures are the same: malathion or dimethoate or possibly ethion (another phosphate spray) for plants that are not dormant.

SOOTY MOLD. A black coating on surface of leaves composed of dark mycelium of a saprophytic fungus (Capnodium, Fumago or Scorias) living on insect honeydew. Aphids, mealybugs, whiteflies, and scale insects all secrete a sticky material attractive to the fungus which harms the rose only indirectly, in appearance and in preventing some photosynthesis. The aphids and scales need not be on the roses themselves. The honeydew may drop down from tulip trees, birches, maples or elms in the vicinity. Control is directed at cleaning up the insect, not the fungus.

SPOT ANTHRACNOSE (*Elsinoë rosarum*). A leaf and cane spot reported from Maine to Florida, Texas to Kansas and Arkansas, and on the Pacific Coast. It is more common on climbing roses with glossy foliage than on hybrid teas. I saw it frequently when I lived in upper New York State but I have seldom seen it in the vicinity of New York City. Leaf spots are scattered or grouped, sometimes running together, usually circular, up to ¼ inch across. Young spots are red, varying to brown or dark purple on upper leaf surface, showing up two to six days after inoculation but not visible on the under surface for two to four weeks, then dull reddish-brown to pale purple. On aging, the center of the spot turns ashen white, with a dark red margin. Leaves may turn yellow or reddish around the spots, may have slits or perforations as the centers fall out.

Cane spots are circular to elongated, raised, brown or purple, with depressed light centers and dark fruiting bodies. The fungus winters in cane spots; spores are produced and spread only in rainy periods. A single leaf lesion may produce 10,000 spores within an hour after wetting and will continue production as long as the rain lasts.

Prune out, so far as possible, infected canes in spring. Keep foliage protected as for blackspot with zineb, maneb or captan or the older sulfur and copper.

THRIPS. Of the several species attacking roses the flower thrips is most important. Thrips are piercing-rasping insects, very small and slender, about as wide as a fine needle, with two pairs of narrow wings edged with long hairs like bristles.

FLOWER THRIPS (*Frankliniella tritici*). The insects enter the developing flower buds and feed on the tender parts, causing petals to be flecked and discolored, the flowers deformed. On roses, the most conspicuous symptom is the failure of a bud, after it is fully formed and shows color, to open. It stays tightly closed with the petals seemingly stuck together. Other buds open part way, but the flowers stay balled with the edges of the petals brown. The young thrips are lemon colored, seen only by opening the rose and looking carefully at the base of the petals. The adults are brownish yellow. This species breeds in various grasses, weeds, and infests tree flowers, fresh batches coming over to roses every day. The life cycle takes only two weeks.

The Western Flower Thrips (*Frankliniella occidentale*) is found in California and the Florida Flower Thrips (*F. bispinosa*) in that state.

GREENHOUSE THRIPS (*Heliothrips haemorrhoidalis*). Worldwide, outdoors in warm climates, in greenhouses everywhere on many plants, including roses. Foliage is silvery, dotted with dark bits of excrement.

ONION THRIPS (*Thrips tabaci*). Probably the most widely distributed thrips, found in all onion-growing sections, and attacking nearly all garden plants and many weeds. Roses have their petals spotted and streaked.

Thrips control is exceedingly difficult because the insects are hidden and protected by the petals so much of the time. Also, with the insects continually coming to opening buds from tree and grass flowers round about, a weekly spray does little good. Thrips have been found swarming through the atmosphere 65 feet up and as many as 400 on a single rose. But even a few insects on a rose can cause typical injury and no sprays yet are good enough to give the required 100 percent control. Spraying with dimethoate is recommended, or dieldrin or lindane or soil treatment with Di-Syston (Scope) or phorate (Thimet) but the last not for amateurs. Workers at the U.S. Department of Agriculture have found a way to exclude thrips from individual rose blooms by inverting quart-sized ice-cream containers, attached to stakes, over individual canes pruned to 1 bud. The cartons are ventilated by cutouts covered with white organdy cloth. Thrips are controlled in greenhouses by screening the vents with cloth dipped in dieldrin. Thrips are usually worse in early summer, autumn roses being much less injured. Some rose varieties are more susceptible than others. In tests with color cards the flower thrips has been particularly attracted to yellow.

TREEHOPPERS. Sucking insects closely related to leafhoppers, with the thorax replaced by a pronotum enlarged with knobs or horns in a grotesque effect.

BUFFALO TREEHOPPER (*Stictocephala bubalus*). Sometimes lays eggs in rose canes, making a double row of curved slits in the bark which offer entrance to brand and other canker fungi. This treehopper is green, triangular, with a two-horned enlargement, and appears in August. Where possible, wounded canes should be cut out.

VIRUS DISEASES. These have not been considered of major importance in the United States on rose but a rose wilt and dieback, due to a virus, is very serious in Australia, New Zealand, and Italy and stringent quarantine measures have been adopted to keep this disease out of our country.

ROSE MOSAIC, INFECTIOUS CHLOROSIS. Usually on greenhouse roses in eastern and central states, on garden roses on the Pacific Coast. Chlorotic areas feather away from midribs of leaflets, often with local distortion, sometimes with ring, oakleaf, and watermarked patterns. Plants are dwarfed with buds often bleached, on short stems. *Rosa manetti,* used for greenhouse understock, is very susceptible. Stock should come from a virus-free source. No insect vector is known. Another form, yellow mosaic, forms bright yellow patterns on green leaves, is found on garden roses from the West Coast. Roses for propagation can be cured of mosaic by holding potted bushes for four weeks in incubators kept at 33° to 36°C.

ROSE ROSETTE; WITCHES' BROOM. On species roses, reported from California, Nebraska and Wyoming. Leaflets and flower parts are misshapen, stems dwarfed, with precocious growth of lateral buds, indefinite chlorotic pattern in leaves, increased thorniness of stems. The general effect resembles 2,4-D injury. The virus is graft transmissible but the disease develops slowly. The Nebraska disease, called witches' broom, may be largely due to eriophyid mites.

ROSE STREAK. On rose in eastern United States. Leaves have brownish or reddish ring and vein-banding patterns; stems have ring patterns and sometimes necrotic areas near inserted buds, causing girdling, wilting of foliage. Transmission is by budding or grafting.

Although these virus diseases may reduce plant vigor they have not been very alarming because they are apparently spread only in propagation, since no insect vectors are known. That means you need not remove an infected plant from your garden but must remember not to take any cuttings from it. In many cases, especially in late summer, rose leaves show patterns that are physiological abnormalities and not due to a virus.

We really know very little about how much toll virus diseases presently take of roses. Work toward the development of methods for the certification of virus-free nursery stock has been started by the state of California in cooperation with the U.S. Department of Agriculture. If such procedures prove feasible they will necessarily increase the price of a healthy rose bush for the ultimate consumer.

WEATHER. Probably the most disastrous thing that can happen to a rose is a sudden sharp drop in temperature in autumn before the plant has hardened off for winter. An early freeze of 18° to 20°F. kills and splits more canes than a winter freeze down to zero. Avoid late summer feeding and excess watering that will delay the hardening process. If mounding with soil for winter, do it early.

Late winter and early spring freezes kill shoots forced during warm days of late winter. Minimize the danger by doing no pruning in autumn and delay spring pruning until danger of very hard frost is past. The buds forced prematurely will then be on the top portions of canes and you are going to cut these off anyway.

Weather is closely linked with spray injury, with plants suffering from drought more susceptible to chemicals. Liquid sprays from emulsions with an oil base are apt to be injurious in hot weather; sulfur and Karathane are tricky above 85°F.; copper may be injurious below 55°F.

WEEVILS. These are really snout beetles and the Imported Long Horned Weevil has been discussed under Beetles. The Cribrate Weevil (*Brachyrhinus cribricollis*) was reported in California in 1929, the larvae feeding on roots, the adults on buds and foliage of many ornamentals, including rose. The Japanese Weevil (*Pseudocneorhinus bifasciatus*) is found at scattered locations in the East, notching leaves of many ornamentals in from the margin. The Pea Leaf Weevil (*Sitona lineata*) has been reported in Oregon nearly defoliating miniature roses. The small grayish brown adults eat U-shaped notches in margins of leaves.

WHITEFLIES. Compared to their importance on gardenias and ligustrum, whiteflies are rather inconsequential on roses.

GREENHOUSE WHITEFLY (*Trialeurodes vaporarium*). The most common species in greenhouse or garden, occasional on rose. The young are oval, flat, pale green, looking like thin scales on underside of leaves. The tiny, white mothlike adults are very lively, flying out in clouds when disturbed. Sooty mold usually grows in the honeydew. If whiteflies become a problem on roses, spray with malathion or dimethoate.

WILT. A systemic disease. *Verticillium albo-atrum,* a fungus causing wilt of many trees, chrysanthemums and other ornamentals occurs on rose and can be transmitted by the budding process. Ragged Robin, Odorata, and Multiflora are understock susceptible to wilt; Dr. Huey is less susceptible and Manetti is said to be resistant. Verticillium blackens the vessels, giving a black ring when the stem is cut across.

EQUIPMENT FOR CHEMICAL CONTROL
OF ROSE ENEMIES

Dusting is the application of a fine dry powder. *Dusters* vary from a cheesecloth bag beaten with a stick to a power machine equipped with a gasoline motor. Rose dusts sometimes come in a small carton supposed to be worked as a duster but after a few tries in humid weather the dust is thankfully transferred to a small dust gun. Plastic squeeze dusters have replaced many of the cardboard cartons on dealers' shelves but they are little improvement and the dust contained in them, usually only 8 ounces, is very expensive supplied in such a gadget.

Far more satisfactory is a midget rotary duster. It may cost nearly $10 but lasts for years and can be filled by dust purchased inexpensively in large quantities. Be sure to ask for an extension tube with the duster and direct the dust from the ground up. All the advertisements of this duster show it in use pointed down, which is entirely wrong for roses. For very large rose gardens there is a heavy crank-type duster or a bellows duster holding 3 or 4 pounds of dust. For very small gardens there are inexpensive plunger-type dust guns, available in pint and quart sizes. They are a little harder to work than the small rotary but quite satisfactory if provided with an extension tube.

Advantages of dusting are that it is quicker than spraying, that you can leave the dust in the machine from one application to the next, that you don't have to mix up chemicals every time you want to cover a few roses (and are more apt to do the job on time); that most dusters are lighter and easier to operate than sprayers, and they don't have to be cleaned after use. Disadvantages are the uneven distribution of dust, the film of powder dulling the beauty of flowers, that dusts do not have as long a residual effect as most sprays, are not as effective in controlling aphids, mites and powdery mildew, and that some people are somewhat allergic to dusts.

Spraying means the application of chemicals in liquid form, a fine mist. Advantages of spraying are that the washing action provides a better control of aphids, mites and mildew, that there is a longer residual action, usually less unsightly residue on flowers, and that you can, in emergencies, spray when the foliage is slightly wet more safely than you can dust wet foliage. Although many directions say to dust plants when they are wet with dew, this is a horrible thing to do to roses for the dust sticks in uneven lumps, is most unsightly and may even burn.

Sprayers vary from the small pressurized bombs and 1-quart atomizers to power-driven estate sprayers. The bombs, so-called aerosols, can serve in an emergency for killing aphids on buds and shoots but they are not very satisfactory for disease control. It is too difficult with outdoor air currents to get complete coverage of all leaf surfaces and in trying to cover rear foliage you may have to get too close to that in front and end up by burning it. The small atomizers are much too hard work for anything over half a dozen bushes.

For backyard gardens the usual equipment is a compressed air sprayer of 2 to 4 gallons capacity. It comes equipped with 2 or 3 feet of hose and an extension rod with an adjustable nozzle to facilitate reaching underside of foliage. Some of these sprayers are mounted on carts or can be rolled along the ground but they all have to be pumped up, which is arduous, and they must be shaken as they are used for they have no agitators.

Knapsack sprayers, designed to be carried on the back, are held in place by shoulder straps and operated by pushing a lever up and down with one hand while directing the spray rod with the other. Once you have hoisted the heavy sprayer on your back the operation is fairly effortless and you can keep up a steady pressure giving even coverage of all plant surfaces. Such a sprayer, with a diaphragm pump, has an agitator but it is more difficult than a compressed air sprayer to clean properly.

If you have a garden assistant with a good right arm a very efficient way to spray the rose garden is by means of a wheelbarrow or Paragon type sprayer with a tank of 12 to 15 gallons capacity, mounted on a one- or two-wheel truck. You don't have to fill it, for it operates as well for 3 gallons as for 8, which is about all you can put in the 12-gallon sprayer and maneuver around the garden without spilling. Such sprayers usually come with 10 feet of spray hose but by exchanging this for 20 or 25 feet it is easy to reach climbers and specimen shrubs at some distance from garden paths. Extra extension rods make it easy to reach even the tallest climber. The nozzle of such a sprayer is designed to give a fine mist but the abrasive action of chemicals continually enlarges the hole. If you seem to be using more spray than usual or getting more residue on foliage put on a new nozzle. It costs a lot less than the extra spray material.

For twenty-five years I happily used this type of sprayer for my clients' roses and my own. With a good assistant it was completely satisfactory. But after giving up spraying for others I no longer had help to spray my own roses nor energy enough to work a compressed air sprayer. So I reluctantly turned to a hose-end sprayer, thinking it just another "gadget" and being pleasantly surprised to find that it works very well for all kinds of mixtures, even wettable powders and the three-way Triogen. The spray is somewhat coarser than with the Paragon type, about like that from a compressed air sprayer. The kind I have used for several seasons is the Hayes 6 Spray Gun (also sold as Ortho Queensize). This has an extension tube with a deflector at the end, so that underside of foliage can be covered, and it has a shut-off at the jar, not back at the faucet. The chemicals for a certain number of gallons are put in the jar —mixed with a little water if they are wettable powders—and then water is added to the proper line on the jar. I usually mix in a separate jar and then strain into the hose jar through a wire tea strainer. This helps to prevent clogging. The jar top, with a siphoning tube, is screwed onto the hose and then onto the jar. As water flows through from the hose the concentrated chemical is picked up in the right proportion. If there is sufficient water pressure and care is taken in getting the hose around the beds this is a very good lazy man's way to spray. It takes no longer than dusting (about half an hour for my present 300 roses) and the apparatus is quickly cleaned after use.

With regular sprayers, the remaining liquid should be immediately emptied and tank, hose and spray nozzle rinsed with at least two changes of water. At the end of the season, and sometimes during it, more extensive cleaning is in order. Use trisodium phosphate (ask at the hardware store for the stuff used by painters) or a handful of washing soda, and put it in the tank filled with water. Let the rods soak in this mixture while nozzle parts and strainer are cleaned with kerosene. Use a bottle brush for the strainer and run heavy wire through the rods. Scrub the side of the tank with a stiff brush on a long handle. Rinse the separate parts with water, reassemble the sprayer and pump through a mild solution of vinegar to clean the rubber hose which should not be touched with either washing soda or phosphate. Then rinse again with pure water. At the end of the season store the parts separately, oiling the rods and wrapping in newspaper, then tying all the parts on to the sprayer so they will not get lost before spring.

Empty the dusters you have used at the end of the season; store in a dry place until spring.

THE CHEMICALS

There are now hundreds of basic chemicals used for pesticides and these are available in thousands of combinations and under vast numbers of trade names. Here is an alphabetical list of chemicals that have been suggested for control of rose pests. Most of the chemicals are listed by their coined common name, with the long chemical name in parentheses. Either may be given on the label which, according to law, requires the listing of all active ingredients of a pesticide, together with uses, proper directions for use, and precautions to be taken in use. Common names are listed in lower case; where there is no approved common name the trade name is used and this is capitalized.

Acti-dione PM (Cycloheximide). An antibiotic, prepared from *Strep-tomyces griseus,* with a safener and spreader, specifically for control of powdery mildew on rose and other ornamentals.

allethrin. A synthetic pyrethrum, contact insecticide of very low toxicity to mammals.

Aramite® (2-(p-*tert*-butylphenoxy) isopropyl 2-chloroethyl sulfite). A miticide, very effective for red spiders on ornamentals at rate of 1 tablespoon 15 percent wettable powder to 1 gallon of water. Safe to handle but possibly carcinogenic so not allowed on vegetables. Included in many combination rose pesticides; not compatible with alkaline materials.

BHC = benzene hexachloride. More often used on roses in the gamma isomer form. See Lindane.

captan (n-trichloromethylthiotetrahydrophthalimide). Fungicide, sold as Orthocide, included in various proprietary combinations. Controls blackspot but not powdery mildew. Compatible with most insecticides; do not use with oil sprays or lime.

carbaryl (1-naphthyl-N-methyl-carbamate). Sevin®. Broad-spectrum insecticide of low mammalian toxicity but toxic to bees and many beneficial insects. Highly effective for Japanese beetles, recommended for some caterpillars, bagworms, sawflies, but may increase mites. Use 2 tablespoons of 50 percent wettable powder to 1 gallon of water.

chlordane (1,2,4,5,6,7,8,8-octachloro-3a,4,7,7a-tetrahydro-4,7-methanoindane). Contact insecticide usually used as a soil treatment for ants, beetle grubs, earwigs, grasshoppers, but included in one or two all-purpose pesticides for roses. Available as an emulsion, wettable powder, or dust.

copper. Fungicide for blackspot and other leaf spots powdrey mildew and cankers. Copper is injurious in cool, cloudy weather. Bordeaux mixture (copper sulfate and lime) at normal strength may defoliate roses. Fixed coppers (e.g. Copper oxychloride sulfate-C-O-C-S) are considered somewhat safer but may injure under certain conditions. Ammoniacal copper (as in Tri-ogen) is usually safe as is copper oleate (as in Mildew King). A dust mixture of 3.4 percent copper with 90 percent sulfur has been widely used for roses in the Southwest but has been replaced to some extent by the newer organics.

Cygon®. See Dimethoate.

D-D Mixture® (1,3-dichloropropene and 1,2-dichloropropane). Dowfume N. Excellent nematocide for *fallow* soil. Apply in holes 6 inches deep staggered 18 inches apart, at rate of ⅓ ounce per hole. Wait 2 to 4 weeks before planting. Handle with caution.

DDT (1,1,1-trichloro-2,2-bis(*p*-chlorophenyl)ethane). Broad spectrum insecticide with long residual effect. Controls Japanese beetles, roseslugs, leafhoppers, caterpillars and rose midge, thrips to some extent, but greatly increases red spiders. As a spray use 1 to 2 tablespoons 50 percent wettable powder to 1 gallon of water. DDT is included in many combination rose pesticides.

diazinon (*O,O*-diethyl *O*-(isopropyl-6-methyl-4-pyrimidyl) thiophosphate). An organic phosphate less dangerous than some others but to be used with caution. Recommended for lawn problems, also for some leaf chewers and whiteflies.

dichlone (2,3,dichloro-1,4-naphthoquinone). Fungicide sold as Phygon, used to some extent for blackspot control but may be slightly injurious. It is included in some aerosol bombs and is apparently safer in that form.

dieldrin (not less than 85 percent of 1,2,3,4,10,10-hexachloro-6,7-epoxy-1,4,4a,5,6,7,8,8a-octahydro-1,4-*endo-exo*-5,8-dimethanonaphthalene). Contact and stomach insecticide; poisonous, handle with caution. Recommended mostly for soil treatment for grubs, sometimes for thrips.

dimethoate (*O,O*-dimethyl *S* (*N*-methylcarbamoylmethyl)phosphorodithioate). Sold as Cygon®. Systemic acaricide (miticide) and insecticide, less hazardous than most other phosphates but to be used with caution. Recommended for aphids, mites, leafhoppers, thrips, whiteflies and scale insects.

Dimite® (1,1-bis(*p*-chlorophenyl)ethanol). Acaricide only, effective for red spiders but possibly injurious to roses.

Di-Syston® (O,O-diethyl S-2-(ethylthio)ethyl phosphorodithioate). Systemic acaricide and insecticide, *highly* poisonous. Also sold as Scope® in 2 percent granules, to be worked into soil around roses to control aphids, thrips, etc. Use with great caution.

Dyrene® (2,4-dichloro-6-(*o*-chloroanilino)-*s*-triazine). Fungicide, very effective for rose blackspot but probably too phytotoxic.

Ethylene dibromide, Dowfume® W 85. Fumigant, nematocide, for soil treatment, safer than methyl bromide for home gardens.

ferbam (tris(dimethyldithiocarbamate) iron). Fermate®. Fungicide, a black wettable powder, effective for blackspot and perhaps rust but not for powdery mildew; included in some combination rose dusts and sprays, often with sulfur.

folpet (N-(trichloromethylthio)phthalimide). Phaltan®; Rosimide®. Fungicide highly effective for control of blackspot, helpful against mildew. Use 1 to 1¼ tablespoons of 75 percent wettable powder to 1 gallon of water; can be combined with Isotox but do not add any sticker or spreader.

Glyodin (2-heptadecyl-2-imidazoline acetate). Fungicide, fairly effective for rose blackspot and included in a few combination sprays. When Karathane has been included in the mixture there has been some phytotoxicity.

Karathane® (dinitro (1-methylheptyl) phenyl crotonate). Mildex. Fungicide specifically for powdery mildew; included in many combination rose sprays and dusts. Be cautious with the dosage—½ to 1 teaspoon of wettable powder to 1 gallon of water; do not use when temperature is above 85°F.

Kelthane® (1,1-bis(*p*-chlorophenyl) 2,2,2-trichloroethanol). Acaricide or miticide safe for home garden use. Included in some combination rose pesticides; sold at farmers' supply outlets.

Lead arsenate. Stomach poison for chewing insects. Less popular now than formerly but an insecticide I still use (in Tri-ogen) in preference to DDT for control of beetles and rose-slugs.

Lime sulfur. Aqueous solution containing calcium polysulfides. Use as a dormant spray, 1 part of liquid to 9 of water, for control of rose scale and of possible help against blackspot and cankers. Orthorix is a summer foliage spray, also of calcium polysulfides, used for mildew and rust control.

lindane (gamma isomer of 1,2,3,4,5,6-hexachlorocyclohexane of 99 percent purity). Insecticide for aphids, thrips, and some beetles, especially the spotted cucumber beetle. Use 1 tablespoon of 25 percent wettable powder to 1 gallon of water. Included in many combination rose pesticides.

malathion (*O,O*-dimethyl dithiophosphate of diethyl mercaptosuccinate). Another broad-spectrum insecticide, one of the phosphates but safe to handle. Effective for aphids, mealybugs, whiteflies, crawling stages of some scale insects, some beetles. Sometimes recommended for mites but in many cases it merely encourages them by killing their enemies.

maneb (manganese ethylene bisdithiocarbamate). Manzate®; Dithane® M22. Fungicide good for black spot and Cercospora leaf spot but not for powdery mildew. Use 1 tablespoon of the wettable powder to 1 gallon of water; included in some combination rose pesticides. Dithane® M45 is a combination of zinc iron with maneb.

methoxychlor (1,1,1-trichloro-2,2-bis (*p*-methoxyphenyl) ethane). Marlate®, Analog of DDT, safer for mammals but with about the same effect on beneficial insects. Replaces DDT in some rose sprays and dusts.

Methyl bromide. Bromethane. Highly toxic fumigant for soil insects and nematodes; extremely hazardous by inhalation and without special odor to give warning; to be used only by expert operators under special covers.

Morocide®, binapacryl (2-*sec*-butyl-4-6-dinitrophenyl-3-methyl-2-butenoate). Relatively new fungicide, not much used for roses but in one or two combinations.

Natriphene® (o-phenyl phenol). Bactericide, fungicide, sometimes recommended for powdery mildew.

Nemagon® (1,2-dibromo-3-chloropropane). DBCP, also sold as Fumazone®. Fumigant nematocide that can be used around living plants.

Nicotine sulfate. An old and still excellent control for aphids. Use 1 to 1½ teaspoons of Black Leaf 40® and 1 ounce of soap to 1 gallon of water.

Oil sprays. Dormant oils are sometimes used to control rose scale in the North and summer oils, such as Volck, for scales and whiteflies in the South. Lime sulfur is more efficient for rose scale and malathion or dimethoate often replaces summer oils.

ovex (p-chlorophenyl p-chlorobenzenesulfonate). Ovotran®. Effective for egg stage of spider mites but sometimes slightly injurious to roses.

parathion (O,O-diethyl O-p-nitrophenyl phosphorothionate). Acaricide and insecticide, a violent poison not to be used except by experienced operators. A phosphate readily absorbed through skin and lungs.

Pentac® (Bis(pentachloro-2,4-cyclopentadien-l-yl). Acaricide proving helpful in mite control on roses and other crops in greenhouses.

Perthane® (1,1-dichloro-2,2-bis(p-ethylphenyl) ethane). Insecticide of great safety but not often recommended for roses.

Phaltan®. See folpet.

Phygon®. See dichlone.

piperonyl butoxide and **piperonyl cyclonene.** Very complex organic chemicals used as synergists and activators for pyrethrum, especially in aerosol sprays.

phorate (O,O-diethyl S-ethylthiomethyl phosphorodithioate). Thimet®. Systemic acaricide, insecticide, acutely poisonous, to be used only by professionals. Helpful in control of thrips and mites.

Pipron (3(2-methylpiperidino) propyl-3,4-dichlorobenzoate). A new fungicide, promising for control of powdery mildew.

pyrethrum. A contact poison, prepared from flowers and nonpoisonous to man, providing a quick paralysis of beetles and aphids but having little residual effect. Used in many aerosols.

Rosimide®. See folpet.

rotenone. A contact and stomach insecticide derived from the roots of derris and other plants, available as a dust and in sprays, often combined with pyrethrum. Safe for warm-blooded animals but very toxic to fish.

Sevin®. See carbaryl.

Sulfur. Wettable sulfur, used as a spray at 3 heaping tablespoons per gallon of water, and sulfur dust, containing 75 to 90 percent sulfur, control blackspot, rust and mildew but may burn plants if temperature is above 85°F.

TDE, DDD (2,2-bis(p-chlorophenyl)-1,1-dichloroethane). Rhothane®. An analog of DDT, less toxic to man but only occasionally used for roses.

Tedion®. See tetradifon.

TEPP (Tetraethyl pyrophosphate). A phosphate insecticide and miticide that is number 1 on the toxicity list and the cause of several accidental deaths. Not recommended for backyard gardeners. One drop of undiluted chemical on your skin could be extremely hazardous.

tetradifon (p-chlorophenyl 2,4,5-trichlorophenyl sulfone). Tedion.® Acaricide useful in home gardens; of low mammalian toxicity. An ingredient in Isotox and some other combination pesticides.

Vapam® (sodium methyldithiocarbamate). Soil fumigant and nematocide of low mammalian toxicity but to be used only in preplanting treatments; not safe around living plants. Sometimes recommended for treating soil containing crown-gall bacteria.

V-C-13 Nemacide® (*O,O*-diethyl *O*,2,4-dichlorophenyl phosphorothi-
oate). Acaricide, insecticide, nematocide for soil treatment; a liquid
safe around living plants.

Zectran® (4-dimethylamino-3,5-xylyl methylcarbamate). Systemic insecticide recommended for slugs and snails, also for scale insects,
thrips and mites.

zineb (zinc ethylene bisdithiocarbamate). Dithane® Z-78; Parzate®.
Fungicide, sold as a wettable powder; a standard control for rose
blackspot but does not control mildew; recommended for rose rust.

ziram (zinc dimethyl dithiocarbamate). Zerlate®. Another zinc fungicide, used chiefly for vegetables but has been included in one or two
rose dusts.

COMBINATION ROSE PESTICIDES

The ingredients of "all purpose" combinations sold under brand names
are subject to change without notice. The same trade name may, in 1965,
cover a different formulation than the one sold in 1964, at the time this
list is being compiled. So do not trust the sampling presented here too
far; read the labels and find out exactly what you are purchasing. The
formulae given here are taken from the 1964 *Pesticide Handbook* and
from sample labels obtained from nurseries. They have been chosen to
show the various types of chemicals offered and are not recommended
over others not included. The nursery from which you order your roses
may also be your best source of a combination spray or dust to take care
of those roses.

The labels on pesticides often give long chemical names instead of
common names or trade names. I have taken the liberty, in many cases, of
translating that chemical name into one more readily recognized.

Acme Quality Paints, Inc., 8250 St. Aubin Avenue, Detroit 11, Michigan.
ACME ROSE DUST. Captan 7%, Karathane 0.75%; DDT 5%; malathion
4%.
ACME ROSE & FLOWER SPRAY. Dichlone 0.12%, Karathane 0.113%;
methoxychlor 0.3%, pyrethrins —.02%, rotenone 0.1%.

Bonide Chemical Co., Inc., 383 N. Genesee St., Utica 4, N.Y.
  BONIDE ROSETOX. Captan 6, sulfur 23.4%; DDT 5%, malathion 5.09%,
  Sevin 1%.

Boyle-Midway, Inc., S. Ave. & Hale St., Cranford, N.J.
  ANTROL ROSE SPRAY FLOWER BOMB. Captan 0.5%, Karathane 1.25%;
  lindane 1%, rotenone 0.2%, pyrethrins 0.02%.
  ANTROL ROSE AND FLOWER DUST. Captan 4%, sulfur 25%; methoxychlor 5%, malathion 4%.

Breck's—Jos. Breck & Sons, 100 Breck Building, Boston 10, Mass.
  BRECK'S ROSE AND FLOWER SPRAY DUST. Ferbam 5%, sulfur 33%; DDT
  5.1%, lindane 1%, rotenone 0.75%, rotenoids 1.5%.
  BRECK'S ROSE AND FLOWER SPRAY. Dichlone 0.12%; pyrethrins 0.025%,
  rotenone 0.128%, piperonyl cyclonene 0.256%.

California Chemical Co., Ortho Div., Lucas St. & Ortho Way, Richmond,
  Calif.
  ORTHO ROSE DUST. Phaltan 7.5%; sulfur 30%; DDT 5%, lindane 1%.
  ORTHO PHALTAN ROSE & GARDEN FUNGICIDE. Folpet (Phaltan) 75%.
  ORTHOCIDE GARDEN FUNGICIDE. Captan 50%.
  ORTHO ROSE & FLOWER BOMB. Phaltan 0.5%; Ovex 0.124%, lindane
  0.5%, rotenone 0.2%.
  ISOTOX GARDEN SPRAY. DDT 5%, lindane 5%, malathion 10%, Tedion
  3%.

Canada Rex Spray Co., Ltd., Brighton, Ontario, Canada.
  BLACK LEAF ROSE DUST. Captan 5%; DDT 3%, malathion 2%.
  BLACK LEAF ROSE & FLORAL SPRAY. Pyrethrins 0.25%, piperonyl butoxide
  0.25%, rotenone 0.128%.

Carbola Chemical Company, Natural Bridge, New York.
  CCC ROSE DUST & SPRAY. Captan 7.5%, sulfur 20%; DDT 5%, rotenone 0.75%, rotenoids, 1.5%, lindane 0.5%.

Chemical Formulators, Inc., P.O. Box 26, Nitro, W. Virginia.
  CHEMFORM ROSE DUST. Maneb 6.4%, sulfur 20%; Sevin 2%, lindane
  1%, Tedion 0.5%.
  ERSKIN'S ROSE & FLORAL DUST. Ferbam 10%, sulfur 20%; malathion
  4%, roteonone 1%, rotenoids 1.85%.

Conard-Pyle Company, West Grove, Pennsylvania.
STAR ROSE DUST. Phaltan 5%; Sevin 5%, Kelthane 1.85%, Pindane 1%.
STAR ROSE SPRAY. Phaltan 10%; Sevin 10%, Kelthane 3.7%, lindane 2%.

Destruxol Corp., 495 S. Arroyo Parkway, Pasadena 1, Calif.
DESTRUXOL ROSE DUST. Copper zinc chromate complex 2%, sulfur 30%;
pyrethrins 0.06%, piperonyl butoxide 0.6%.
DESTRUXOL ROSE SPRAY. Copper 5%; ethylene dichloride 4%; nicotine
6.4%.

Doggett-Pfeil Co., 191 Mountain Ave., Springfield, N.J.
ROSE-ALL. Glyodin 12.4%; Aramite 2.6%, lindane 2.9%, pyrethrins
0.05%, piperonyl butoxide 0.5%.

E. I. du Pont de Nemours and Co., Inc., Wilmington 98, Del.
DU PONT DEENALL. Folpet (Phaltan) 7.5%; carbaryl (Sevin) 5%,
Kelthane 3%.

E-Z Flo Chemical Co., P.O. Box 808, Lansing 3, Mich.
E-Z-FLO ROSE GUARD. Captan 10%, Karathane 0.93%; malathion 6.2%,
DDT 9.3%.

Faesy and Besthoff, Inc., 143 River Road, Edgewater, New Jersey.
F & B ROSE DUST. Phaltan 7.5%; DDT 5%, Kelthane 1.48%, malathion
5%.
F & B ROSE SPRAY LIQUID. Glyodin; Kelthane, lindane, dieldrin.

Florida Agricultural Supply Co., P.O. Box 658, Jacksonville 1, Fla.
IDEAL BRAND ROSE DUST. Zineb 6%, sulfur 30%; chlordane 3%, DDT
3%, lindane 1%.

J. M. Harris & Co., P.O. Box 411, Roanoke 3, Va.
DRAGON ROSE DUST. Zineb 6%, sulfur 25%; Aramite 1.5%, DDT 5%,
lindane 1%.

Hayes-Sammons Chemical Co., Inc., 123 Auditorium Circle, San Antonio
5, Texas.
MISSION BRAND ROSE DUST. Captan 6%, sulfur 15%; lindane 1%, methoxychlor 5%.

Inter-State Nurseries, Hamburg, Iowa.

INTER-STATE ROSE DUST. Phaltan, 7.5%; Aramite, 1.5%, lindane 1%.

INTER-STATE ROSE SPRAY. Phaltan 0.7%; Sevin 1%; pyrethrins 0.0256%, rotenone 0.128%, piperonyl butoxide 0.256%.

Jackson & Perkins Co., Newark, New York.

J AND P ROSE DUST. Rosimide (folpet, same as Phaltan) 2%, ferbam 1.5%; Sevin 2.5%, Aramite 1.5%, Karathane 0.675%.

J AND P ROSE SPRAY. Rosimide 5%, ferbam 7.5%; maneb 2.5%, zineb 5%, Karathane 2%; DDT 15%, Aramite 2.5%, pyrethrins 0.5%, rotenone 2%.

J AND P SPECIAL ROSE SPRAY. Rosimide 15%, ferbam 15%; Sevin 12.8%, Aramite, 1.5%, endosulfan 2.5%.

BEETLE-DOWN SPRAY BOMB. Rosimide 0.7%; Sevin 1%; pyrethrins 0.025%, rotenone 0.128%.

Krider Nurseries, Inc., Middlebury, Indiana.

KRIDER'S ROSE DUST. Phaltan 7.5%, sulfur 30%; DDT 5%, lindane 1%.

KRIDER'S MULTI-PURPOSE SPRAY. Ferbam 7%, sulfur 30%, copper quinolinolate 10%; DDT 10%, rotenone 3%.

Lebanon Chemical Corp., Lebanon, Pa.

LEBANON ROSE DUST OR SPRAY. Ferbam 7.5%, sulfur 25%; DDT 5%, lindane 1.25%, Aramite 2%.

LEBANON ROSE-EVERGREEN SPRAY. Glyodin 5%, Karathane 1.44%; lindane 5%, malathion 12.5%, Kelthane 3%.

LEBANON ROSE-FLORAL SPRAY. Maneb 15.4%, Karathane 4.95%; DDT 11%, malathion 5.5%, Tedion 2.75%.

Earl May Seed & Nursery Company, Shenandoah, Iowa.

ROSE & FLORAL DUST. Phaltan 7.5%; DDT 3%, malathion 4%.

Niagara Chemical Div. Food Machinery & Chemical Corp., Middleport, N.Y.

NIAGARA HORTICULTURAL PRODUCTS ROSE DUST. Sulfur, arsenic, nicotine.

Nott Manufacturing Co., Box 832, Poughkeepsie, N.Y.

TRI-OGEN 3 WAY ROSE SPRAY (Kit). No. 1—Lead Arsenate 11.7%, Ferbam 3.75%; No. 2—rotenone 1.3%, pyrethrins 0.17%, Aramite 2.4%; No. 3—ammonical copper complex 0.8%.

TRI-OGEN 3 IN 1 ROSE SPRAY. Ammoniacal copper complex 0.8%, ferbam 7.5%; rotenone 0.5%, pyrethrins 0.17%, Aramite 2.4%.

Parsons Chemical Works, P.O. Box 146, Grand Ledge, Mich.

PARSONS ROSE DUST. Ferbam; malathion, methoxychlor.

Pearson-Ferguson Chemical Co., Inc., 1400 Union Avenue, Kansas City 1, Mo.

PATTERSON'S ROSE DUST. Zineb 3.9%, Karathane 1%; DDT 5%, lindane 1%, Kelthane 1.48%.

PATTERSON'S ROSE SPRAY. Malathion, methoxychlor, Kelthane.

Pearson & Co., P.O. Box 431, Mobile, Alabama.

PEARSON'S ROSE DUST. Copper 3.7%, sulfur 20%; DDT 5%, rotenone 0.75%.

B. G. Pratt Co., 204 21st Avenue, Paterson 21, N.J.

PRATT'S ROSE DUST OR SPRAY. Copper sulfate 3.4%, sulfur 30%; pyrethrins 0.03%, rotenone 0.128%, rotenoids 0.75%.

PRATT'S LIQUID ROSE SPRAY. Glyodin 12.5%; dieldrin 4%, lindane 3%, Kelthane 3%.

Roseway Nurseries, 2935 S.W. 234th Ave., Beaverton, Oregon.

KXL ALL PURPOSE YEAR ROUND SPRAY. Copper oleate 1%; pyrethrins 0.50%, rotenone 1%, other cube resins 2%, ethylene dichloride 9.75%.

Swift and Co., 115 W. Jackson Blvd., Chicago 4, Illinois.

END-O-PEST ROSE DUST. Captan 7.5%, Karathane; DDT 5%, malathion 4.5%.

END-O-PEST ROSE AND GARDEN SPRAY (Aerosol). Dichlone 0.12%; methoxychlor 0.3%, pyrethrins 0.02%, rotenone 0.1%.

Thompson Chemicals Corp., 3600 Monon St., Los Angeles 27, Calif.

ROSE AND GARDEN BOMB. Captan 0.5%, Karathane 0.2%; pyrethrins 0.025%, rotenone 0.128%.

Tobacco States Chemical Co., P.O. Box 479, Lexington, Kentucky.

TOBACCO STATES BRAND ROSE DUST. Zineb 6%, Karathane 0.9%; DDT 5%, lindane 1%, Aramite 1.5%.

United Co-operatives, Inc., P.O. Box 836, Alliance, Ohio.
UNICO ROSE & FLORAL DUST. Phaltan 5%, sulfur 25%, zineb 5%; DDT 5%, lindane 1%.
UNICO ROSE AND FLORAL SPRAY POWDER. Zineb 12.5%, sulfur 20%; DDT 12.5%, lindane 3%.

Woolfolk Chemical Works, Ltd., Box 922, Fort Valley, Ga.
SECURITY BRAND ROSE DUST. Copper 5.2%, sulfur 80%; DDT 5%, lindane 1%.

Melvin E. Wyant, Rose Specialist Inc., Johnny Cake Ridge, Mentor, Ohio.
WYANT'S DELUXE MIXTURE (dust). Phaltan 5%; malathion 4%, Aramite 2%.

These formulations have been given to you in the full realization that some may have been changed by the time this book gets into print. The list does give you some idea of the range covered by combination pesticides and some addresses. To know what is actually in the pesticide you buy at your local garden center you must read the label and be able to translate the long chemical name into a trade or common name that means something to you. The list of chemicals, starting on page 188, may help in this line.

BIBLIOGRAPHY

This book list, like the variety list, is strictly personal. It is a selection from the well-thumbed volumes in my own library and omits many fine treatises I do not yet own. Most of these books are still in print and may be purchased through the American Rose Society; some may have to be borrowed from the Society.

ALBERA, A. E. *Making Roses Behave.* 127 pp., 6 illus. Borden Publishing Company, Los Angeles, California. 1960. Concise treatment from planting to the rose show.

ALLEN, HAROLD H. *Roses—Growing for Exhibiting.* 175 pp., 67 line drawings. D. Van Nostrand Company, Inc., Princeton, N.J. 1961. By a prize-winning exhibitor who can transmit his enthusiasm and knowledge.

ALLEN, R. C. *Roses for Every Garden.* 218 pp., 32 illus. in color, line drawings. M. Barrows and Company, Inc., New York. 1948, revised 1956. A standard rose book by a former Secretary of the American Rose Society, now Director of Kingwood Center. Excellent drawings clarify planting, pruning, and other operations. There are chapters on roses for special climates, propagation and hybridization, exhibiting, and fun with roses.

AMERICAN ROSE SOCIETY, 4048 Roselea Place, Columbus, Ohio 43214. Membership in the Society, for $5.50 yearly dues, brings exciting reading in the *American Rose Annual* and the monthly *American Rose Magazine.* A valuable part of the *Annual* is Proof of the Pudding, an unbiased evaluation of new roses as they grow in home gardens across the country. Other privileges of the Society include help on your own problems from consulting rosarians, lists of gardens open to members, and use of the lending library. Free, even if you are not a member, are the booklets, "A Guide for Beginners on Growing Roses" and the "Guide for Buying Roses." The latter gives national ratings of rose varieties and is revised each year. The best way to acknowledge my debt to the Society for the past thirty years is to give you an urgent invitation to join us.

AMERICAN ROSE SOCIETY. *What Every Rose Grower Should Know.* 84 pp.,

19 illus., 6 in color. American Rose Society, Columbus, Ohio. Revised 1965. Excellent, concise exposition of rose characteristics and culture. Drawings differentiating bud and flower forms are especially helpful.

BAIRD, BESSIE MARY. *Roses for Southern Gardens*. 96 pp., 8 illus. in color. University of North Carolina Press, Chapel Hill. 1948. A delightful book with common sense sugar-coated with humor. Oriented for the South but hitting us all with such characterizations as "The flower arranger who thinks one rose with a long stem in the house is worth two on the bush. Pretty soon she won't have a bush."

BECHTEL, EDWIN DE T. *Our Rose Varieties and Their Malmaison Heritage*. 20 pp., 12 illus. New York Botanical Garden, New York. 1949. Story of the Empress Josephine and the history of rose hybridization.

BOLTON, ELEANOR REED. *Dried Flowers with a Fresh Look*. 210 pp., 24 illus. in color. D. Van Nostrand Company, Inc., Princeton, N.J. 1958. Winter cheer from summer flowers, including roses.

BURKE, EMILIA. *Let's Arrange Roses*. 124 pp., 40 illus. J. Horace McFarland Company, Harrisburg, Pa. 1951. The first book devoted exclusively to rose arrangements.

COATS, PETER. *Roses—Pleasures and Treasures*. 128 pp., 118 illus. G. P. Putnam's Sons, New York. The rose in history, medicine, literature, and art. A beautiful book, printed in Italy.

EDWARDS, JOHN PAUL. *How to Grow Roses*. 88 pp., illus. Lane Publishing Company, Menlo Park, California. 1955. 2nd ed. Guide to western rose growing; many pictures.

EMSWELLER, S. L. AND PHILIP BRIERLEY. *Roses for the Home*. 24 pp. U.S. Department of Agriculture Home and Garden Bulletin No. 25. Rev. 1963. 15 cents. For sale by Superintendent of Documents, U.S. Government Printing Office, Washington, D.C. 20402.

FAIRBROTHER, F. *Roses*. 185 pp., 105 illus. Penguin Books Inc., Baltimore, Md. 1958, rev. 1963. Prepared in Great Britain but useful to Americans.

FOOTE, HARRIET RISLEY. *Mrs. Foote's Rose Book*. 164 pp., 22 illus. Charles T. Branford Company, Boston. 1948. Written by the first woman to receive the Gold Honor Medal of the American Rose Society for "the beautiful rose gardens she has made" and the one largely responsible for the introduction of hybrid tea roses into the United States. Testing more than 2000 varieties in her own garden—a mecca for visitors from all over the world—Mrs. Foote was a firm believer in deep soil preparation and in planning to avoid disease.

FREAR, D. E. H. Editor, compiler. *Pesticide Handbook*. 314 pp., 16th ed. 1964. College Science Publishers, State College, Pennsylvania (paper bound). This *Handbook* is revised every year to give much information about pesticides—thousands of products—under trade, common and chemical names.

I used it to check formulations for this edition of the rose book. You can use future editions of the Handbook to check changes in rose pesticides.

GAMBLE, JAMES ALEXANDER. *Roses Unlimited.* 82 pp., 12 illus. Publ. by the author. Available from American Rose Society. Dr. Gamble was particularly interested in breeding fragrant roses and left a large bequest to the American Rose Foundation for work in that line.

GORDON, JEAN. *Pageant of the Rose.* 232 pp., 100 illus., 14 color plates. Thomas Y. Crowell Company, New York. 1953. History of the rose in art, romance, poetry, legend, heraldry, religion, symbolism, fairy tales, fashion, fragrance, cosmetics and cookery.

GORDON, JEAN. *Rose Recipes.* 100 pp. Red Rose Publications, Woodstock, Vermont. 1958. Roses for flavor and fragrance.

HARVEY, N. P. *The Rose in Britain.* 181 pp., 23 color plates. Plant Protection Ltd. and D. Van Nostrand Company, Inc., Princeton, N.J. 1953. For English and American gardeners with wonderful color photographs.

JENKINS, DOROTHY H. *The Complete Book of Roses.* 114 pp. Bantam Books, New York, 1956. A lot of solid information and ideas.

KEAYS, MRS. FREDERICK LOVE. *Old Roses.* 222 pp., 56 illus. Macmillan Company, New York. 1935.

KORDES, WILHELM. *Roses.* Translated and edited by N. P. Harvey. 240 pp., 16 illus. in color. Reinhold Publishing Corp., New York. 1964. By the beloved German hybridizer, creator of Crimson Glory and the Kordesii shrub roses.

LESTER, FRANCIS. *My Friend the Rose.* 90 pp., 16 illus. J. Horace McFarland Company, Harrisburg, Pa. 1942, reprinted 1953. Francis Lester and his roses were friends and I'll never forget the day I spent with them in California. He liked old roses best.

LEWIS, C. H. *The Judging of Roses.* 89 pp., illus. The American Rose Society, Columbus, Ohio. 1959. Official judge's manual with many hints for exhibitors.

McFADDEN, S. E., H. N. MILLER, L. C. KUITERT, A. M. WILSON. *Roses in Florida.* University of Florida Agricultural Extension Service Bulletin 180. 55 pp., 23 illus. Gainesville, Fla. 1963. Excellent specialized information for the Deep South.

McFARLAND, J. HORACE. *Memoirs of a Rose Man.* 144 pp., 22 illus. Rodale Press, Emmaus, Pa. 1949. Tales from Breeze Hill, home of the man who, more than any other, popularized the rose in America, and source of 50,000 photographs.

J. HORACE McFARLAND COMPANY AND AMERICAN ROSE SOCIETY, compilers. *Modern Roses V.* 471 pp. J. Horace McFarland Company, Harrisburg, Pa. 1958. Descriptive list of 7562 varieties and 333 species of roses now in commerce or of historical interest. Standard reference for rosarians, edited by Roy Shepherd. *Modern Roses 6* due in 1965.

MILTON, JOHN. *Rose Growing Simplified*. 128 pp., 58 illus., 15 in color. Hearth-side Press, Inc., New York. 1962. Concise information with helpful draw-ings.

PARK, BERTRAM. *The Guide to Roses*. 288 pp., 64 color plates, 32 half-tones. D. Van Nostrand Company, Inc., Princeton, N.J. 1956. An English book with superexcellent illustrations of rose varieties and their problems.

PINNEY, MARGARET E. *The Miniature Rose Book*. 149 pp., numerous sketches, 8 color plates. D. Van Nostrand Company, Princeton, N.J. 1964. Detailed descriptions of more than 150 miniatures grown by the author.

PYENSON, LOUIS. *Keep Your Garden Healthy*. 256 pp., 41 illus. E. P. Dutton & Co., Inc. New York. 1964. Very practical pest control for roses and other plants.

REUSCH, GLAD AND MARY NOBLE. *Corsage Craft*. 192 pp., illus. D. Van Nos-trand Company, Inc. Princeton, N.J. 1951, rev. 1960. Roses to wear.

ROCKWELL, F. F. AND ESTHER C. GRAYSON. *The Rockwell's Complete Book of Roses*. 332 pp., 44 color illus., numerous half-tones and line drawings. Doubleday & Company, Inc., Garden City, N.Y. 1958. Most of the fine photographs are by the authors who have spent years growing, arranging, and exhibiting roses.

SHARP, MORRIE L. AND DEAN COLLINS. *Roses Illustrated*. 160 pp., 353 illus., 71 in color. Western Trail Publishers, Portland, Ore. 1951. Brief text on rose culture and exhibition, profusely illustrated. Sponsored by the Portland Rose Society.

SHEPHERD, ROY E. *History of the Rose*. 264 pp. The Macmillan Company, New York. 1954. Important history of all known classes of roses.

SHEPHERD, ROY E. *Roses*. 96 pp., line drawings. Rinehart & Company, Inc. New York. 1954. Brief summary of rose culture.

TAYLOR, GEORGE M. *The Book of the Rose*. 176 pp., 33 illus. in color, 16 halftones. Winchester Publications, Lt. London. 1949. Adaptability and utility of the rose, review of cultural methods.

THOMSON, RICHARD, editor. *Handbook on Roses*. 76 pp., numerous halftones and line drawings. Brooklyn Botanic Garden, Brooklyn, N.Y. 1955. All kinds of condensed information.

THOMSON, RICHARD. *Old Roses for Modern Gardens*. 154 pp., 26 illus. in color, 16 halftones. D. Van Nostrand Company, Inc., Princeton, N.J. 1959. You have to grow some old roses after reading this book.

THOMSON, RICHARD AND HELEN VAN PELT WILSON. *Roses for Pleasure*. 207 pp., 8 illus. in color, 16 halftones. D. Van Nostrand Company, Inc., Prince-ton, N.J. 1957.

THOMPSON, M. M. *Rose Pruning with Pictures*. 56 pp., 75 illus. Mary Lynn & Associates, Los Angeles, California. 1960. A "how-to" book, mostly in photo-graphs.

WESTCOTT, CYNTHIA. *Are You Your Garden's Worst Pest?* 305 pp., 23 line drawings. Doubleday & Company, Inc., Garden City, N.Y. 1961. Things not to do to your roses; safe use of pesticides.

WESTCOTT, CYNTHIA. *The Gardener's Bug Book.* 625 pp., 95 line drawings, 36 color plates. Doubleday & Company Inc. Garden City, N.Y. 3rd ed. 1964. Includes descriptions of a great many pests recorded on roses.

WHITING, JOHN R., editor. *How You Can Grow Beautiful Roses.* 143 pp., numerous illus. Arco Publishing Company, Inc., New York. 1959.

WHITSITT, EDNA. *Roses and Home Flower Arranging.* 48 pp., 36 illus. in color. Greystone Press, New York, 1951. Basic rules for arranging flowers, with roses featured in illustrations.

WILSON, HELEN VAN PELT. *Climbing Roses.* 212 pp., 8 illus. in color, 55 half-tones. M. Barrows and Company, Inc., New York. 1955.

INDEX

Boldface type indicates illustrations.